Keys to Good Language

TEACHER'S EDITION

Phoenix Learning Resources, LLC.

910 Church Street • Honesdale, PA 18431
1-800-228-9345 • Fax: 570-253-3227 • www.phoenixlr.com

Item# 1173   ISBN 978-0-7915-1173-2

Contents

KEYS TO GOOD LANGUAGE OVERVIEW

For nearly half a century, **Keys to Good Language**™ has been providing students across the country with the basic skills used in effective communication. This edition of the program continues the tradition of careful instruction and extensive practice in language skills. In addition, the program has been enriched by new content and art that today's students will find stimulating and motivating.

Keys to Good Language is a complete program of concept and skill development in mechanics, usage, grammar, speaking, and composition. The student text–exercise book offers the explanations and examples needed for understanding concepts as well as the practice activities needed for mastery. The Teacher's Edition provides lesson procedures and additional activities for practice, extension, and review of the lessons. Duplicating masters are available for additional practice and a complimentary testing program provides evaluation.

Carefully structured development is the key to skill building. **Keys to Good Language** begins with the basic applications of capitalization, punctuation, parts of speech, and sentence development and gradually builds to the development of more complex sentences, paragraphs, and varied composition forms. Frequent lessons and reminders encourage students to develop standard language usage habits. Formal reviews after each unit assure retention.

The overall goal of **Keys to Good Language** is to provide students with instruction in the essential language skills and to provide the opportunities to use these skills in developing clear, well-structured written and oral communication.

Program Objectives

1. To encourage in students an appreciation for the English language through the study of structure, use, and oral and written composition.
2. To provide students with the important language skills in mechanics, usage, and grammar.
3. To help students develop good writing through the study and practice of basic language skills and structured composition activities.

Student Book

The student book is organized into six units, each consisting of sixteen or seventeen lessons. Each lesson is designed to be completed in one class period and contains additional activities that may be used at the teacher's discretion for student reinforcement at home or in another class period. The student book is designed to be completed in one school year.

The Text section is a unique feature, found in the center of each student book. This section is a complete handbook of the accepted forms and uses of the English language. A simple numbering system keys these rules to each lesson. This "key section" is used for instruction, reinforcement, and reference.

Three indexes are provided for student use. The first, *Index of Lessons,* lists the skills developed in the student book. The *Index of Lessons* can be used to locate and review skills already studied or to preview skills of special importance. The second index, *Index of Informational Topics and Stories in Lessons,* shows the wide range of subjects used as vehicles for instruction and can be used to generate discussion of topics of student interest. The third index, *Index of The Text,* lists the contents of the key section in alphabetical rather than numerical order.

The Lesson Page

Every lesson in the student book appears in a regular, predictable format.

At the top of each lesson page are the key symbol and numbers. The numbers refer to those keys that explain the lesson skills and provide examples of their use.

Many lessons contain illustrations, which are provided for two reasons: first, the illustrations provide interest and motivation for students; second, the illustrations are used as a basis for oral language development through the feature known as *Broadcasting.* Explained in the Teacher's Edition, *Broadcasting* provides an opportunity for students to discuss experiences and ideas and to relate this discussion to the content of the lesson.

Each lesson begins with an explanation of the skill being introduced or a short selection used to illustrate the skill. This introduction to the lesson activity is frequently followed by a short summary statement, stating the rule or generalization presented in the key section.

The lesson activities provide ample practice with the skills introduced. The forms of activities include fill-in, matching, sentence completion, sentence combining, complete sentence answers to questions, story writing, letter writing, and much more. In addition, each lesson activity centers around a theme or topic to provide students with additional motivation and enjoyable reading. Answers for the lesson activity items are given in the Teacher's Edition.

Teacher's Edition

Every lesson in **Keys to Good Language** has a corresponding lesson plan in the *Instructional Plans* section of the Teacher's Edition. This section is followed by the text of the complete student book with annotated answers for activities. The last section of the Teacher's Edition contains full-sized reproductions of the **Keys to Good Language** Student Test Booklet pages, with annotated answers.

Using the Instructional Plans

Keys The teacher is reminded of the key numbers that will be used in the course of the lesson. These keys should be reviewed by the teacher prior to instruction. This review will help the teacher to concentrate on the skills and examples of greatest value to the class.

Key Objectives The goals and expected outcome of each lesson are clearly stated in each lesson. They relate directly to the skills taught or reviewed.

Procedures A complete guide for lesson implementation is provided in the *Procedures* section. When the student lesson is accompanied by an illustration, the *Procedures* section is divided into two parts: *Broadcasting* and *Explaining the Lesson.* When no illustration is provided, the *Broadcasting* section is not included.

Broadcasting Questions that encourage students to examine and discuss the illustrations in the student book are included in the Teacher's Edition. These questions are meant only as suggestions; the teacher should take the opportunity to ask additional questions, use new vocabulary, and introduce appropriate concepts as student interest develops. Students themselves should be encouraged to ask each other questions concerning the illustrations. The goal of the *Broadcasting* section is to use concrete experiences to help students develop oral communication skills.

Explaining the Lesson The teacher is given complete information for conducting the lesson. The students are first asked to turn to the key section indicated on the lesson page. The skill information and examples in the keys should be read aloud. The teacher should then discuss the information with the class to be sure that all the students understand the concepts.

After turning back to the lesson page, many students will be able to read and complete the lesson activities with no difficulty; however, to be certain that students successfully transfer their understanding of the keys to the lesson activity, the teacher should read the information and directions at the top of the page with the students. When all students demonstrate an understanding of the lesson, they can complete the activity page themselves, with the teacher available for individual help.

When the students have completed the lesson, the teacher may want to read the answers to the class, allowing the students to correct their answers and discuss misunderstandings. The students should then record their scores at the top of the page and on the chart on the inside back cover of their books.

Supplementary Exercises For students who need reinforcement of the lesson skills, additional exercises are provided in a format similar to the lesson activity. The *Supplementary Exercises* may be written on the chalkboard or duplicated and distributed to the students. Answers to all items are included in the Teacher's Edition.

Supplementary Activities Additional reinforcement and extension activities are provided for the teacher. These activities employ a variety of techniques and appear in one or more of the following categories.

1. *More Practice*—activities for further reinforcement for groups or individuals
2. *Instructional Variation*—ideas for games, art projects, learning centers, and other varied approaches that extend and reinforce concepts and skills
3. *Using Resources and Materials*—suggestions for library visits, guest speakers, field trips, and composition activities that require additional preparation or materials

Review Lessons and Student Tests

The final lesson of every unit, *Remembering What We Have Learned,* provides the teacher with information about how well students have learned the skills and concepts in the unit. The teacher should have the students complete the activity independently, allowing them to refer to the indicated keys as necessary. Review and discussion of the students' answers are most beneficial. The teacher can explain concepts that are still unclear and note the skills that may need additional review.

In addition, the **Keys to Good Language** Student Test Booklets are available from Bowmar/Noble Publishers. These tests are reproduced full-sized and with annotations in the last section of this Teacher's Edition. Two tests are provided for each unit in the student book: a pretest and a post test.

Pretests Pretests are administered before beginning a unit to evaluate the students' knowledge of the concepts and skills to be encountered. The teacher should administer the pretest without giving assistance. A check of the tests will indicate general class readiness for instruction, individual weaknesses that may require additional instruction and reinforcement during completion of the unit, and individual strengths that may allow certain students to concentrate on extension activities.

Post Tests Administered after completion of the *Remembering What We Have Learned* lessons, post tests evaluate student mastery of unit concepts and skills. An analysis of student performance on the post tests will provide valuable information about class development and the need for reinforcement or instruction for individuals.

The students should mark their pretest and post test scores in the spaces provided on the chart at the back of their books. For additional encouragement, the teacher should take the opportunity to point out to students the improvement in post test scores over pre-test scores.

Duplicating Masters

Additional reinforcement of skills is provided by **Keys to Good Language Duplicating Masters,** available from Bowmar/Noble Publishers. The duplicating masters are cross-referenced to lesson skills and can be used prescriptively when the students' performance indicates the need for extra practice. The activities provided are similar in format to the lesson activities and can be completed independently by the students.

SCOPE AND SEQUENCE

Grammar/Usage

Sentences

Recognizing and writing sentences
    Writing effective sentences 1, 17, 82, 98
    Recognizing and writing declarative sentences 2, 5, 6, 16, 17, 44, 70, 90, 98
    Recognizing and writing interrogative sentences 2, 5, 6, 16, 17, 44, 90
    Recognizing and writing exclamatory sentences 2, 5, 6, 16, 17, 44, 90, 98
    Recognizing and punctuating sentences in a paragraph 18, 55, 70, 83
    Combining short sentences 68, 69, 86, 91, 98
    Separating run-on sentences 18, 55, 70, 71, 91
    Recognizing and writing topic sentences 35, 36, 85
Recognizing subjects and predicates
    Recognizing simple subjects 7
    Recognizing complete subjects 19
    Recognizing complete predicates 19

Parts of Speech

Nouns
    Recognizing nouns 8, 44, 47, 93, 98
    Forming plurals of singular nouns 9, 16, 47, 76, 93, 98
    Forming possessives of nouns 10, 16, 47, 76, 98
    Recognizing proper nouns 8, 44, 47, 93, 98
Verbs
    Recognizing verbs 20, 47, 93, 98
    Identifying principal parts of verbs 21, 32, 98
    Using proper verb forms 15, 16, 21, 22, 24, 30, 31, 32, 43, 46, 49, 62, 65, 81, 82, 89, 96, 97, 98
    Drink, drank, and *drunk* 22, 31, 96
    Is and *are* 14, 23, 46, 89, 96
    Lay, lie, and *laid* 30, 31, 32, 46, 81
    Sit, sat and *set* 30, 31, 32, 46
    Write, wrote, and *written* 22, 31, 65, 66
    Using helping verbs 24, 96
    Avoiding double negatives 79, 82
    Writing contractions 29, 32, 47, 76, 93, 98
Adjectives
    Recognizing and using adjectives 67, 73, 82, 98
    Using demonstrative adjectives *these* and *those* 61, 88
Pronouns
    Recognizing pronouns 11, 47, 59, 93, 98
    Using personal pronouns *I, he, she, we,* or *they* to tell who did something 12, 13, 15, 16, 59, 66, 95
    Placing nouns and pronouns that name others before the pronouns *I* and *me* 60, 66, 95, 98
    Using *me, him, her, us,* or *them* after *told, give, heard, from, to, for, by,* or *with* 12, 13, 15, 16, 66, 95, 98
    Using *I, he, she, we,* or *they* after *it is, it was, is it,* or *was it* 14, 15, 16, 59, 95, 98
    Using *them, these,* and *those* 61, 66, 88, 95
    Using *himself, themselves, their* and *there* 80, 95, 97
    Using pronouns in pairs 13, 15, 16, 59, 95, 98
Conjunctions
    Using conjunctions 68, 69, 82, 86, 91
    Avoiding too many *ands* 71
Prepositions
    Using prepositions *in* and *into* 88, 89

Composition

Speaking, Listening

Speaking and listening to other people
    Participating in class discussions 6, 27, 36, 39, 46, 50, 51, 54, 56, 57, 62, 64, 67, 68, 69, 73, 84, 85, 93
    Presenting oral reports 4, 6, 8, 15, 48, 59, 92
    Telling a story 18, 21, 83
    Broadcasting — (students discussing pictures and personal experiences in preparation for the lesson) 3, 5, 7, 12, 14, 18, 19, 20, 23, 26, 28, 35, 37, 38, 43, 45, 58, 59, 61, 67, 70, 77, 79, 81, 86, 87, 90, 93, 97

Writing

Recognizing and writing sentences
    Writing declarative sentences 2, 16, 17
    Writing interrogative sentences 2, 16, 17
    Writing exclamatory sentences 2, 16, 17
    Avoiding too many short sentences 68
    Avoiding run-on sentences 18, 55, 70, 71
Writing outlines 34, 37, 48, 49, 84
Writing paragraphs 37, 48, 49, 73
Writing stories 83
Writing letters 54, 55, 56, 66
Writing friendly letters 53, 54
Writing business letters 55, 56
Writing addresses 54, 55, 56, 57, 66
Addressing envelopes 57
Writing reports 85
Writing direct quotations 26, 32, 50
Writing indirect quotations 50

Mechanics

Capitalization

Writing names
    Capitalizing names of persons 4, 28, 32, 45, 72, 87, 92, 98
    Capitalizing names of pets 72, 92, 98
    Capitalizing days of the week 28, 58, 92, 98
    Capitalizing names of holidays and special days 4, 28, 92, 98
    Capitalizing months of the year 4, 28, 32, 45, 55, 58, 72, 87, 92, 98

Vocabulary

Dictionary

Pretest—Unit I

Before beginning Unit I, administer the pretest for this unit. Pretests for all units are at the back of the Teacher's Edition. The results should indicate the students' preliminary competency levels for concepts and skills presented in the unit. Instructions for administration and ways to use the pretests appear in the introduction to the Teacher's Edition.

Lesson **1** (page 3)

Effective Sentences

 41

Key Objective The student will be able to select the more effective sentence from a given pair of sentences.

Procedures

Write the following sentences on the chalkboard:
1. While riding to the museum, the clock struck two.
2. The clock struck two while they were riding to the museum.
3. Ann lost her wallet at the museum, which had several dollars in it.
4. At the museum Ann lost her wallet, which had several dollars in it.
5. They saw so many interesting exhibits that they are hard to describe.

Ask the students to open their books to Lesson 1. Then read the title of the lesson and call the students' attention to the key number. Have them find the key referred to in Lesson 1, Key 41. Have one student read the key information and examples aloud while the other students read silently.

Ask the students to read the first two sentences on the chalkboard. Then ask, "Which of these sentences expresses a thought clearly?" Help the students see that the meaning of the second sentence is clear; the first sentence gives the impression that the clock is riding to the museum. Work in the same way with sentences 3 and 4. Then have one student rewrite sentence 5 so that its meaning is clearly expressed. The student might write a sentence similar to the following: It is hard for them to describe the exhibits because they saw so many interesting ones.

Have the students turn again to Lesson 1. Read the information and the directions for part I and part II. Be sure they understand the directions. Then have them work independently.

Most students will be able to read the exercises without difficulty, but if there are slow readers in the group, give them assistance in their reading.

When the work is completed, discuss the sentences in part I and have the students explain which sentences are clear in meaning. Let several students read aloud the sentences they wrote in part II. After you have checked the answers to the exercises, have the students record their scores on the line at the top of the page and on the score chart at the back of their books. Have the students correct their errors so that they will see their mistakes when they review the lesson.

Supplementary Exercises

The following exercises may be assigned to students who need further practice in writing clear, effective sentences. Write the directions and exercises on the chalkboard.

I. Write the letters *A, B,* and *C,* in a column on your paper. Decide which sentence in each pair below expresses a thought clearly. If you think the first sentence is more effective, write *1* beside the A on your paper. If you think the second sentence is more effective, write *2* beside the A on your paper. Work in the same way with groups B and C. (Score: 3)

<u>(2)</u> Group A

1. Bill gave his report to the teacher that he had written.
2. After Bill had written his report, he gave it to the teacher.

<u>(2)</u> Group B

1. We looked inside the caterpillar's cocoon, which we saw had become a beautiful moth.
2. When we looked inside the cocoon, we saw that the caterpillar had become a beautiful moth.

<u>(2)</u> Group C

1. They met so many people that it is hard to remember their names.
2. They met so many people that it is hard for them to remember each person's name.

II. Rewrite the sentences below to make them clear and effective. (Score: 6—2 for each sentence)

1. The ball went over the wall that he threw. (The ball that he threw went over the wall.)
2. Running toward the house, the storm began. (The storm began while we were running toward the house.)
3. He usually eats more than his brother. (He usually eats more than his brother does.)

Supplementary Activities

More Practice: Have the students write effective sentences for the following: directions from school to the student's home; directions for the student's favorite recipe; and a description of what the student is wearing.

Instructional Variation: Have each student write a clear, effective sentence on a sentence strip. Then have the students cut their sentences after each word, mix up the word cards, and gather them together with a paper clip. Have the students exchange their word cards with each other to see if other students can form the word cards into effective sentences.

Using Resources and Materials: Have the students find newspaper headings and rewrite them as effective sentences.

Lesson **2** (page 4)

Kinds of Sentences
 41 b, c, d

Key Objectives The student will be able to identify declarative, interrogative, and exclamatory sentences from a given series of sentences.

Procedures

Write the following sentences on the chalkboard:
1. Luis has read many books.
2. Has Luis read many books?
3. How many books Luis has read!

Ask the students to open their books to Lesson 2 and read the title of the lesson. Have them find parts b, c, and d of Key 41 in the text section. Have one student read the key information and examples aloud while the other students read silently.

Have the students read the sentences on the chalkboard. Then ask: Which sentence would you use if you wanted to ask whether or not Luis has read many books? Which would you use to exclaim about the many books Luis has read? Have several students tell which sentence is declarative, which is interrogative, and which is exclamatory.

Ask the students to turn back to Lesson 2. Read the directions for the exercises, read the examples, and answer any questions about procedure. Then have the students complete the exercises independently.

You may check each individual's work or let the students check their own work after a discussion of each sentence. After the answers are checked, have the students record their scores on the line at the top of the page and on the score chart at the back of their books. Remind the students to correct their errors.

Supplementary Exercises

Place an *S* after each statement, or declarative sentence, a *Q* after each question, or interrogative sentence, and an *E* after each exclamation, or exclamatory sentence. (Score: 6)
1. What did the American colonists write about? (Q)
2. The settlers wrote about their progress in their new homes. (S)
3. Did the colonists write any poetry? (Q)
4. "Day of Doom," written by Michael Wigglesworth, is an example of early American poetry. (S)
5. Sarah Kemble Knight wrote about travel in the colonies. (S)
6. How amusing her "Journal" is! (E)

NOTE: A sentence that ends with a preposition is considered natural, correct, and even desirable by many grammarians.

Supplementary Activities

More Practice: Have the students write sentences that describe how life is in their city or town. Have them write three declarative sentences, three interrogative sentences, and three exclamatory sentences.

Instructional Variation: Have the students play the game, "Guess What I Am." To prepare for this game, draw on separate index cards a period, a question mark, or an exclamation point. Pin one card on each student's back, making sure the students do not know what punctuation cards are pinned to their own backs. Have the students speak to each other using sentences that reflect the punctuation mark they see on a student's back. For example, students will use only exclamatory sentences to speak to the student who is wearing an exclamation point. Continue until the students correctly guess which punctuation marks are pinned to their own backs.

Using Resources and Materials: Have the students choose a paragraph from a reading book, a newspaper, or a magazine. Have them change the declarative sentences into interrogative or exclamatory sentences.

Lesson **3** (page 5)

Ending Sentences Correctly
 7a, 8a, 9a

Key Objective The student will be able to place

a period at the end of a declarative sentence, a question mark at the end of an interrogative sentence, and an exclamation point at the end of an exclamatory sentence.

Procedures

Broadcasting

Have the students open their books to the text section and direct their attention to Keys 53 and 54 on page 68. Read the explanatory material aloud as the students read silently. Then have the students turn back to Lesson 3 and look at the picture. Begin a discussion of Lesson 3 by asking the following questions: Why do people add salt to their food? Salt used to be used as money. Why do you think salt was so valuable? What do you think the expression ''salt of the earth'' means?

Explaining the Lesson

Write the following sentences on the chalkboard:
1. Salt has been found on land many miles from the ocean
2. Is the salt carried in the air
3. How far the salt travels

Review with the students what they have learned about three kinds of sentences. Ask the following questions: What are the names of the three kinds of sentences? What does a declarative sentence do? An interrogative sentence? An exclamatory sentence?

Have the students turn to Lesson 3, read the lesson title, and find the correct key numbers. When they have found Keys 7a, 8a, and 9a in the text section, read and discuss the key information and examples with them. Have them note that each example begins with a capital letter and that the different kinds of sentences end with different kinds of punctuation marks.

Direct the attention of the students to the sentences on the chalkboard. Have them determine what kinds of sentences they are. Then have a student volunteer to punctuate the sentences while the rest of the class checks the work.

Have the students turn back to Lesson 3 and read the directions to the exercises. As soon as they understand the directions, let them work independently. After they check the answers to the exercises, have the students record their scores at the top of the page and on the score chart at the back of the book. Then have them correct their mistakes.

Supplementary Exercises

Place the correct punctuation mark at the end of each sentence. Write an *S* after each statement, or declarative sentence, a *Q* after each question, or

interrogative sentence, and an *E* after each exclamation, or exclamatory sentence. (Score: 18)
1. Workers once received salt as wages (.) (S)
2. How valuable the salt was then (!) (E)
3. Salt in liquid form is called brine (.) (S)
4. Have you ever looked at dry salt under a microscope (?) (Q)
5. What an interesting sight it is (!) (E)
6. Each salt crystal is the shape of a cube (.) (S)
7. Will salt melt ice or snow (?) (Q)
8. A mixture of salt and ice has a lower freezing point than water (.) (S)
9. Is that why salt is used in freezing ice cream (?) (Q)

Supplementary Activities

More Practice: Have each student write a declarative, an interrogative, and an exclamatory sentence about their favorite food. Choose some of the sentences and rewrite them on the chalkboard omitting the end punctuation marks. Have several students go to the chalkboard and place the correct punctuation marks at the ends of the sentences.

Instructional Variation: Have a story or series of sentences recorded on a tape for the listening center. Have the speaker narrate the tape without inflection and have the students identify which sentences are declarative, interrogative, or exclamatory.

Using Resources and Materials: Have the students listen to a news report or a speech on the radio or television. Have the students tell the class how many times the reporter or speaker used declarative, interrogative, or exclamatory sentences.

Lesson **4** (page 6)

Using Capital Letters
 1a, g, h, i, j, 5

Key Objectives The student will be able to identify the following words to be capitalized: the first word of a sentence; names of persons, holidays, months, and days of the week; particular places or things; and words made from the names of places.

Procedures

Write the following sentences, without capital letters or punctuation marks, on the chalkboard:

the colonists left their homes in england to seek a new life in america could they survive in the american wilderness what courage the first settlers had

Have the students open their books to Lesson 4. The students should remember to read the title of the lesson and find the correct keys in the text section. When all students have followed this routine, read Keys 1a, g, h, i, j, and 5 with them.

Ask a student to read the paragraph on the chalkboard. Place capital letters and punctuation marks where they are needed. Then have the student read the paragraph again. Help the students recognize that capital letters and punctuation marks make reading easier by asking: Which way is the paragraph easier to read? Why?

Be sure the students understand the directions in Lesson 4 before they work the exercises independently. After answers to exercises have been checked and scores recorded, have the students correct their mistakes.

For practice in writing sentences, assign the activity suggested in Other Things to Do at the bottom of Lesson 4. Remind the students to begin each sentence with a capital letter and to end it with the appropriate punctuation mark. Then let them work independently.

Supplementary Exercises

Rewrite the following sentences, using capital letters where they are needed. (Score: 23)

1. a group of people came from england to america in 1587. (A group of people came from England to America in 1587.)
2. this was several years before the *mayflower* crossed the atlantic ocean. (This was several years before the *Mayflower* crossed the Atlantic Ocean.)
3. they settled on roanoke island, near north carolina. (They settled on Roanoke Island, near North Carolina.)
4. in august a little girl named virginia dare was born. (In August a little girl named Virginia Dare was born.)
5. she was the first english child born in america. (She was the first English child born in America.)
6. but the settlement at roanoke did not last. (But the settlement at Roanoke did not last.)
7. no one knows what happened to that english settlement. (No one knows what happened to that English settlement.)

Supplementary Activities

More Practice: Have several students volunteer to speak to the class. Have the speakers tell their names, addresses, and the names of any brothers or sisters. Have the rest of the class write the information on a piece of paper, remembering to use capital letters where they are needed.

Instructional Variation: Record a story or series of sentences for the listening center. Be sure the tape uses names of persons, places, months, holidays, and other words that need to be capitalized. On a sheet of paper have the students write the story or sentences using capital letters and punctuation marks correctly.

Using Resources and Materials: Have the students use the encylopedia or other resource material to find more information on early American settlements. Have the students make a list of early settlements as well as the countries the settlers came from. Remind the students to use capital letters where they are needed.

Lesson **5** (page 7)

Punctuating Sentences
 1c, f, g, i, 7, 8a, 9a

Key Objectives The student will be able to:
1. Place the correct punctuation mark at the end of a sentence.
2. Place a period after initials and abbreviations.
3. Identify given words that can be abbreviated, and write their abbreviations, using a period at the end of each abbreviation.

Procedures

Broadcasting

Have the students read and review Keys 53 and 54 in the text section. Then have them turn back to Lesson 5 and look at the picture. Begin a discussion of Lesson 5 by asking the following questions: Why do people put stamps on letters? Do you know anyone who has a stamp collection? What kinds of stamps do people collect? Can you describe some of the stamps you have seen?

Explaining the Lesson

Write the students' responses to the questions above on the chalkboard. Omit punctuation marks in the sentences and at the end of each sentence. Try to vary the sentences so there will be declarative, exclamatory, and interrogative sentences. Have several students go to the chalkboard and punctuate the sentences correctly.

Have the students read the title of the lesson. Have a student explain why capital letters and punctuation marks are used in writing. Then read and discuss Keys 1c, f, g, i, 7, 8a, and 9a with the students.

Be sure the students understand the directions for parts I and II in Lesson 5 before they work the exercises independently. After answers to the exercises have been checked and scores recorded, have the students correct their mistakes.

NOTE: Point out that abbreviations of days, months, directions, states, etc., are not used in formal writing but that they may be used for informal writing, such as notes, lists, etc.

Mention also that there are two ways of writing the abbreviations of states and that this lesson requires the form used for lists and maps. Make the students aware that the two-letter, postal form presented in Key 7f is used only to address letters and envelopes.

Supplementary Exercises

I. Rewrite the following sentences, placing punctuation marks where they are needed. (Score: 14)

1. What a beautiful stamp this is (What a beautiful stamp this is!)
2. Didn't Maria buy it from Dr Woods (Didn't Maria buy it from Dr. Woods?)
3. No, it was given to her by E S Hays (No, it was given to her by E. S. Hays.)
4. This red stamp shows a picture of Samuel F B Morse (This red stamp shows a picture of Samuel F. B. Morse.)
5. Didn't Mr Morse invent the telegraph (Didn't Mr. Morse invent the telegraph?)
6. This stamp has a picture of Stephen F Austin on it (This stamp has a picture of Stephen F. Austin on it.)
7. He was an early settler in Texas (He was an early settler in Texas.)

II. Write the abbreviations of the words below that can be abbreviated. Put an X by the words that cannot be abbreviated. (Score: 6)

8. Tuesday (Tues.)   11. Miss (X)
9. Boulevard (Blvd.)   12. Saturday (Sat.)
10. May (X)   13. Utah (X)

Supplementary Activities

More Practice: Have the students make a list of several of the streets and highways in their city or town. Have them abbreviate words wherever possible.

Instructional Variation: Have the students design and draw a stamp honoring their state. Have the students read and study Key 44, and then write a paragraph on the history of the state. Remind the students to punctuate their sentences correctly.

Using Resources and Materials: Arrange for the class to visit the post office and get a catalogue of commemorative stamps. Then have the students choose one of the stamps in the catalogue and write a report on the person, place, or event pictured on the stamp. Have the students read and study Key 45 before they plan and write their report. Remind the students to punctuate their sentences correctly.

Lesson **6** (page 8)

Recognizing Sentences
🔑 7a, 8a, 9a, 41

Key Objectives   The student will be able to:
1. Distinguish sentences from sentence fragments.
2. Identify groups of words that are sentences.
3. Place the correct punctuation marks at the end of sentences.

Procedures
Write the following sentences on the chalkboard:
1. Devon sang.
2. The star of the play sang in a clear voice.
3. Raisins are good to eat.
4. The tree was hit by lightning.

Explain to the students that every simple sentence has two parts: one part tells who or what the sentence is about; the other tells something about what that person, place, or thing is or does. Explain that a thought is not complete unless it has these two parts. Ask one student to read the first sentence on the chalkboard. Ask the student who or what the sentence is about. Then have the student look at the rest of the sentence to see whether it tells who or what Devon is, what he does, or what is done to him. Explain to the students that both parts of this short sentence are necessary to make a complete thought. Follow a similar procedure with the other sentences, showing that each part of a sentence may contain several words.

Direct the students' attention to Keys 41, 7a, 8a, and 9a, in that order. Have them read the information and be sure they understand it. After this the students should be ready to turn to Lesson 6, read the directions, and work the exercises without difficulty.

After answers to the exercises have been checked and the class has discussed the sentences and sentence fragments, direct the attention of the group to the suggestions under Other Things to Do at the bottom of the exercise page. Have the students read the directions silently. Then remind them that each sentence must have two parts. Have one student tell the group about the two parts of a sentence. Be sure the student explains that one part tells who or what the sentence is about and that the other part tells something about what that person, place, or thing is or does.

Help the students understand that they are to determine what part of a sentence is missing from each sentence fragment and to add that part so that the group of words expresses a complete thought.

Supplementary Exercises

Assign the following exercises to students who need further practice in sentence recognition. After writing the directions and the exercises on the chalkboard, have the students decide whether each group of words expresses a complete thought. Explain that they should try to think of a way to complete each sentence fragment so that it makes a complete sentence about the subject.

Write *Yes* if the group of words is a sentence. Write *No* if it is not a sentence. Punctuate each sentence. (Score: 17)

1. Air is a mixture of various gases (Yes) (.)
2. One gas found in air is carbon dioxide (Yes) (.)
3. Where does the carbon dioxide in air come from (Yes) (?)
4. From the air breathed out of your body (No)
5. Also sent into the air by burning fuels (No)
6. Decaying bodies of dead plants and animals (No)
7. How many uses carbon dioxide has (Yes) (!)
8. Carbon dioxide bubbles make bakery products light and fluffy (Yes) (.)
9. A very cold substance in its solid form (No)
10. Used to keep ice cream frozen hard (No)
11. Carbon dioxide is used by all living things (Yes) (.)

Supplementary Activities

More Practice: Write the following questions on the chalkboard:

1. What materials are needed and what is done with them to perform the experiment about carbon dioxide?
2. What are the results of the experiment?
3. What are the reasons for these results?

Have the students write three paragraphs giving information about performing an experiment with carbon dioxide. Suggest that the students study Keys 44 and 45 before writing. Direct their attention to the questions on the chalkboard and explain that these questions should be answered in the paragraphs. Students may use the information on page 8 of their books. The first paragraph should answer the first question with information from exercises 3, 4, 5, and 10; the second paragraph should answer the second question with information from exercises 8 and 12; and the third paragraph should answer the third question with

information from exercises 9, 14, 15, 16, and 17. Have the students use their own words in giving the information and remind them to write sentences, to use capital letters where they are needed, and to punctuate their sentences correctly. Remind them to write an appropriate title at the top of the report.

Instructional Variation: Have some students volunteer to organize and present a demonstration of the experiment explained on page 8 of their books. Have the students read and study Key 52a before they plan their presentation. Have the rest of the class act as an audience for the demonstration, and have them read and discuss the suggestions for listening found in Key 52c. Suggest that each student identify and make a note of one declarative, one interrogative, and one exclamatory sentence used by the demonstrators. After the demonstration, help the class evaluate the presentation according to the suggestions in Key 52c.

Using Resources and Materials: Have the students make individual science experiments in the classroom or at home and ask them to make written reports about their equipment, procedure, and results. Refer them to Key 45 for information about writing reports. Instruct the students to be sure to use at least one declarative, one interrogative, and one exclamatory sentence in each report. The following books may be helpful in this activity: *Experiments in Science*, by Nelson F. Beeler and Franklyn M. Branley; *First Book of Science Experiments*, by Rose Wyler; *It's Fun to Know Why*, by Julius Schwartz; *Science Experiences*, by Bertha M. Parker; and *The Real Book of Science Experiments*, by Joseph Leeming.

Lesson **7** (page 9)

Recognizing Subjects of Sentences
14, 41a

Key Objectives The student will be able to:
1. Explain that a person, a place, or a thing is the subject of a sentence.
2. Identify the subjects in a given series of sentences.

Procedures

Broadcasting

Have the students turn to Lesson 7 in their books and look at the picture on the page. Then ask the students the following questions: What animal is pictured in Lesson 7? What other animals does it look like? Where do you think this animal lives?

Explaining the Lesson

Write the following sentences on the chalkboard:

1. The okapi ran into the forest.
2. Part of the okapi's body is striped.
3. Have you ever seen an okapi in the zoo?
4. The zoo has many interesting animals.

Briefly review sentences by asking the following questions: What is a sentence? How can you tell whether or not a group of words is a sentence? Ask the students to read the sentences on the chalkboard. Follow the procedure used in Lesson 6 to discuss the sentences. Then have several students draw one line under the subject of the sentence. Explain that the underlined words are called *nouns*.

Read and discuss Keys 14 and 41a. Make sure the students understand the directions before they work the exercises in Lesson 7. After answers to the exercises have been checked and scores recorded, have the students correct their mistakes.

If time permits, have various students read the sentences in Lesson 7 and tell the subject of each sentence and what the subject does.

Assign the activity suggested in Other Things to Do at the bottom of Lesson 7.

Supplementary Exercises

At the end of each sentence write the name of the person, place, or thing that the sentence is about. (Score: 5)

1. The jungle is an interesting place. (jungle)
2. The trees are very large. (trees)
3. The sunlight barely comes through them. (sunlight)
4. Long vines hang from the limbs. (vines)
5. The weather is often hot and damp. (weather)

Supplementary Activities

More Practice: Have the students choose two paragraphs from a reading book and make a list of the subjects found in each sentence of the paragraphs.

Instructional Variation: Have students use clay or papier-mâché to make models of various animals and paint them as naturally as possible. Have them simulate the animal's natural environment with twigs, sand, etc. Then have the students write a paragraph describing where the animal lives, its habits, its diet, its enemies, and other interesting facts about the animal. Tell the students to underline the subject of each sentence. Have the students read Key 44 before writing the paragraph.

Using Resources and Materials: Have students write reports on protective coloration of animals. They may get necessary information from encyclopedias and such books as *Animal Mas-*

querade, by I. E. Green; and *Animal Clothing*, by G. F. Mason. Read and discuss Key 45 with them before they plan and write their reports. Have the students proofread their reports, checking for sentences, correct spelling, capitalization, and punctuation. Tell the students to underline the subject of each sentence in their reports.

Lesson **8** (page 10)

Recognizing Nouns

 14

Key Objective The student will be able to identify nouns in given sentences.

Procedures

After the students have turned to Lesson 8, ask someone to explain what steps should be taken before the exercises are worked. The student should mention reading the title, noting the key number, finding the key in the text section, and reading and discussing key information and examples.

Ask the students to name common nouns and proper nouns. Then say the following words and have several students tell whether or not each one is a noun: *car, child, sing, leaf, with, and,* and *city.*

Be sure the students understand the directions before they work the exercises in Lesson 8. After answers to the exercises have been checked and scores recorded, have the students correct their mistakes.

Supplementary Exercises

After each sentence list the nouns in the sentence. (Score: 13)

1. John Smith wrote a book. (John Smith, book)
2. John Smith traveled all over the world. (John Smith, world)
3. He wrote about his life in America. (life, America)
4. His book tells about Jamestown. (book, Jamestown)
5. One story tells how Pocahontas saved his life. (story, Pocahontas, life)

Supplementary Activities

More Practice: Have the students make a list of ten nouns found in the classroom. Have them use each noun in a sentence. Suggest that their sentences discuss the noun in a setting other than the classroom.

Instructional Variation: Have the students plan and draw a picture or construct a model of the

Jamestown settlement. Then have them write a few sentences describing their picture. Have the students underline the nouns in their sentences.

Using Resources and Materials: Have the students use the encyclopedia or other resource material to get more information about John Smith and/or Jamestown. Have the students write a report and present it to the class. Have the students read and study Keys 45 and 52a before writing their reports. Tell the students to underline the nouns in their reports.

Lesson **9** (page 11)

Singular and Plural Nouns

 15

Key Objectives The student will be able to write the plural form of given singular nouns.

Procedures

Write the following words on the chalkboard:

1. chair	5. baby
2. inch	6. monkey
3. leaf	7. foot
4. life	8. sheep

As you say each of the following words, have the students tell whether it means one object or more than one: *geese, day, knives, children, deer,* and *berries.* Be sure they understand that they cannot tell whether *deer* means one or more than one unless the word is used in a sentence. Explain that nouns that name one thing are *singular* and nouns that name more than one thing are *plural.*

Tell the students that there are several ways to form plurals of singular nouns and that they will learn the main ways in this lesson. Read and discuss Key 15 with them and be sure that they understand each rule.

NOTE: There are exceptions to the rule stated in Key 15c, but only words in which *f* is changed to *v* in the plural form are used in the student's book.

Have someone read word 1 on the chalkboard and write its plural form beside it. Have other students follow the same procedure with the other words.

When the students understand the directions in Lesson 9 let them work the exercises independently. After answers to the exercises have been checked, have several students read the sentences in part I and spell the words in the blanks.

Supplementary Exercises

If the underlined word in each sentence below is a singular noun, write the plural form at the end of the sentence. If the underlined word is plural, write the singular form at the end of the sentence. (Score: 6)

1. Tom's <u>family</u> always eats healthy foods. (families)
2. Tom packed his lunch <u>box.</u> (boxes)
3. He put in a carrot <u>stick.</u> (sticks)
4. There were also two <u>sandwiches.</u> (sandwich)
5. He cut the sandwiches with a <u>knife.</u> (knives)
6. There were also some <u>berries</u> for Tom to eat. (berry)

Supplementary Activities

More Practice: Have the students find ten singular nouns in their reading books. Have them list the ten nouns and write their plural forms beside them.

Instructional Variation: Have the students play a spelling game with singular and plural nouns. Divide the class into two teams and have a student from each group go to the chalkboard. Say a singular or plural noun and have the two students at the chalkboard write its opposite form. Continue this procedure until all students from both teams have had an opportunity to go to the chalkboard. The team that gets the most answers correct wins the game.

Using Resources and Materials: Invite a member of the Dairy Council or a local nutritionist to speak to the class about a nutritious, balanced diet. Have the students plan a nutritious breakfast, lunch, or dinner. Refer them to cookbooks, restaurant menus, or the food section of the newspaper for ideas. After the students have planned their meals, have them prepare a menu similar to one found in a restaurant. On a separate piece of paper have the students change singular nouns to plural nouns, and change plural nouns to singular nouns in the menu. Suggest that some students may wish to prepare a special nutritious snack at home and share it with the class.

Lesson **10** (page 12)

Progressive Forms of Nouns

 16

Key Objective The student will be able to:
1. Form the possessive of a singular noun or a plural noun not ending in *s* by adding an apostrophe and an *s* ('s).
2. Form the possessive of a plural noun ending in *s* by adding an apostrophe only (').

Procedures

Write the following words on the chalkboard:

1. toy
2. Jess
3. boys
4. women

Briefly review nouns and their plural forms by asking: What is a noun? How do you form the plural of most nouns? How do you form the plural of a noun that ends in *ch, sh, s, x,* or *z*? How do you form the plural of a noun that ends in *f* or *fe*? How do you form the plural of a noun that ends in *y* with a consonant before it? What other ways do you know to form plurals of nouns? Have the students give examples each time they answer a question.

Read and discuss Key 16 with the students. Be sure they understand what is meant by a *possessive noun*. Then say the following phrases and have the students restate them using possessive words: *the tail of the dog, the horn of the cow, the shirt that belongs to Bill, the brakes of the cars, the hats that belong to the women,* and *hands of the artist*. Ask someone to read word 1 on the chalkboard and change it to the possessive form. Have other students form the possessives of the other words on the chalkboard.

As soon as the students understand directions for the exercises in Lesson 10, let them work independently. After answers have been checked and scores recorded, have the students correct their mistakes.

Supplementary Exercises

Rewrite the following phrases using a possessive word in each. (Score: 6)

1. the tail of the dog (the dog's tail)
2. the tails of the dogs (the dogs' tails)
3. the wings of the birds (the birds' wings)
4. the wool of the sheep (the sheep's wool)
5. the pencil that belongs to Chris (Chris's pencil)
6. hoofs of horses (horses' hoofs)

Supplementary Activities

More Practice: Have the students find five phrases, containing possessive nouns, in their reading books. Have them rewrite each phrase without a possessive word. For example, if someone finds the phrase *the rabbit's tail*, the student should write *the tail of the rabbit*.

Instructional Variation: Write each student's name on an index card and place the cards in a box at a learning center or in a separate area of the classroom. Have the students pick a card from the box and write a sentence that tells something they like or admire about the student whose name they have picked. Have them use a possessive noun in each sentence. You may use the following sentences as examples: "I like Sergio's warm smile." "I think Leah's outfit is very nice." "Robin's helpfulness is appreciated."

Using Resources and Materials: Have the students look through magazines and newspapers for scenes which include people. Then have them cut out only the faces of the people in the pictures and replace them with drawings or photographs of themselves, their family, or their friends. Have the students write a description or news story for their new picture. Suggest that the students use possessive forms of nouns wherever possible.

Lesson 11 (page 13)

Recognizing Pronouns
 17b

Key Objectives The students will be able to:

1. Recognize a pronoun as a word used in place of a noun.
2. Identify the pronouns in given sentences.

Procedures

Read and discuss Key 17b, paying particular attention to the examples so that the students understand the functions of personal pronouns and the need for them. Let the students practice substituting personal pronouns for nouns. After you say each of the following sentences, have several students restate it, using pronouns in place of some of the nouns: *Ann* took *Ann's* book to *Ann's* room. *Bill* ran to get *Bill's* book. The dog ran to *Brenda and Sam. Ann and Sue* went to see a movie, and *Ann and Sue* enjoyed *the movie*.

Be sure the students understand directions for the exercises in Lesson 11 before they work independently. After answers to the exercises have been checked and scores recorded, have the students correct their mistakes.

Assign the activities suggested in Other Things to Do at the bottom of Lesson 11. The object of substituting nouns for pronouns is to impress the students with the importance of clear pronoun references. Help them with this activity to make certain they have substituted the correct noun or nouns for each pronoun. The noun *people* may be substituted for the pronoun *we* in sentences 11, 12, and 17; and *people* or the name of an individual may be substituted for *you* in sentence 24.

Supplementary Exercises

After each sentence list the pronouns used in the sentence. (Score: 12)

1. Did you enjoy *The Covered Bridge* as much as I did? (you, I)
2. I thought that it was a very good book. (I, it)
3. Connie and her friends spent much of their time working. (her, their)
4. They also had many good times. (they)
5. We enjoyed reading about them. (We, them)
6. Peter did his work very well. (his)
7. Sometimes he helped Connie with her work too. (he, her)

Supplementary Activities

More Practice: Have the students choose five sentences from their reading books and list the pronouns used in the sentences. Then, next to the pronouns, have the students write the nouns that the pronouns refer to.

Instructional Variation: Read a story, a poem, or an article to the class and have them raise their hands, clap, or stand up when they hear a pronoun being used.

Using Resources and Materials: Have each student cut out an article from a newspaper or magazine. Then have the students rewrite the article substituting the correct noun for each pronoun used in the article.

Lesson **12** (page 14)

Using *We* and *Us* in Sentences
 18a, c

Key Objectives The student will be able to:
1. Explain when to use the pronoun *we* or *us* in a sentence.
2. Complete a series of sentences by filling in blank spaces with the pronoun *we* or *us*.

Procedures

Broadcasting
What is the child in the picture doing? Have you ever carved an object out of soap? Out of a potato? Out of soft wood? Describe a craft project you enjoy doing.

Explaining the Lesson
Read and discuss Key 18a and c with the students. Then have several students give sentences about an art or craft. Tell them to use *we* or *us* as they are used in the examples in Lesson 12. Use the following sentences as examples: *We* made

ceramic bowls. Miss Blair showed *us* how to model clay.

Help the students understand how to check the proper use of these pronouns. Write the following sentences on the chalkboard:
1. Sam and (we, us) went to the library.
2. The librarian showed craft books to (we, us) children.

Cover *Sam* while the students read sentence 1, and cover *children* while they read sentence 2. Point out that they will not make mistakes in the use of *we* and *us* if they use these pronouns without the nouns that go with them.

Be sure the students understand the directions before they work the exercises in Lesson 12.

Supplementary Exercises

Underline the pronoun in parentheses that properly completes each sentence. (Score: 7)
1. Several of (we, us) enjoy making pottery. (us)
2. (We, Us) use clay to make the pottery. (We)
3. Ms. Teal helped (we, us) plan our designs. (us)
4. She showed (we, us) how to mold the clay. (us)
5. (We, Us) placed our pottery in a kiln. (We)
6. (We, Us) knew how hot the kiln should be. (We)
7. The teacher helped (we, us) take the pottery out of the kiln. (us)

Supplementary Activities

More Practice: Have the students write three sentences using *we* and three sentences using *us*. Give the following sentences as examples: "*We* are studying pronouns." "Sometimes it is hard for *us* to decide which pronoun to use."

Instructional Variation: Write sentences on individual sentence strips, leaving a blank space where the pronoun *we* or *us* should be placed. Give each student two index cards and have them write the pronoun *we* on one card, and the pronoun *us* on the other card. Hold up a sentence strip so the class can read it. Tell the students to hold up the pronoun card which properly completes the sentence. Continue this procedure using the remainder of the sentence strips.

Using Resources and Materials: Have the students think of a craft project or game they enjoy doing. Then have them write directions for making the project or playing the game. Remind them to use the pronouns *we* or *us* wherever possible. Suggest that some students may wish to have the class participate in making their project or learning how to play their game.

Lesson **13** (page 15)

Using Pronouns in Pairs

 18a, b, c

Key Objectives The student will be able to:
1. Explain that the pronoun *I, he, she,* or *they* is used when someone does something.
2. Explain that after such words as *told, give, heard, from, to, for, by,* or *with,* the pronoun *her, him, them,* or *me* is used.
3. Select the pronoun from a pair of pronouns that properly completes the given sentences.

Procedures

Read and discuss the key information and examples in Key 18a, b, and c. Point out that students almost always use these pronouns correctly when they use them singly but that when they use the pronouns in pairs they can make mistakes. Tell them that when they wish to use pronoun pairs they should think of each pronoun alone. Then they are likely to choose the proper forms.

Be sure the students understand the directions before they work the exercises in Lesson 13. After answers to the exercises have been checked and scores recorded, have several students read the sentences aloud, using the pronouns they have underlined.

Before assigning the activity suggested in Other Things to Do, briefly review the rules for plurals of nouns. The students may use nouns other than those listed, but they should use words that form their plurals in the same way.

Supplementary Exercises

Underline the correct pronoun in parentheses that properly completes each of the following sentences. (Score: 14)
1. Sergio showed a picture of Niagara Falls to (he, him) and (she, her). (him, her)
2. (He, Him) and (she, her) saw that the water was colored. (He, she)
3. Sergio told (he, him) and (I, me) that the picture was taken at night. (him, me)
4. Sergio told (they, them) and (I, me) that colored lights are turned on the falls. (them, me)
5. (They, Them) and (I, me) thought that Niagara Falls were beautiful. (They, I)
6. Did Sergio go with (he, him) and (she, her)? (him, her)
7. (They, Them) and (I, me) heard about his boat trip to the falls. (They, I)

Supplementary Activities

More Practice: Have the students write nine sentences using pronouns in pairs. Have them use one of the following words in each sentence: *told, give, heard, from, to, for, by, asked,* and *with.*

Instructional Variation: At a learning center or in a separate part of the classroom, have travel brochures and posters showing other cities and towns. Have the students choose a place they would like to visit. Then have them plan and write a report about the area, writing the report as if they had already made the trip with a friend. Have them discuss the local customs, food, clothing, landmarks, and other interesting facts about the area they have chosen. Remind the students to use pronouns in pairs when writing their report. Have them read and study Key 52a before they write their report.

Using Resources and Materials: Using the lesson mentioned above, have the students select a special food, a piece of clothing, a custom, or a game that is indigenous to the city or country they chose for their report. Then have the students prepare a demonstration and present it to the class. Suggest that some students may wish to prepare one of the foods, wear a costume, or teach a game that comes from the city or country they chose for their report. Remind the students to use pronouns in pairs when making their presentation.

Lesson **14** (page 16)

Using Pronouns After *Is* and *Was*

 18d

Key Objective The student will be able to:
1. Recognize that the pronouns *I, he, she, we,* or *they* are used after the words *it is, it was, is it,* or *was it.*
2. Select the pronoun from a pair of pronouns that properly completes the given sentences.

Procedures

Broadcasting

The plant pictured in Lesson 14 is a pitcher plant. Why do you think it is named "pitcher plant"? Can you think of other plants whose names describe how they look? Name some plants that grow in your neighborhood.

Explaining the Lesson

Begin the lesson with a brief review of pronoun usages that were presented in Lessons 11, 12, and 13. Write the following sentences on the chalkboard:

1. (We, Us) learned about pronouns yesterday.
2. The teacher told (we, us) which pronoun to use.
3. (He and I, Him and me) used the word properly.
4. Did you hear (he and I, him and me)?

Ask one student to explain what a pronoun is and to give examples of pronouns. Then ask another student to go to the chalkboard and draw a line under the pronoun in sentence 1 that properly completes the sentence. Have the student explain how the pronoun was chosen. Follow a similar procedure with the other sentences, reviewing the rules and usages which they represent.

Tell the group that they are ready to learn more about the use of pronouns and direct their attention to Key 18d. After the key information and examples have been read, demonstrate the use of pronouns after *is* or *was*. Tell the students to use *it is* or *it was* and a pronoun to answer each of your questions. Hand a book to someone and ask, Who took the book? The student should answer, It *was I.* Continue to ask such questions as: Who sits near the window? Who is the president of our class? Who was in the fourth grade last year?, until the group understands these pronoun usages.

After these questions and answers, the group should turn to Lesson 14, read the directions, and work the exercises.

NOTE: Some grammarians accept the use of pronouns in the objective case after *is* or *was*, stating that *It is him, It was me,* etc., are often used in informal situations and are therefore acceptable. If you wish to follow this approach, make the following alterations in the procedure suggested above. Explain to the group that in informal situations, such as talking with friends or members of the family, using *It was him,* etc. is acceptable. But in more formal situations, such as writing a class report, or giving an oral presentation, they should use *It was he,* etc. Set up a number of hypothetical situations and help the group decide whether they should use the formal or the informal expression. Then explain to the students that the sentences in the book are formal and instruct them to follow the directions on the page.

Supplementary Exercises

Assign the following exercises to students who need further practice in pronoun usage. Note that the informational subject given in the exercises is a continuation of the subject used in the student's book. After writing on the chalkboard the directions and the exercises given below, tell the students that they can learn more about insect-eating plants by working these exercises.

Draw a line under the pronoun in parentheses that properly completes each sentence. (Score: 7)
1. It was (she, her) who said that several plants

trap insects. (she)
2. Was it (they, them) who said that such plants live in moist places? (they)
3. Bob said it was (he, him) who learned about the sundew plant. (he)
4. But it was (us, we) who knew about the sticky hair on sundew leaves. (we)
5. Wasn't it (they, them) who told that the sticky hair catches flies? (they)
6. It is (we, us) who said the sundew's leaf curls around the insect. (we)
7. Is it (him, he) who wants to find out about Venus's-flytrap? (he)

Supplementary Activities

More Practice: Make up a series of questions similar to those used in the procedures, and have the students answer the questions using *it is* or *it was* and a pronoun. Ask questions such as: Who is wearing blue pants and a white shirt today? Who has a birthday on September 29? Who was the winner of the relay race yesterday? The students should answer the questions by saying *It is* (*was*) *I,* or by pointing to a classmate and saying, *It is* (*was*) *she* or *It is* (*was*) *he.*

Instructional Variation: Organize a game in which the expressions *Is it he, Is it she,* or *Is it they* are used. Have a student volunteer to be "It" and leave the room while the class selects someone to be student X. When "It" returns to the room have a student tell one thing about student X, such as, "Student X has brown hair." "It" points to a person who fits the description and asks, "Is it (he, she)?" That person then answers, "It is I," or "It is not I." If the person is not student X, he or she tells another fact about student X. This procedure continues until student X is identified. The student who gives the information that identifies student X is "It" for the next game.

Using Resources and Materials: Have the students collect pictures, make drawings, and/or write reports about unusual and interesting plants. Suggest that they use the encyclopedia or other resource material to find more information about this subject. Tell the students to write sentences that use pronouns after *is* and *was.* Tell them that they may write sentences similar to those in Lesson 14.

Lesson **15** (page 17)

Using Proper Word Forms
 18, 25, 26, 27

Key Objective The student will be able to properly complete sentences by selecting one of the following pairs of words: *may–can, teach–learn, a–an, they–them, he–him, she–her, we–us, themselves–theirselves, himself–hisself.*

Procedures

Write the following sentences on the chalkboard:
1. Ray attends (a, an) art class.
2. Mrs. Taylor will (teach, learn) him about painting.
3. (May, Can) I take art lessons, Mom?

Review pronoun usage by reading and discussing Key 18. Then study Keys 25 to 27 with the students. Point out that *an* is used before words that begin with all vowel sounds except long *u* and that *a* is used before all other words. Be sure the students are aware of words, such as *honor* and *hour,* that begin with silent consonants. Explain that the proper use of *may, can, teach,* and *learn* depends on the meaning of the sentence. Ask someone to read sentence 1 on the chalkboard and draw a line under the proper word form in parentheses. Have the student explain why the word is underlined. Follow the same procedure with sentences 2 and 3.

As soon as the students understand the directions, let them work independently to complete the exercises in Lesson 15. After answers to the exercises have been checked and scores recorded, let several students read the sentences aloud, tell which words are underlined, and explain why the underlined words are correct.

Supplementary Exercises

Choose the proper word in parentheses to write in the blank. (Score: 8)
1. (May, Can) _____ birthday cards be made with blueprints? (Can)
2. (learn, teach) Aaron will _____ us how to make the cards. (teach)
3. (a, an) He cut _____ unusual design out of paper. (an)
4. (She, Her) _____ and I put the design on blueprint paper. (She)
5. (them, they) Was it _____ who made a print of the design? (they)
6. (May, Can) "_____ I write a verse for the card?" asked John. (May)
7. (him, he) He read the verse to _____ and them. (him)
8. (learn, teach) We were glad to _____ how to make these cards. (learn)

Supplementary Activities

More Practice: Have the students write ten sentences about an art activity they enjoy. Have the students include ten of the word forms reviewed in the lesson.

Instructional Variation: Write all the words being reviewed on the chalkboard. Have the students compose a chain story by telling part of a story and stopping in the middle of a sentence so that the next student will continue the story. Encourage the students to use the words on the chalkboard. The last student in the sequence must end the story.

Using Resources and Materials: Have the students find out about other ways of making simple prints, such as sponge printing and gadget printing. Suggest they get ideas from the art teacher or check out some arts and crafts books from the library. Then have the students prepare a demonstration for the class, explaining their printmaking procedure in sequence. Have the students write the procedures in list form. Tell the students to use several of the word forms mentioned in Lesson 15 when writing their procedures.

Lesson **16** (page 18)

Remembering What We Have Learned

Key Objective   The student will be able to apply the skills taught in Unit I.

Procedures

Have the students open their books to Lesson 16 and read the title of the lesson. Explain that this lesson will help them remember what they learned in Unit I and prepare for the post test that follows. Make sure that everyone understands the directions for the exercises and explain that each person should find the keys and review the information.

Since the exercises are subjective, let several students read their answers aloud. Then direct a discussion of the material being reviewed, covering the following:
1. Recognition of sentences
2. Three kinds of sentences: declarative, interrogative, and exclamatory
3. Recognition of nouns and pronouns
4. Plurals and possessives of nouns
5. Use of capital letters for first words of sentences; sacred names; names of persons, particular places and things, months, and holidays; and words made from the names of places
6. Use of periods after declarative sentences, abbreviations, and initials
7. Question marks after interrogative sentences
8. Exclamation points after exclamatory sentences

9. Proper use of *I* and *me*, *we* and *us*, *he* and *him*, *she* and *her*, *they* and *them*, *a* and *an*, *may* and *can*, and *teach* and *learn*

Post Test—Unit I

At the conclusion of Unit I, administer the post test for this unit. Post tests for all units are at the back of the Teacher's Edition. The results of the post test should indicate which students have mastered the concepts and skills in the unit. Instructions for administration of post tests appear in the introduction to the Teacher's Edition.

Pretest—Unit II

Before beginning Unit II, administer the pretest for this unit. Pretests for all units are at the back of the Teacher's Edition. The results should indicate the students' preliminary competency levels for concepts and skills presented in the unit. Instructions for administration and ways to use the pretests appear in the introduction to the Teacher's Edition.

Lesson 17 (page 19)

Writing Sentences
 Key 41

Key Objectives The student will be able to:
1. Write effective declarative sentences, interrogative sentences, and exclamatory sentences.
2. Capitalize first words of sentences and place correct punctuation marks at the ends of sentences.

Procedures

On the chalkboard write the following sentences without capital letters or end punctuation.

have you read about the world's first great library at alexandria, egypt this library contained thousands of manuscripts from many countries what priceless volumes were lost when the library was destroyed

Have several students place capital letters and punctuation marks where they are needed in the sentences on the chalkboard. Ask the students to identify the kinds of sentences written. Have them review Key 41 to see whether their identification was correct.

Have the students turn to Lesson 17. Read the information and examples with them. Let the students suggest logical answers to the example sentences. Help them see that the second sentence is a statement and the first two questions do not really ask for the information wanted; only the last

question would be effective in gaining the desired information. Use these examples to illustrate the importance of knowing what you want to say and then saying it effectively.

Be sure the students understand the directions for the exercises. Then let them work independently.

After you have checked the exercises and students have recorded their scores, have several students read their sentences aloud. Have a class discussion of ways in which each sentence might be made more effective.

Supplementary Exercises

Have the students write effective sentences for the following three topics: (Score: 15)
1. You need to write the Chamber of Commerce in your state's capital to ask for information about historical monuments in your state. Write a sentence that asks for the information you need. (Score: 5)
2. A friend is planning to visit you at your home after school. Write a sentence that gives the directions from school to your home. (Score: 5)
3. You are sleeping very soundly when a loud noise suddenly awakens you. Write a sentence that expresses your feelings. (Score: 5)

Supplementary Activities

Instructional Variation: Have each student write a question on an index card that asks for information about something the class has studied in social studies or science. Put the cards in a box and have each student pull out a card. Then have the students write a sentence that answers the question on the card. Repeat this procedure five times. You may wish to vary the setting by placing the box in a learning center or another part of the classroom and letting the students do this as an independent activity.

Using Resources and Materials: Have each student cut out three advertisements that begin with a sentence in headline-size type. Display the ads and ask the class to decide which sentences are most effective. Which sentences make you stop and read the ad?

Lesson 18 (page 20)

Recognizing Sentences in Paragraphs
 Key 41a, b, c, d

Key Objectives The student will be able to:
1. Recognize sentences in paragraphs.

2. Indicate that the first word of a sentence should be capitalized.
3. Place correct punctuation marks at the ends of sentences.

Procedures

Broadcasting

What is the person pictured in Lesson 18 doing? When do you think this picture took place? Paul Revere was a silversmith. Why do you think he became involved in the Revolutionary War?

Explaining the Lesson

Review important points about sentences by asking the following questions: What is a sentence? Why do we use sentences when we speak and write? What kind of sentence would you use to tell that you had been to a movie? What kind of sentence would you use to find out if your friend saw the movie? What kind of sentence would you use to show a sudden or strong feeling, such as excitement or anger? Have several students go to the chalkboard and write examples of declarative, interrogative, and exclamatory sentences. Be sure they use capital letters and punctuation marks correctly.

After the students have studied Key 41a, b, c, d, read the directions for Lesson 18 with them. Caution them to use capital letters and punctuation marks so that each group of words makes a sentence. Have them work independently. As soon as answers have been checked and scores recorded, have several students read the paragraphs aloud, indicating by expression and voice inflection how they have separated and punctuated the sentences. Point out that the purpose of writing is to communicate and that capital letters and punctuation marks are important in making the meaning clear.

To give further practice in recognizing pronouns and determining pronoun references, assign the activity suggested in Other Things to Do.

Supplementary Exercises

Rewrite the following paragraphs, using capital letters and punctuation marks where they are needed. There should be four sentences in each paragraph. (Score: 16—1 for each capital letter and 1 for each punctuation mark)

didn't Helen and Scott go to a museum they saw many things that Paul Revere had made there was a beautiful silver teapot that they liked there were also some silver cups

they also saw an old church tower in Boston it was the tower where Paul Revere's friend had hung a lamp when Paul Revere saw the lamp, he knew that the British army was coming he rode swiftly to tell other Americans to be ready to fight

(Didn't Helen and Scott go to a museum? They saw many things that Paul Revere had made. There was a beautiful silver teapot that they liked. There were also some silver cups.

They also saw an old church tower in Boston. It was the tower where Paul Revere's friend had hung a lamp. When Paul Revere saw the lamp, he knew that the British army was coming. He rode swiftly to tell other Americans to be ready to fight.)

Supplementary Activities

More Practice: Rewrite a paragraph from a reading book, leaving out punctuation marks and not capitalizing letters. Have the students rewrite the paragraph adding the correct punctuation marks and capitalizing the first words of sentences. Have the students check their work by finding the correctly written paragraph in their reading books.

Instructional Variation: Have the students make up verbal signals for the period, the question mark, and the exclamation point. The signals may be nonsense words or just funny sounds. Have them also make up a physical signal, such as standing up or raising their hands, for the first word of a sentence that starts with a capital letter. Then have several students read short paragraphs from their reading books, doing the signal for capitalizing the first word of a sentence and using one of the punctuation mark sounds after every sentence.

Using Resources and Materials: Have the students read the poem "Paul Revere's Ride," by Longfellow. Have them tell the story in their own words by writing a paragraph or by giving an oral presentation. If they write a paragraph, remind them to punctuate the paragraph correctly and capitalize the first words of sentences. If they choose to tell the story orally have them read and study Key 52b before giving their presentation.

Lesson **19** (page 21)

Recognizing Parts of Sentences
🔑 14, 17, 18, 19

Key Objectives The student will be able to:
1. Identify the complete subject of given sentences.
2. Identify the complete predicate of given sentences.

Procedures

Broadcasting

What is the name of the animal pictured in Lesson 19? The octopus is related to the squid. How are the squid and the octopus the same? How are they different?

Explaining the Lesson

Write the following sentences on the chalkboard:
1. The squid swam.
2. It is a good swimmer.
3. It can swim long distances.
4. It swims many miles every day.

Read and discuss Keys 14 and 17 to 19 with the students. Remind them that every simple sentence has two parts: the complete subject tells who or what the sentence is about; the complete predicate tells something about what that person, place, or thing is, does, or has done to it. Explain that a thought is not complete unless it has these two parts. Ask someone to read sentence 1 on the chalkboard. Ask the student what the complete subject of the sentence is. Then have the student look at the rest of the sentence to see whether it tells who or what the squid is, what it does, or what is done to it. Show the students that both parts of this sentence are necessary to make a complete thought. Follow a similar procedure with the other sentences, showing that each part of the sentence may contain several words.

After the students have worked the exercises in Lesson 19, checked their answers, and recorded their scores, have several students read the sentences aloud and tell the parts of each.

Supplementary Exercises

Draw one line under the complete subject of the sentence. Draw two lines under the complete predicate. (Score: 12)

1. The octopus lives in the ocean. (The octopus lives in the ocean.)
2. Its body is usually small. (Its body is usually small.)
3. The squid has ten arms. (The squid has ten arms.)
4. The octopus has only eight arms. (The octopus has only eight arms.)
5. They often hide in underwater caves. (They often hide in underwater caves.)
6. An octopus may try to bury itself in sand. (An octopus may try to bury itself in sand.)

Supplementary Activities

More Practice: Have each student write five sentences about a subject that interests them, and then exchange their sentences with a classmate. Next have the students draw one line under the complete subjects of their classmate's sentences and two lines under the complete predicates in the sentences. Return the sentences to the students who wrote them, and have them check the work.

Instructional Variation: Have the students write sentences on long strips of paper. Then have them cut the strips in two, so that one part tells what the sentence is about and the other part tells what that person or thing does. Have the pupils make new sentences by combining the complete subjects and complete predicates.

Using Resources and Materials: Have students use the encyclopedia and other resource materials to find information on how sea animals and fish protect themselves from their enemies. Have them write a report or draw a picture with captions on the information they obtain.

Make arrangements for the class to visit an aquarium. After the visit, have each student write a report on the exhibit that interested them the most. Have the students read and study Key 52a before writing their reports. Tell the students to draw one line under the complete subject and two lines under the complete predicate of each sentence in their reports.

Lesson **20** (page 22)

Recognizing Verbs
 19

Key Objectives   The student will be able to:
1. Explain that a verb is a word that shows action, being, or state of being.
2. Identify verbs in sentences.

Procedures

Broadcasting

The instrument pictured near the top of Lesson 20 is a harpsichord. What other instrument does it look like? Name other instruments besides a piano that have a keyboard. Describe the kind of music you enjoy listening to. What instruments are used to perform your favorite music?

Explaining the Lesson

Read and discuss Key 19 with the students paying particular attention to the examples. Then ask a student to name a verb of action. Have the student combine the verb with a noun or a pronoun to make a sentence. Of course, other words may be used to modify the noun or pronoun and the verb in order to make the sentence complete. Have other students name verbs, including verbs of action, being, and state of being, and make sentences with them.

Be sure the students understand directions for the exercises in Lesson 20 before they work independently. After answers to the exercises have been checked and scores recorded, have everyone correct their mistakes. Next, have several students read the sentences aloud, name the verbs, and explain who or what each verb tells about. For example, in sentence 1 a student should name *singing* and *dancing*; then explain that it is *people* who sing and dance.

Supplementary Exercises

After each sentence below write any verbs that are used in the sentence. (Score: 9)
1. The Virginia reel is the name of a dance. (is)
2. People first danced the Virginia reel many years ago. (danced)
3. Do you know the song "My Old Kentucky Home?" (know)
4. Stephen Foster wrote this song after he traveled in the South. (wrote, traveled)
5. "Casey Jones" is a favorite American folk song. (is)
6. It tells a story about a railroad engineer. (tells)
7. People sometimes sang this song as they built railroads. (sang, built)

Supplementary Activities

More Practice: Have the students choose five sentences from their reading book and write them on a separate piece of paper. Have the students draw one line under the noun or pronoun in each sentence and two lines under each verb.

Instructional Variation: Form two teams and give each team a list of verbs to pantomime. Have the students on each team take turns pantomiming the verbs until members of the other team guess the answer. Continue until all students have a chance to pantomime a verb.

Using Resources and Materials: Have the students use the encyclopedia or other resource material to get more information about early American music. Have some students listen to American folk songs and tell the stories in their own words. Try to get musical recordings of early American music and have the students compare them to the current music they enjoy.

Have the students write the lyrics of their favorite songs on a separate piece of paper. Tell them to draw one line under the noun and two lines under the verb in each sentence of the song.

Have a caller from a local square dance club visit the class and teach the students some of the early American dances such as the Virginia reel.

Lesson **21** (page 23)

Principal Parts of Verbs
21

Key Objectives The student will be able to:
1. Explain that verbs have three principal parts.
2. Write the principal parts of given verbs.
3. Select the principal part of a verb that properly completes a sentence.

Procedures

Write the following sentences on the chalkboard:
1. I do my work in school.
2. I did my work yesterday.
3. I have done my work every day this week.

Briefly review verbs by asking the students to explain what verbs are. Have several students name verbs of action, being, and state of being. Then read and discuss Key 21 with the students. Explain that knowing the principal parts of verbs helps us use them properly. Direct the students' attention to the sentences on the chalkboard. Ask someone to read the sentences aloud and name the verb in each. Point out that these sentences show the use of the three principal parts of the verb *do*.

Be sure the students understand the directions for the exercises in Lesson 21 before they work independently. After answers have been checked and scores recorded, have everyone correct their mistakes.

NOTE: If you wish to teach the names of the principal parts of verbs, have the children write *present* above the first column in Part I, *past* above the second column, and *past participle* above the third column.

Supplementary Exercises

Choose the proper verb form in parentheses to write in each blank space. (Score: 6)
1. (came, come) The soldiers at Valley Forge were glad when spring _____. (came)
2. (saw, seen) They were happy when they _____ the snow melt. (saw)
3. (ate, eaten) All winter they _____ very little food. (ate)
4. (gave, given) But they knew Washington had _____ them all the food he had. (given)
5. (saw, seen) All winter the soldiers had _____ the British soldiers in Philadelphia. (seen)

6. (ate, eaten) The British soldiers had _____ well during the winter. (eaten)

Supplementary Activities

More Practice: Have the students write the principal parts of the following verbs, and write sentences using each of the words: *eat, write, run, come, go.*

Instructional Variation: Read sentences to the class. Have students volunteer to repeat the sentence using a different principal part of the verb used in the sentence.

Using Resources and Materials: Have the students use the encyclopedia or their social studies books to get more information about the Continental Army's experiences at Valley Forge in 1777. Suggest that some of the students write and perform a skit depicting the hardships the soldiers experienced. Some students may wish to pretend they are news reporters and write or give a report on how the soldiers spent the winter at Valley Forge in 1777. Tell the students to use the three principal parts of the same verb in their reports.

Lesson **22** (page 24)

Using Proper Verb Forms
 21

Key Objective The student will be able to complete sentences by selecting the proper form of the verbs *drink* or *write.*

Procedures

Write the following sentences on the chalkboard:
1. Who _____ my lemonade?
2. Have you _____ your report?

Review principal parts of verbs by reading and discussing Key 21. Have the students find the principal parts of *drink* and *write.* Ask someone to read sentence 1 on the chalkboard and supply the principal part of *drink* that properly completes the sentence. Have the student explain why the principal part was chosen. Let another student fill the blank in sentence 2 with the principal part of *write* that properly completes the sentence. Have the student explain why the principal part was chosen.

Be sure the students understand directions for the exercises in Lesson 22 before they work independently. After answers have been checked and

scores recorded, have the students correct their mistakes.

Supplementary Exercises

Choose the word form in parentheses that properly completes each sentence and write it in the blank. (Score: 8)
1. (wrote, written) Steven _____ a report about the city's water. (wrote)
2. (drank, drunk) He knew that the water people _____ was pure. (drank)
3. (drank, drunk) The water was purified before people _____ it. (drank)
4. (wrote, written) Steven has _____ about ways that water is made clean. (written)
5. (drank, drunk) People often have _____ boiled water. (drunk)
6. (wrote, written) Steven _____ that boiled water is safe to drink. (wrote)
7. (drank, drunk) Some cities add chemicals to water before it is _____. (drunk)
8. (wrote, written) Steven _____ that chemicals kill germs in the water. (wrote)

Supplementary Activities

More Practice: Have the students write their own sentences using the three principal parts of the verb *drink* and the three principal parts of the verb *write.*

Instructional Variation: Give each student six index cards and have them write the principal parts of the verbs *drink* and *write* on each card. Read sentences which use the principal parts of those verbs, but omit the verb when reading the sentences. Have the students hold up the word card which is the proper verb form to complete each sentence.

Using Resources and Materials: Arrange for the class to visit the local water plant to observe how the city's water supply is purified for drinking. After the trip, have the students write reports based on their observations. Tell the students to use the principal parts of the verbs *drink* and *write* in their reports.

Lesson **23** (page 25)

Using *Is, Are, Was,* and *Were*
 20a, b

Key Objective The student will be able to select the proper verb forms, *is* or *are* and *was* or *were,* to complete sentences.

Procedures

Broadcasting

The girls pictured in Lesson 23 are doing an experiment with air. Are you heavier or lighter than air? Can anyone name some things that are lighter than air? What kind of weather makes air feel heavy?

Explaining the Lesson

Write the following sentences on the chalkboard:
1. The _____ is ripe.
2. The _____ are ripe.
3. The _____ was hungry.
4. The _____ were hungry.

Ask a student to explain the difference between a singular noun and a plural noun. Tell the class that verbs also are singular and plural and that singular verbs must be used with singular nouns or pronouns while plural verbs must be used with plural nouns or pronouns.

Read and discuss Key 20a, b with the students to clarify agreement of subjects and verbs. Then ask someone to read sentence 1 on the chalkboard and to fill the blank with the singular or plural form of *apple*. Have the student explain the choice of using the singular noun or the plural noun. Let other students fill the blank in sentence 2 with the singular or plural form of *apple* and the blanks in sentences 3 and 4 with *child* or *children*.

As soon as the students understand the directions for the exercises in Lesson 23, let them work independently. Make sure that everyone corrects their mistakes after the answers to the exercises have been checked and scores recorded.

Supplementary Exercises

Choose the word form in parentheses that properly completes each sentence and write it in each blank space. (Score: 7)
1. (was, were) Jeannie and Pat _____ amazed when they saw the can. (were)
2. (is, are) They _____ eager to do the experiment again. (are)
3. (Is, Are) _____ there water in the can? (Is)
4. (was, were) The can _____ placed on the stove. (was)
5. (was, were) The stopper on the can _____ loose. (was)
6. (was, were) They _____ surprised to see what happened. (were)
7. (was, were) The stopper of the can _____ suddenly pushed out. (was)

Supplementary Activities

More Practice: Have the students write their own sentences using the words *is, are, was* and *were.*

Instructional Variation: Write the words *is, are, was* and *were* on four index cards, put them in envelopes and pass them out to four students. Write four sentences on the chalkboard or on sentence strips and leave a blank space where the words *is, are, was,* and *were* should be written. Give a signal for the four students to look at their word cards and stand next to the sentence that is completed by the word on their card. Have the class check the students' answers. Repeat this procedure, writing new sentences and giving the word cards to other students.

Using Resources and Materials: Arrange to have the experiment discussed in Lesson 23 demonstrated in class. Have the science teacher visit the class and discuss the principles of air pressure with the students. Have the students write about the experiment using their own words. Tell the students to include the words *is, are, was,* and *were* when they write about the experiment.

Lesson **24** (page 26)

Using Proper Verb Forms

 20, 30

Key Objective The student will be able to complete sentences by selecting the proper verb forms, *has* or *have, hasn't* or *haven't,* and *doesn't* or *don't.*

Procedures

Read and discuss Keys 20a, b and 30 with the students. Ask several students to give sentences, using *doesn't, don't, has, hasn't, have,* and *haven't.* Have them tell whether the noun or pronoun they tell about in each sentence is singular or plural. Then have them tell whether the verb is singular or plural.

Be sure the students understand the directions before they work the exercises and that they correct their mistakes after answers have been checked and scores recorded.

Supplementary Exercises

Choose the proper verb form in parentheses to write in the blank space. (Score: 7)
1. (has, have) Perhaps you _____ heard about Benjamin Franklin's experiments. (have)
2. (doesn't, don't) Amos _____ enjoy Ben's experiments. (doesn't)
3. (has, have) Don't Amos and Ben _____ a kite? (have)

4. (Hasn't, Haven't) _____ Ben tied a key to the kite? (Hasn't)
5. (has, have) Then Amos _____ a ride on the kite. (has)
6. (doesn't, don't) But Amos _____ enjoy the ride. (doesn't)
7. (has, have) Lightning _____ almost hit the kite. (has)

Supplementary Activities

More Practice: Have the students write their own sentences using the verb forms *has, have, hasn't, haven't, doesn't,* or *don't.*

Instructional Variation: Using the same procedure mentioned in instructional variation for Lesson 23, write the words *has, have, hasn't, haven't, doesn't,* and *don't* on six individual index cards, put them in an envelope, and hand them out to six students. Write six sentences using each of the words mentioned above but omit the words when writing the sentences on the chalkboard or on sentence strips. Give a signal and have the six students look at their cards and stand next to the sentence which is completed by the word on their card. Repeat this procedure by writing new sentences and allowing other students to have the word cards.

Using Resources and Materials: Have the students use an encyclopedia or other resource material to find more information about Benjamin Franklin's accomplishments and inventions. Have the students choose an incident from Franklin's life and write a story as if they were with Franklin when the incident took place. Suggest to the students that they read and study Key 47 before they plan and write their stories. Tell them to use the verb forms *has, have, hasn't, haven't, doesn't,* and *don't* in their stories.

Lesson 25 (page 27)

Expressions to Be Avoided
 33

Key Objective The student will be able to complete sentences by selecting the proper word form.

Procedures

Write the following sentences on the chalkboard:
1. Jack might of drawn them pictures.
2. Jack might have drawn those pictures.

Have the students read the sentences on the chalkboard. Let someone tell which is the better sentence. Read Key 33 with the students being careful to stress that the first expression is better to

use than the second expression. Tell the students to read carefully each sentence in Lesson 25 before they underline the proper word in parentheses.

After answers to the exercises have been checked, scores recorded, and mistakes corrected, let several students read the sentences aloud, using the proper word form in parentheses.

For practice in using the principal parts of *eat, come, see,* and *do,* assign the activity suggested in Other Things to Do at the bottom of Lesson 25.

Supplementary Exercises
Choose the proper word form in parentheses to write in the blank space. (Score: 6)
1. (knowed, knew) Daniel Boone _____ how to live in the wilderness. (knew)
2. (drawn, drawed) He was _____ to the new lands in the West. (drawn)
3. (grew, growed) After he _____ up, he went to live in Kentucky. (grew)
4. (Isn't, Ain't) _____ it true that he lived there by himself? (Isn't)
5. (bought, buyed) There were no stores where he could have _____ food. (bought)
6. (of, have) You may _____ read some stories about Daniel Boone. (have)

Supplementary Activities

More Practice: Have the students write a list of expressions to be avoided. Each time one of the expressions is used by the students, have them write it on their lists with the preferred expression beside it. Encourage the students to observe their speech and correct their mistakes. Suggest that they check their lists once a week to determine whether or not they have eliminated poor expressions from their speech.

Instructional Variation: Read a story to the class, or dictate a tape for the listening center. Have the students indicate they have heard an expression to be avoided by raising their hand or standing up and telling the preferred expression. If they are listening to a tape, have them write the preferred expression on a separate piece of paper.

Using Resources and Materials: Have students use the encyclopedia or other resource material from the library to find more information about Kentucky. Have them make a list or write a report on significant dates, events, and places in Kentucky. Suggest that some students draw a replica of Kentucky's state flag or make a travel poster for the state. Tell the students to write their reports carefully using clear and effective expressions.

Lesson **26** (page 28)

Writing Quotations
 6, 7h, 8b, 9b, 10f, 42

Key Objectives The student will be able to:
1. Place quotation marks around the exact words of a speaker.
2. Punctuate sentences by supplying commas, question marks, and exclamation points where needed.
3. Identify words in sentences that should begin with a capital letter.

Procedures

Broadcasting
What sport is pictured in Lesson 26? Describe the skills you need to learn to ski. What kind of equipment do you need? Describe the skills you need to have to learn another sport.

Explaining the Lesson
Read and discuss Keys 6, 7h, 8b, 9b, 10f, and 42 with the students. Be sure they understand that a direct quotation is the exact words of a speaker. Give practice in distinguishing between direct and indirect quotations by reading the following sentences and letting the students tell whether they are direct or indirect quotations:
1. Larry said, ''I am sorry.''
2. Larry said that he is sorry.
3. ''Are you going to the library?'' asked Ann.
4. Ann asked whether you are going to the library.
5. Bob said, ''Mary likes to play bingo.''
6. Bob said that Mary likes to play bingo.
7. John asked, ''Bill, will you go to the show with me?''
8. John asked Bill to go to the show with him.

Be sure the students understand the directions before they work the exercises on page 28. After answers to the exercises have been checked and scores recorded, have the students correct their mistakes.

Supplementary Exercises
Rewrite the sentences below, using punctuation marks and capital letters where they are needed. (Score: 31)
1. What a beautiful thing I saw in Vermont said Tony. (''What a beautiful thing I saw in Vermont!'' said Tony.)
2. Many people went to the top of a mountain she explained. (''Many people went to the top of a mountain,'' she explained.)
3. Tony added, it was a cold, dark night. (Tony added, ''It was a cold, dark night.'')
4. each person had a blazing torch, Tony explained. (''Each person had a blazing torch,'' Tony explained.)
5. one by one they skied down the mountain, she added. (''One by one they skied down the mountain,'' she added.)
6. Tony said soon there were bright, moving lights all over the mountain. (Tony said, ''Soon there were bright, moving lights all over the mountain.'')
7. Could you see the people on skis Carol asked. (''Could you see the people on skis?'' Carol asked.)
8. No, only the torches could be seen Tony replied. (''No, only the torches could be seen,'' Tony replied.)
9. She exclaimed how quickly the torches moved (She exclaimed, ''How quickly the torches moved!'')

Supplementary Activities

More Practice: Have the students find examples of direct and indirect quotations in their reading books. Let several students read the sentences aloud and tell how the sentences are punctuated. Have the students note that a new paragraph is begun for each new speaker.

Instructional Variation: Have two students plan a skit portraying an exciting moment of a sporting event. Have them plan a brief dialogue for the skit. Then have the other students in the class write the skit after they have watched it. Tell them to write the direct quotations as they remember them. Remind them to begin a new paragraph each time a different speaker's words are quoted directly.

Using Resources and Materials: Have students clip interviews from newspapers or magazines and underline each direct quotation in the interview. Next, have the students rewrite the interview changing direct quotations to indirect quotations. Explain that rewording will be necessary.

Lesson **27** (page 29)

Using Punctuation Marks
 7a, c, h, 8, 9, 10

Key Objectives The student will be able to:
1. Place a comma between the day of the month and the year, and a comma between the year and the remainder of the sentence.

2. Use a comma to separate the names of a city and a state when they are written in a sentence.
3. Place a comma between the name of the state and the remainder of the sentence when the city and state are written in a sentence.
4. Place punctuation marks after titles of courtesy.
5. Place correct punctuation marks at the end of sentences.

Procedures

Briefly review direct and indirect quotations by asking the following questions: What is a direct quotation? Can you give an example of one? What is an indirect quotation? Can you give an example of one? How do you punctuate direct quotations? Do you use quotation marks around indirect quotations?

Read and discuss Keys 7a, c, h, and 8, 9, and 10 with the students, clarifying any questions they have. Make sure that everyone understands directions for the exercises in Lesson 27. Then let the students work independently.

After the students have completed the exercises, ask someone to read sentence 1, tell what punctuation marks were used, and explain the use of each mark of punctuation. Call on others to follow the same procedure with the other sentences. Then have the students correct their mistakes.

Assign the activity suggested in Other Things to Do at the bottom of Lesson 27.

Supplementary Exercises

Rewrite the following sentences, placing punctuation marks where they are needed. (Score: 31)
1. Ira did you know that each state has a different flag asked Carol. ("Ira, did you know that each state has a different flag?" asked Carol.)
2. Yes many of the flags are very interesting replied Ira. ("Yes, many of the flags are very interesting," replied Ira.)
3. He asked Does the Texas California or New York flag have a bear on it. (He asked, "Does the Texas, California, or New York flag have a bear on it?")
4. I believe that is the California flag Ira said Carol. ("I believe that is the California flag, Ira," said Carol.)
5. The Texas flag is red white and blue said Ira. ("The Texas flag is red, white, and blue," said Ira.)
6. Wasn't December 29 1845 the date when Texas became a state asked Ira. ("Wasn't December 29, 1845, the date when Texas became a state?" asked Ira.)
7. I saw the Texas flag when I visited in Austin Texas he said. ("I saw the Texas flag when I visited in Austin, Texas," he said.)

Supplementary Activities

More Practice: On sentence strips have each student write the sentence, "I was born on (month) (day), (year), in (city), (state)." Rewrite the sentences on the chalkboard leaving out the punctuation marks. Have a student go to the chalkboard to fill in the missing punctuation marks. If the students know the day of the week they were born, have them include that information in their sentences. For variety, you may wish to start the names of the month, city, or state with a lowercase letter when rewriting the sentence on the chalkboard. Then have the students capitalize those words as well as adding the correct punctuation marks.

Instructional Variation: Hold a quiz show called "Great Events." Have each student write a sentence giving the date and the place of a familiar historical event; for example, "On October 12, 1492, Columbus landed in America." Give the students time to look up the exact dates and places. Put all the answers in a pile. Choose one student to be the emcee. Have the emcee select an answer, write the date and place on the chalkboard, and ask the class to guess the event. Repeat this procedure, giving other students an opportunity to be the emcee.

Using Resources and Materials: Have the students use the encyclopedia or other resource material to find pictures of early American flags or flags from different states. Have the students draw replicas of the flag. Have the students label the early American flags with the dates they were made, and have them label the state flags with the date the state was admitted to the Union. Remind the students to place commas correctly when writing the dates.

Lesson **28** (page 30)

Using Capital Letters
 1, 2, 5

Key Objective   The student will be able to identify words in sentences that should begin with capital letters.

Procedures

Broadcasting

What is the woman pictured in Lesson 28 doing? Explain some of the differences between making cloth in colonial times and making cloth today.

Look at labels on clothing. What kinds of material are clothes made of today?

Explaining the Lesson

Read and discuss Keys 1, 2, and 5 with the students, clarifying any questions they have. Make sure they understand the directions for the exercises in Lesson 28. Then let them work independently.

After the students have completed the exercises, checked their answers, and recorded their scores, ask someone to read sentence 1, telling which words were capitalized, and why. Have several students follow the same procedure with the other sentences. Then have the students correct their mistakes.

Assign the activity suggested in Other Things to Do at the bottom of Lesson 28.

Supplementary Exercises

Rewrite the sentences below, using capital letters where they are needed. (Score: 24)

1. mr. j. f. boat told maggie and me about rayon. (Mr. J. F. Boat told Maggie and me about rayon.)
2. rayon looks very much like silk. (Rayon looks very much like silk.)
3. people in europe, america, and asia had tried to make silk. (People in Europe, America, and Asia had tried to make silk.)
4. a french man named chardonnet made artificial silk. (A French man named Chardonnet made artificial silk.)
5. one saturday last june i saw a rayon factory. (One Saturday last June I saw a rayon factory.)
6. The factory had been built on the housatonic river. (The factory had been built on the Housatonic River.)
7. cotton was brought from mississippi and georgia. (Cotton was brought from Mississippi and Georgia.)
8. The rayon made from cotton and wool was sold in america and europe. (The rayon made from cotton and wool was sold in America and Europe.)

Supplementary Activities

More Practice: Copy two paragraphs from a reading book, newspaper, or magazine changing capital letters to lowercase letters. Reproduce the paragraphs for each student or copy the paragraphs onto the chalkboard and have the students indicate which words should begin with capital letters.

Using Resources and Materials: Let students bring samples of several kinds of cloth and give reports about the source of each fabric and its manufacture. Remind the students to study Key 52a before making their reports. Tell the students to check their reports for correct capitalization.

Lesson **29** (page 31)

Using Contractions

 11a, 22

Key Objectives   The student will be able to:

1. Write contractions of given words.
2. Complete sentences by writing contractions of given words.

Procedures

Write the following sentences on the chalkboard:
1. Did not the team play baseball today?
2. Didn't the team play baseball today?

Have someone read the two sentences aloud. Then ask: Do the two sentences say the same thing? What is the difference between them? Which one sounds more natural? After these questions have been answered, read and discuss Keys 11 and 22 with the students. To demonstrate the fact that the apostrophe stands for the omitted letters, write *are not* on the chalkboard. Below these words write *arenot*; then erase the *o* and insert an apostrophe. Remind the students not to use this procedure in writing a contraction.

After the students have worked the exercises in Lesson 29, checked their answers, and recorded their scores, have someone read the sentences, substituting the words in parentheses, using the contractions in the blanks. Be sure that the listeners note the more natural quality of the second reading.

Supplementary Exercises

Following each sentence below, write the contraction formed from the underlined words. (Score: 8)

1. I have enjoyed reading "The Big Tree." (I've)
2. It is a story that covers many centuries. (It's)
3. Sometimes it seems that the tree will not live. (won't)
4. Did not a great fire almost destroy the tree? (Didn't)
5. Yes, that is one thing that happened to it. (that's)
6. Perhaps you have seen a copy of "Giant Tree." (you've)
7. You will enjoy the beautiful pictures in the book. (You'll)

8. <u>Is not</u> the book written by Mary and Conrad <u>Buff</u>? (Isn't)

Supplementary Activities

More Practice: Have the students read several pages in their reading books, newspaper or magazine articles and make a list of the contractions.

Instructional Variation: Make a gameboard or use the gameboard of an existing game in which the players move markers on squares from start to finish. Write on game cards two words that can be made into contractions. Players may move from square to square when they pick a card and write the correct contraction of the two words.

Using Resources and Materials: Have students use the encyclopedia or other resources to find information about sequoia trees. Have the students draw pictures that contrast the height differences of various sized buildings and the height of a giant sequoia. For example, they might draw a picture of a skyscraper standing next to a giant sequoia to show how small the skyscraper would look. Have the students write sentences which describe their pictures. Tell the students to use contractions in their sentences.

Lesson **30** (page 32)

Using *Sit* and *Set*, *Lie* and *Lay*
 21, 28, 29

Key Objectives   The student will be able to:
1. Explain that the verb *sit* means to be seated and the verb *set* means to place or put something.
2. Explain that the verb *lie* means to rest or recline, and the verb *lay* means to place or put something.
3. Complete sentences by selecting the proper verb forms, *sit* or *set*, *sat* or *set*, *lie* or *lay*, *lay* or *laid*, *lain* or *laid*.

Procedure

Write the following sentences on the chalkboard:
1. Please _____ in that chair.
2. Will you _____ the box on the table?
3. I want to _____ on the bed.
4. They will _____ the board on the ground.

Read and discuss Keys 21, 28, and 29 with the students. Point out the meanings of *sit, set, lie,* and *lay* and be sure the children know the three principal parts of each word. Ask a student to read sentence 1 on the chalkboard, fill in the blank space with *sit* or *set,* and explain the choice. Let other

students fill in the blank space in sentence 2 with *sit* or *set* and in sentences 3 and 4 with *lie* or *lay*.

Be sure the students understand the directions before they work the exercises in Lesson 30. After answers to the exercises have been checked, scores recorded, and mistakes corrected, have several students read the sentences aloud so that the class can listen to these words and develop a feeling of naturalness in using them properly.

Supplementary Exercises
Choose the proper word in parentheses to write in each blank. (Score: 10)
1. (sat, set) King Midas _____ and counted his gold. (sat)
2. (laid, lay) At night King Midas _____ on a comfortable bed. (lay)
3. (sit, sat) One day the king _____ and wished for the golden touch. (sat)
4. (set, sit) Soon it was time to _____ down and eat. (sit)
5. (set, sat) The food was _____ on the table before him. (set)
6. (set, sat) When the king _____ down, the food turned to gold. (sat)
7. (laid, lain) That night he had _____ down on his bed. (lain)
8. (laid, lay) But the bed turned to gold when he _____ on it. (lay)
9. (set, sat) When his daughter _____ by him, she turned to gold. (sat)
10. (sit, sat) When the golden touch was gone, King Midas _____ happily in his chair. (sat)

Supplementary Activities

More Practice: Have the students write seven sentences using the verb forms, *sit, sat, set, lay, lie, laid,* and *lain.* Have the students review Keys 28 and 29 before writing their sentences.

Instructional Variation: Play a game to complete sentences with the words, *sit, sat, set, lay, lie, laid,* and *lain.* Make two sets of seven word cards using the words mentioned above. Divide the class into two teams and give each team a set of cards. Write two sentences on sentence strips or on the chalkboard that use the words, *sit, sat, set, lie, lay, laid,* and *lain,* but omit the words when writing the sentences. Give a signal and have each team send a representative with the word card that properly completes one of the sentences. Score one point for each team that properly completes their sentence, and one point for the team that completes their sentence first. Repeat this procedure until all members of both teams have had an opportunity to complete a sentence.

Using Resources and Materials: Have the students visit the library to find pictures of early American quilts and modern day quilts. Have them find information about quilt making in pioneer America, and how quilts are made today. Suggest that each student bring a square of cloth to school and participate in making a class quilt that can be displayed in the classroom. Have the students write sentences about quilts or quilt making. Tell the students to use the verb forms, *sit, sat, set, lay, lie, laid,* and *lain* in their sentences.

Lesson **31** (page 33)

Using Proper Verb Forms
🔑 20, 21, 28, 29, 30

Key Objective The student will be able to properly complete sentences by choosing between forms of the verbs *give, write, drink, go,* and *do;* between singular and plural forms of the verb *to be;* and between the verbs *sit* or *set,* and *lay* or *lie.*

Procedures

Help the students recall information they have learned about verbs. Direct a discussion by asking the following questions: Can you name the three principal parts of the verb *drink*? With which principal part of a verb is a helping word needed? Can you name a singular and a plural verb? In a sentence how can you tell whether you should use a singular or plural verb? Have several students write sentences on the chalkboard to illustrate the use of the principal parts of verbs and singular and plural verbs.

Review the information and examples in Keys 20, 21, and 28 to 30. Answer the students' questions about this information. Then let everyone work independently to complete the exercises in Lesson 31.

To check the answers to the exercises, have several students read the exercises aloud using the words they underlined in the sentences and explaining the reason for the choice. If other students disagree with the answers, have them explain the reasons for their objections.

Supplementary Exercises

Choose the proper verb form in parentheses to write in each blank space. (Score: 9)

1. (gave, given) The fifth grade _____ a play about famous Americans. (gave)
2. (was, were) Molly Pitcher _____ one person the play told about. (was)
3. (drank, drunk) She carried water that the soldiers _____ . (drank)
4. (lying, laying) Then she saw her husband _____ on the ground. (lying)
5. (sit, sat, set) She _____ the pitcher of water on the ground. (set)
6. (saw, seen) Molly _____ that the soldiers needed her help. (saw)
7. (went, gone) She _____ to help them shoot the cannon. (went)
8. (did, done) Many women have _____ brave things for America. (done)
9. (Doesn't, Don't) _____ you know the story about Dolley Madison? (Don't)

Supplementary Activities

More Practice: Have the students write original sentences using the three principal parts of the verbs, *give, write, drink, go, sit,* and *do.*

Instructional Variation: Have a "sentence bee" to give students practice in using proper verb forms. Write the principal parts of the verbs, *give, write, drink, go, sit,* and *do* on index cards or on the chalkboard. Divide the class into two teams and alternately give each team one of the verb forms to use in a sentence. Limit the time each team has to say a sentence or write a sentence on the chalkboard. If one team is not able to think of a sentence for a particular verb form within the time allotted, the other team is given an opportunity to think of a sentence for that verb form. Score one point for the team that produces a sentence within the given time period.

Using Resources and Materials: Have the students use resources from the library to find more information about women who played a leading role in America's history. Have the students write a report on the contributions of one woman. Suggest they read *Liberty's Women,* published by the G. and C. Merriam Company to learn more about American women in history before they write their report. Have the students read and study Key 52a before writing their report. Tell the students to use principal parts of the verbs, *give, write, drink, go, sit,* and *do* in their sentences.

Lesson **32** (page 34)

Remembering What We Have Learned

Key Objectives The student will be able to apply the skills taught in Unit II.

Procedures

Explain that the exercises in Lesson 32 will help the students remember what they learned in Unit II and prepare for the post test that follows. Point out that no score or grade will be recorded for this lesson. Make sure the students understand the directions for the exercises and have them find and review the information in the keys mentioned after every exercise.

Have several students read their answers aloud and correct their mistakes. Then direct a discussion of the following that is being reviewed:

1. Recognition of verbs, principal parts of verbs, and agreement of subjects and verbs
2. Contractions
3. Capitalization of the word *I*; initials; titles of courtesy; first words of sentences; first words of direct quotations; names of persons, particular places and things, days, months, and holidays; and words made from the names of places
4. Punctuation of direct quotations, dates, addresses, words in series, direct address, and *yes* or *no* at the beginnings of sentences
5. Proper use of *ate* and *eaten*, *came* and *come*, *did* and *done*, *doesn't* and *don't*, *drank* and *drunk*, *gave* and *given*, *has* and *have*, *is* and *are*, *lie* and *lay*, *ran* and *run*, *saw* and *seen*, *sit* and *set*, *was* and *were*, *went* and *gone*, and *wrote* and *written*

To check on oral language skills, have several students tell stories they have read recently.

Post Test—Unit II

At the conclusion of Unit II, administer the post test for this unit. Post tests for all units are at the back of the Teacher's Edition. The results of the post test should indicate which students have mastered the concepts and skills in the unit. Instructions for administration of post tests appear in the introduction to the Teacher's Edition.

Pretest—Unit III

Before beginning Unit III, administer the pretest for this unit. Pretests for all units are at the back of the Teacher's Edition. The results should indicate the students' preliminary competency levels for concepts and skills presented in the unit. Instructions for administration and ways to use the pretests appear in the introduction to the Teacher's Edition.

Lesson **33** (page 35)

Writing Titles
 3, 12a

Key Objectives The student will be able to:

1. Use capital letters to begin the first word and each important word in a title.
2. Underline the titles of books, magazines, plays, motion pictures, and other long works.
3. Put quotation marks around the titles of songs, poems, short stories, chapters, and other short works.
4. Correctly punctuate and capitalize titles that appear in sentences.

Procedures

Read and discuss Keys 3 and 12a with the students. Some of the students may ask how they can tell whether or not a word in a title is important. Explain that there are many little words that are never capitalized in titles unless they are the first word. List the following words on the chalkboard as examples: *a, an, the, and, but, of, by, for, to, from,* and *with.* Caution the students that some little words, such as the pronouns *I, he, it, my,* and *his* and the verbs *is, are,* and *am,* are considered important words in titles and must be capitalized.

Have several students name their favorite song, story, or book. Help them decide which words are important and should be capitalized and let them write the titles on the chalkboard. Follow the same procedure with other members of the class until the distinction between important and unimportant words in titles is clear. Be sure the students understand that titles of books, magazines, plays, and other long works are underlined. Also, be sure the students understand that quotation marks are put around the titles of songs, poems, short stories, chapters, and other short works. Point out that periods belong inside the quotation marks, but exclamation points and question marks go outside quotation marks.

Have the students work independently to complete the exercises in Lesson 33. Have them correct their mistakes after answers to the exercises have been checked and scores recorded.

Supplementary Exercises

Write the following sentences correctly. (Score: 35)

1. Do you know when ''the star-spangled banner'' was written? (Do you know when ''The Star-Spangled Banner'' was written?)
2. I enjoyed reading the book the adventures of robin hood. (I enjoyed reading the book *The Adventures of Robin Hood.*)
3. Did you see the movie peter pan? (Did you see the movie *Peter Pan?*)
4. Helen's favorite magazine is national geographic. (Helen's favorite magazine is *National Geographic.*)

5. oh! susannah is our favorite song. ("Oh! Susannah" is our favorite song.)
6. Sally read the poem old ironsides to us. (Sally read the poem "Old Ironsides" to us.)
7. Did you see the play my fair lady? (Did you see the play _My Fair Lady_?)

Supplementary Activities

More Practice: Have the students write five sentences in which they use the title of a favorite book, story, poem, song, motion picture, or television program. Remind the students to begin important words in the title with capital letters and to pay attention to titles that should be underlined and titles that need quotation marks.

Instructional Variation: Help reinforce the students' knowledge of writing titles by making an activity for a learning center. Write the titles of books, magazines, stories, poems, chapters, songs, motion pictures, and television programs on index cards. Use lower case letters to begin the words in the titles, and omit underlining and quotation marks. Label the cards by writing what the title is, for example write, "charlotte's web, a book," or "home on the range, a song." Place the cards in a box and have the students randomly choose five cards and write the titles correctly using capital letters and punctuation marks.

Using Resources and Materials: Gather several pieces of posterboard and write headings on them such as, "books," "stories," "poems," etc. Have the students write book reports, motion picture reviews, poems, and short stories and put them on the appropriate poster. Some students may wish to illustrate stories or books they have read and put their illustrations on the appropriate poster.

Lesson **34** (page 36)

Outlining
 43

Key Objectives The student will be able to:
1. Explain that an outline is a plan for a report or a story.
2. Arrange given facts about an animal in outline form.

Procedures
On the chalkboard write the following facts:

Has blue feathers
Is about five inches long
Says its name
Stands on my head
Looks in the mirror

Read and discuss Key 43 with the students and call their attention to the example outline. Point out that an outline contains a title, which gives an idea of the subject of the report; paragraph topics, which tell important ideas about the subject; and paragraph subtopics, which give information to be included in each paragraph.

Ask the students to read the information on the chalkboard and tell them that these facts are to be included in a report titled "My Parakeet." Help the students see that the first two facts tell what the parakeet looks like and that the last three facts tell what the parakeet does. Then have several students go to the chalkboard and arrange the facts in outline form. The outline should be similar to the following:

My Parakeet

  I. What it looks like
    A. Has blue feathers
    B. Is about five inches long
  II. What it does
    A. Says its name
    B. Stands on my head
    C. Looks in the mirror

Explain that an outline is a plan for a report or story. It gives the information to be included in a report or story and shows the order in which the information will be presented. The finished report or story presents the information more fully and interestingly.

Be sure the students understand the explanations and directions in Lesson 34 before they work the exercises. After they have correctly outlined the information about the sloth, have them write the report on a separate sheet of paper.

Supplementary Exercises

Use the facts given below about a parrot to make an outline of two paragraphs about this bird. (Score: 20)

Has gray feathers
Sits on a perch
Has a curved bill
Says its name
Has red tail feathers
Laughs at people

NOTE: Answers will vary. Check for proper arrangement, numbering, and capitalization.

Supplementary Activities

More Practice: Have the students outline two or more paragraphs from their reading books, social studies books, or science books.

Instructional Variation: Choose a subject that interests the students and write facts about the subject on sentence strips or index cards. Write facts that will become paragraph subtopics in an outline. Write a title for the outline on the chalkboard and write as many paragraph topics as needed under the title. Arrange the sentence strips on the chalkboard rail and have several students go to the chalkboard and place or rewrite the facts under the appropriate paragraph topics. Have the rest of the class determine if the outline is arranged properly. Have the students write a report or a story using the outline as a plan.

Using Resources and Materials: Suggest that the students consult a dictionary to find meanings of the word *sloth* and its derivatives. Then have the students write one sentence using the word *sloth* to illustrate a meaning other than the name of an animal and to write two sentences using a different derivative of *sloth* in each. Tell the students to make a new outline for the word *sloth* using the information they have read in the dictionary.

Lesson **35** (page 37)

Topic Sentences

 44

Key Objectives   The student will be able to:
1. Explain that a topic sentence introduces the subject of a paragraph.
2. Identify the topic sentences and subjects of two paragraphs.
3. Write a topic sentence for a given paragraph.

Procedures

Broadcasting

What is the name of the animal pictured in Lesson 35? The roadrunner runs very fast. Name other animals that are swift runners. What are the advantages of an animal being able to run very fast?

Explaining the Exercise

On the chalkboard write the following paragraph subjects:
1. Flying in an airplane
2. Learning to ski
3. Traveling in outer space
4. How animals protect themselves

Read and discuss Key 44 with the students. Point out that a paragraph should tell about one main idea, and all the sentences in the paragraph should tell something about that idea. After the students have read the example paragraph in Key 44, ask someone to tell the main idea of the paragraph. Have another student tell whether or not all of the sentences in the paragraph tell about the subject.

Stress that every paragraph should have an interesting topic sentence that introduces the subject of the paragraph. Explain that the topic sentence should give an idea of what the rest of the paragraph is about.

Call the students' attention to the paragraph subjects listed on the chalkboard. Have several students write on the chalkboard topic sentences that would introduce paragraphs about the subjects listed.

Be sure the students understand the directions before they work the exercises in Lesson 35. After answers are checked and scores recorded, have several students read their answers aloud.

Before assigning the activities suggested in Other Things to Do at the bottom of Lesson 35, remind the students that a title should give an idea of the subject of a paragraph, a report, or a story. Suggest that the students review Key 43 before making their outlines.

Supplementary Exercises

Write an interesting topic sentence for a paragraph about each of the subjects below. (Score: 10) Answers will vary.
1. My favorite book
2. How pioneers made soap
3. My favorite game
4. Looking at the stars
5. A trip in a spaceship
6. Exploring a cave
7. Collecting honey from bees
8. Playing in the snow
9. Building a tree house
10. A brave person

Supplementary Activities

More Practice: Have the students find an interesting paragraph in their reader or some other book. Have them write three different titles for the paragraph. Have each student read the paragraph and three titles aloud. Then ask the other members of the class to choose the best title.

Instructional Variation: Give the students practice in limiting subjects for paragraphs and reports. Suggest a general, broad subject and let them think of more specific main ideas about the subjects. For example, you may name "Safety" as a subject, and the students might suggest "Avoiding Fires," "Crossing the Street Safely," and "Rules for Safe Bicycle Riding."

Using Resources and Materials: Have the students choose five paragraphs from a newspaper or a magazine article. Have them identify the topic sentence and subject of each paragraph. Then have the students write a new title for the article.

Lesson 36 (page 38))

Writing Topic Sentences
 44

Key Objectives   The student will be able to:
1. Write effective topic sentences for given subjects.
2. Identify the misplaced topic sentence in a given paragraph.

Procedures

Review the paragraph by asking such questions as: What is a paragraph? Should each sentence in a paragraph tell about the same subject? What is a topic sentence? Suggest that students check their answers to the questions by reading Key 44.

Ask the students to turn to Lesson 36 in their books. Read the information and examples with them. Ask several students to tell whether or not they would want to read paragraphs that began with the example sentences. Some students may find some sentences more interesting than others because of the subject matter introduced.

Help the students see that each example sentence is a good topic sentence, regardless of subject matter, because each sentence introduces a subject in an effective and interesting way.

Read the directions for the exercises with the students. Explain that topic sentences introducing a narrative or story, such as the one in part II, do not necessarily reveal what the story is about. They serve instead to introduce the story and make the reader curious about the situation that will be described.

After the answers to the exercises are checked and scores recorded, have several students read aloud their sentences from part I. Ask the class to give suggestions for making each sentence more interesting and effective.

Supplementary Exercises

Have the students write an effective topic sentence for each of the following subjects: (Score: 30) Answers will vary.
1. River rafting
2. Visiting a foreign country
3. Watching a sports event

Supplementary Activities

More Practice: Have the students write a paragraph using one of the topic sentences they wrote in part I of Lesson 36. Tell the students that each paragraph should have a title written in the students' own words rather than those in Lesson 36.

Remind the students to proofread their writing, checking for complete sentences, proper paragraph form, and correct spelling, capitalization, and punctuation.

Instructional Variation: Omitting the title and topic sentence, read a paragraph aloud. Ask the students to write what they think the subject of the paragraph is. Then ask them to write a title and a topic sentence for the paragraph. Have several students tell what they wrote. Have the class discuss the effectiveness of each title and topic sentence read.

Lesson 37 (page 39)

Writing Paragraphs
 43, 44

Key Objectives   The student will be able to:
1. Write an outline for two paragraphs about a subject.
2. Write two paragraphs about the subject using the outline as a guide.

Procedures

Broadcasting

Where do you think the people in the picture are? Why are they connected to the spaceship by a line? What kind of work could they be doing?

Explaining the Exercise

Have the students discuss possible subjects for a story about the picture in Lesson 37. Next, ask the students the following questions about writing paragraphs: How many subjects are told about in a paragraph? Should each sentence tell about a different topic? Where should the first line of a paragraph begin? Should a title tell anything about the subject of a paragraph? Can more than one paragraph be used to tell about one subject? What is an outline? Suggest that the students check their answers to these questions by reading Keys 43 and 44.

In discussing the key information, stress the characteristics of a paragraph: it must tell about one subject; it must contain only sentences that tell about that subject; it should have a topic sentence that effectively introduces the subject; and the first line must be indented. Explain that a writer may wish to tell more than one important idea about a subject. Help the students see that they will need a separate paragraph to tell about each important idea. You may wish to use the outline in Key 43,

"Making and Flying Your Own Kite," as an example to show that more than one paragraph is needed to tell about a subject.

Before the students write the paragraphs in Lesson 37, be sure that they make outlines on separate paper. Remind them that each outline should contain a title, which gives an idea of the subject of the report or story; the paragraph topics, which tell important ideas about the subject; and paragraph subtopics, which give information to be included in each paragraph.

Remind the students to proofread their paragraphs, checking for correct paragraphing, complete sentences, and correct spelling, capitalization, and punctuation. After answers are checked and scores recorded, let several students read their paragraphs aloud.

Supplementary Exercises
Write the following on the chalkboard:
1. My favorite hobby
2. My favorite person
3. An exciting trip
4. How I made a kite (or other object)
5. The funniest joke I ever heard
6. How I surprised a friend
7. What I found out by watching an animal

Tell the students to write a paragraph about something they have done or something that has happened to them. They may use a subject listed on the chalkboard if they wish. Remind them to be sure that all sentences tell about the main idea and are important to the story. Tell them to proofread their writing, checking for indention of the first line, complete sentences, and correct spelling, capitalization, and punctuation. (Score: 20)

Supplementary Activities

More Practice: Read and discuss Key 52c with the students. Then have them listen as various students read the paragraphs that they wrote in the activity above. Let the class tell the main idea of each paragraph.

Instructional Variation: Select a paragraph written for "Supplementary Exercises" and write each sentence of the paragraph on separate sentence strips. Place the sentence strips in random order on the bulletin board or on the chalkboard ledge. Have the students volunteer to place the sentence strips in the order they think makes the most effective paragraph. Have them tell which sentence is the topic sentence. Repeat this procedure using paragraphs written by the students, or paragraphs from other sources.

Writing Quotations
 6, 7h, 8b, 9b, 10f, 42

Key Objectives The student will be able to:
1. Indicate that the first word of a direct quotation begins with a capital letter.
2. Punctuate sentences correctly using periods, question marks, exclamation points, quotation marks, and commas where they are needed.

Procedures

Broadcasting

What kind of journey do you think the people in the picture are going on? Why do you think the leader is an American Indian? When do you think this journey took place?

Explaining the Exercise

Write the following sentences on the chalkboard:
1. Have you read about early explorers asked Sue
2. Bill said that he had read about exploring the Northwest
3. How brave the explorers were Sue exclaimed
4. Bill said I would like to be an explorer

Conduct a discussion about direct and indirect quotations, using the following questions: What is a direct quotation? Can you give an example of one? What is an indirect quotation? Can you give an example of one? How should a direct quotation be separated from the rest of the sentence?

Read and discuss Keys 6, 7h, 8b, 9b, 10f, and 42 with the students. Be sure they understand that commas, periods, question marks, and exclamation points at the ends of direct quotations should be placed inside the quotation marks. Ask someone to read sentence 1 on the chalkboard, tell whether it is a direct or an indirect quotation, and place punctuation marks where they are needed. Follow a similar procedure with the other sentences.

After the students understand the directions for the exercises in lesson 38, let them work independently. Be sure they correct their mistakes after answers to the exercises have been checked and scores recorded.

Supplementary Exercises
Write the following direct quotations correctly, using capital letters and punctuation marks where they are needed. (Score: 29)
1. Ellen said, there is an interesting story about Sacajawea. (Ellen said, "There is an interesting story about Sacajawea.")

2. When Sacajawea was young, she lived with her family Ellen explained. ("When Sacajawea was young, she lived with her family," Ellen explained.)

3. She continued another tribe took Sacajawea from her home. (She continued, "Another tribe took Sacajawea from her home.")

4. Ellen said she was taken to North Dakota. (Ellen said, "She was taken to North Dakota.")

5. Ellen said years later Sacajawea went with Lewis and Clark. (Ellen said, "Years later Sacajawea went with Lewis and Clark.")

6. They met a tribe of Indians Ellen said. ("They met a tribe of Indians," Ellen said.)

7. Joe asked who do you think was among the Indians? (Joe asked, "Who do you think was among the Indians?")

8. Ellen exclaimed how happy Sacajawea was to see her family (Ellen exclaimed, "How happy Sacajawea was to see her family!")

Supplementary Activities

More Practice: Have the students rewrite sentences 20 to 25 on page 40 as indirect quotations. Explain that rewording will be necessary.

Instructional Variation: Have the students write three jokes that contain conversation. Remind the students to begin a new paragraph each time they quote the words of a different speaker.

Using Resources and Materials: Have the students find direct and indirect quotations in magazine and newspaper articles. Next, have the students change the indirect quotations to direct quotations, and change the direct quotations to indirect quotations. Explain that rewording may be necessary.

Lesson **39** (page 41)

Alphabetizing Words
 38a

Key Objective The student will be able to arrange words in alphabetical order to the first, second, and third letters.

Procedures

Read Key 38a with the students. Then have a short drill on the alphabetical sequence of letters. Have the class recite the alphabet. Say letters at random and let pupils tell what letter comes before and after them. Next, say pairs of words, such as *meal* and *lunch, pheasant* and *quail, stream* and *river,* and *van* and *wagon,* and let several students

tell which word should come first in an alphabetical arrangement.

Explain that sometimes words that begin with the same letter need to be alphabetized and that they are arranged according to their second or third letters. Say pairs of words that begin with the same letter, such as *art* and *act, peach* and *plum, boat* and *bottle,* and *lantern* and *lamp,* and let the students tell which word should come first in an alphabetical arrangement.

After the exercises on page 41 have been worked and checked, have the students correct their mistakes.

NOTE: Alphabetizing to the third letter is presented at this grade level. If students ask about arranging words that begin with the same three letters, explain that they are alphabetized according to succeeding letters. If the problem of alphabetizing such words arises in a class activity, remind the students of the correct arrangement, and let them do the alphabetizing themselves.

Supplementary Exercises

I. Arrange the following words in alphabetical order. (Score: 17)

1. dirigible	7. automobile	13. chariot
2. pony	8. helicopter	14. trailer
3. gondola	9. yacht	15. jitney
4. wagon	10. elevator	16. flatboat
5. biplane	11. kayak	17. locomotive
6. railroad	12. mailplane	

(Answers:)

1. automobile	7. gondola	13. pony
2. biplane	8. helicopter	14. railroad
3. chariot	9. jitney	15. trailer
4. dirigible	10. kayak	16. wagon
5. elevator	11. locomotive	17. yacht
6. flatboat	12. mailplane	

II. Arrange these words in alphabetical order. (Score: 10)

1. fall	5. fail	9. fade
2. favor	6. fate	10. far
3. face	7. fast	
4. fan	8. fame	

(Answers:)

1. face	5. fame	9. fate
2. fade	6. fan	10. favor
3. fail	7. far	
4. fall	8. fast	

Supplementary Activities

More Practice: Have the students alphabetically arrange the first names of the students in the class. If more than one student has the same first name, suggest that the students use the initial of students' last names to place them in the correct alphabetical order.

Instructional Variation: Suggest that the students bring telephone directories to class. Have them examine the directories to see how names are arranged. Point out the alphabetical listing. Have the students observe listings of first and last names, names with initials, and successive last names that are identical. If the directories have guide words, point out that the names at the top of each page and all the other names that can be arranged alphabetically between them appear on that page. Explain that the students can use these guide words to tell at a glance whether the name they are looking for appears on that page.

Choose a name at random from the directory and have the students find the telephone number that appears with the name. The first student to find the correct number should pick the next name. Be sure that everyone in the class has found the name in the directory before another name is chosen. Continue until a number of students have had an opportunity to choose a name.

Using Resources and Materials: Discuss using the telephone. Have the students use the directories they brought to class to find out how to make calls for assistance to the telephone company, the police, the fire department, etc.

Have the students think of rules for using the telephone courteously and write the rules on the chalkboard. They should list rules similar to the following:
1. Answer the telephone promptly.
2. Keep your mouth near the telephone.
3. Speak in a natural tone.
4. Speak clearly.
5. Listen politely.
6. Let the person who calls tell the reason for the call.
7. Do not talk too long.

Let the students make imaginary emergency or friendly calls. Have them use the directory to find the numbers they wish to call.

Have the students write their own list of rules for using the telephone courteously. Tell the students to write their rules in alphabetical order.

Lesson **40** (page 42)

Using the Dictionary

 37, 38

Key Objectives The student will be able to:
1. Write the number of the dictionary page on

which given words can be found.
2. Match words with their definitions.

Procedures

Conduct a brief review of alphabetical order. Let several students recite the alphabet. Say letters at random and have students tell what letters precede and follow in alphabetical sequence. Next say pairs of words that begin with the same first two letters, such as *jar* and *jam*, *phase* and *phrase*, *children* and *chalk*, and *fresh* and *fruit*, and let several students tell which word should come first in an alphabetical arrangement.

Read Key 38 with the pupils. Be sure they understand that two words are located at the top of each page in the dictionary. Explain that these words will guide them to the correct page so that they do not have to read all words but can tell at a glance whether or not a particular word is on the page. Demonstrate the use of guide words in a dictionary by finding words such as *planet, comet,* and *meteor.* Have the students use the guide words at the tops of the dictionary pages to find the words.

Help the students study the directions in Lesson 40 to be sure that they understand what they are supposed to do. Explain that if they are unsure of a definition in part II they may find it in a dictionary or in Key 37. After answers to the exercises have been checked and scores recorded, have the students correct their mistakes.

Supplementary Exercises

I. Beside each word listed below write the number of the dictionary page on which it would be found. (Score: 12)

Page 80	Page 81	Page 95	Page 96
dab–diary	did–dry	pace–pick	piece–place

1. dog (81)
2. pack (95)
3. pig (96)
4. pea (95)
5. damp (80)
6. pin (96)
7. dance (80)
8. pad (95)
9. did (81)
10. dish (81)
11. pile (96)
12. day (80)

II. Before each word in column A write the number of the definition from column B that fits the word. (Score: 6)

	A		B
(1)	dear	1.	a word showing love
(4)	deer	2.	a pit
(3)	fair	3.	honest
(6)	fare	4.	an animal that has antlers
(2)	hole	5.	not broken or cut up
(5)	whole	6.	the price of a trip

More Practice: Have the students use dictionaries to find the following words: *airplane, dinner, hammer, lady, picture,* and *violet.* Tell them to write the two guide words found at the top of the page on which each word is located. Also have them note that the words are divided into syllables and ask them to write each word as it is divided in the dictionary.

Instructional Variation: Divide the class into two teams and give each team a dictionary. Write a word on the chalkboard and have one member of each team find the word in the dictionary as quickly as possible. The team whose member finds the word first receives one point. The other team has an opportunity to earn a point if they can define the word without reading the definition in the dictionary. Continue this procedure until all members of both teams have had a turn at finding a word in the dictionary.

Using Resources and Materials: Have the students use their knowledge of alphabetical order and guide words during other periods of the day. They may use indexes, dictionaries, and encyclopedias while doing reference work in reading, social studies, and science classes.

Lesson **41** (page 43)

Dividing Words into Syllables

 39

Key Objectives   The student will be able to:
1. Divide given words into syllables.
2. Identify one-syllable words.

Procedures

Write the following words on the chalkboard:

1. saddle	4. baby
2. basket	5. real
3. bucket	6. darkness

NOTE: Fifth-graders who have learned to read in a comprehensive basic-reading program will know the rules for the syllabication of words and will be able to use them efficiently in reading situations. This lesson was planned to help students apply an established reading skill to a writing situation rather than to teach them principles of syllabication. Throughout this lesson, emphasize that dictionaries show the correct syllabication of words.

Read and discuss Key 39 with the students. Have them look in their readers and other textbooks to find words that are divided at the ends of

lines. Then have them refer to dictionaries or glossaries to see how words are divided there.

Use the words on the chalkboard to help the students recall the various ways of dividing words. Ask a student to read word 1 and draw a vertical line between its two syllables. The student should explain that words containing double consonants are usually divided between the two consonants that are alike. Have other students divide the other words on the chalkboard to show divisions between two consonants that are not alike, between a vowel and a consonant, between two vowels, and between a root word and a suffix. This activity should help the students recall the syllabication principles that they have learned.

Be sure the students understand the directions before they work the exercises in Lesson 41. Suggest that they divide the words according to syllabication rules and then check their work in a dictionary. If there are not enough dictionaries in the classroom, delay the checking of answers until each student has had an opportunity to use a dictionary.

Supplementary Exercises

Divide the following words into syllables. Put an *X* by one-syllable words. (Score: 15)

1. maple (ma-ple)	9. July (Ju-ly)
2. ever (ev-er)	10. wagons (wag-ons)
3. donkey (don-key)	11. jump (X)
4. timber (tim-ber)	12. pronoun (pro-noun)
5. secret (se-cret)	13. silver (sil-ver)
6. dog (X)	14. vacant (va-cant)
7. open (o-pen)	15. sentence (sen-tence)
8. hungry (hun-gry)	

Supplementary Activities

More Practice: Have the students choose ten words from their spelling lists or from their reading books, and write the words on a separate piece of paper. Next, have them divide the words into syllables and check their work by looking up the words in the dictionary.

Instructional Variation: Make a game board on which three to five players move markers on squares from the start to the finish. Then write vocabulary words on individual game cards and have the players take turns choosing a game card and dividing the word on the card into syllables on a separate piece of paper. Have one of the other players check the syllabication in a dictionary. When students divide a word correctly, they choose a card from another pile which indicates how many spaces to move their markers. Continue this procedure until one player reaches the finish.

Using Resources and Materials: Have the students read magazine articles to find examples of words that have been divided into syllables at the end of a line of type.

Lesson 42 (page 44)

Choosing Homophones
 37

Key Objective The student will be able to complete sentences by selecting the correct homophone.

Procedures

Explain that homophones are words that sound alike but have different spellings and meanings. Ask someone to write the word *to* and two homophones for it on the chalkboard. Then ask the student to write sentences with each of the three words to illustrate their correct use. Let several students name other homophones and use them in sentences. To help the students understand the importance of using the correct homophone, write the following sentence on the chalkboard:

The ranchers (herd, heard) the cattle on the mesa.

Help the students understand that each word in parentheses makes sense in the sentence but that each gives the sentence a meaning altogether different from the other. They should see that the meaning of the sentence depends on the homophone used.

Read Key 37 with the class and discuss the examples, making sure that the meaning of each homophone is clear.

After the exercises in Lesson 42 have been worked and checked and scores have been recorded, have the students correct their mistakes. Then assign the activity suggested in Other Things to Do.

Supplementary Exercises

Choose the correct word in parentheses to write in the blank. (Score: 10)
1. (whose, who's) Alonzo was a boy _____ family lived on a farm. (whose)
2. (know, no) Did Alonzo _____ how to train his oxen? (know)
3. (too, two, to) He spent many hours with the _____ animals. (two)
4. (It's, Its) " _____ fun to work with them," said Alonzo. (It's)
5. (it's, its) The family took good care of _____ animals. (its)

6. (there, their) They knew that _____ animals were valuable. (their)
7. (too, to, two) Alonzo took good care of his oxen, _____ . (too)
8. (too, to, two) Alonzo hoped his family would give a pony _____ him. (to)
9. (one, won) It was the _____ thing he wanted most. (one)
10. (by, buy) How Alonzo wished that he had the money to _____ a pony! (buy)

Supplementary Activities

More Practice: Have the students use each of the following words in sentences:
1. hear, here
2. their, there, they're
3. it's, its

Suggest that the children also write sentences using other homophones that are often misspelled and misused.

Instructional Variation: Have the pupils collect or draw cartoons to illustrate the meanings of various homophones. Ask them to write sentences under the cartoons to show the correct use of the homophones. For example, a cartoon may show a monkey hanging by his tail and also a thick book. Sentences under the cartoon should tell that the monkey hangs by his long tail and that someone has written a long tale about a monkey.

Using Resources and Materials: Have the students read articles in newspapers and magazines and look for examples of homophones used in the articles. Suggest that they read the sentences aloud and have several members of the class volunteer to spell the homophones they hear.

Lesson 43 (Page 45)

Using Proper Verb Forms
 21

Key Objective The student will be able to complete sentences by choosing the proper past forms of the verbs *grow, blow, fly, know,* and *throw.*

Procedures

Broadcasting

Pecos Bill is pictured riding a horse in Lesson 43. What is the horse doing? Why do you think horses buck? Name several places you could go to see someone ride a bucking horse.

Explaining the Lesson

Write the following words on the chalkboard:

1. blew, blown
2. flew, flown
3. grew, grown
4. knew, known
5. threw, thrown

Read and discuss Key 21 with the students. Ask them how they can tell whether the second or the third principal part of a verb should be used in a sentence. They should explain that the third principal part needs a helping verb while the second principal part does not. Have the pupils locate the principal parts of *blow, fly, grow, know,* and *throw.* Then ask someone to read the first pair of words on the chalkboard and use them properly in sentences. Let other students follow the same procedure with the other pairs of words on the chalkboard.

Let everyone work independently to complete the exercises on page 45. After answers have been checked and scores recorded, have the students correct their mistakes.

Supplementary Exercises

Choose the proper verb form in parentheses to write in the blank. (Score: 10)

1. (grew, grown) Sam told how Bill had _____ up in the desert. (grown)
2. (threw, thrown) Bill was _____ from his family's wagon. (thrown)
3. (grew, grown) He _____ up with a family of coyotes. (grew)
4. (knew, known) Bill and his coyote friends were _____ as fast runners. (known)
5. (flew, flown) Often they _____ across the desert. (flew)
6. (threw, thrown) Sometimes Bill _____ his rope at cattle. (threw)
7. (blew, blown) Often the wind _____ very hard in Texas. (blew)
8. (blew, blown) Sand was _____ in the wind. (blown)
9. (knew, known) Do you think Pecos Bill _____ how to stop sandstorms? (knew)
10. (knew, known) He was _____ for the amazing things he did. (known)

Supplementary Activities

More Practice: Have the students write ten sentences about a subject or subjects that interest them. Tell them to use the past forms of the verbs *grow, blow, fly, know,* and *throw* in their sentences.

Instructional Variation: Have twenty students volunteer to play a "proper verb form" game and then divide the students into two groups of ten members. Write one of the past forms of the verbs *grow, blow, fly, know,* and *throw* on each of ten index cards and give a card to each member of one group. Give each member of the other group a sentence strip on which you have written a sentence requiring one of the past forms of the verbs mentioned above, but with a blank where the verb form belongs. Have all students read their sentences and word cards to themselves. After a signal is given, have the group with the sentence strips hold up their sentences so they are visible to the other group. Then have the students holding the index cards find the student whose sentence requires the verb form. The first two students to form a completed sentence win the game. Have the class read the completed sentences and continue the procedure until all students have had an opportunity to play the game.

Using Resources and Materials: Have the students use the library to find additional information about the legend of Pecos Bill. Ask the students to write five sentences about one of Pecos Bill's adventures using five of the verb forms discussed in Lesson 43.

Lesson **44** (page 46)

Reviewing Sentences

🔑 7a, 8a, 9a, 41a, 14, 19

Key Objectives   The student will be able to:
1. Place the correct punctuation mark at the end of a sentence.
2. Distinguish between groups of words that are sentences and groups of words that are not.
3. Identify nouns that are subjects of sentences.
4. Identify the verbs in sentences.

Procedures

Begin the lesson by asking the following questions: What is a sentence? How can you tell whether or not a group of words is a sentence? What is a noun? What is a verb? What three kinds of sentences do you know about? What punctuation mark is used at the end of each different kind of sentence? Tell the students to check their answers to the questions by reviewing Keys 7a, 8a, 9a, 41a, 14, and 19, in that order.

After the exercises in Lesson 44 have been worked, answers checked, and scores recorded, have the students correct their mistakes. Then tell the students to punctuate each sentence in part II.

Supplementary Exercises

I. Place the correct punctuation mark at the end of each sentence. (Score: 5)

1. What bright flashes the cannons made (!)
2. Anxiously, Francis Scott Key looked toward the shore (.)
3. Was the American flag still flying (?)
4. Yes, there it was (!) or (.)
5. It meant that the Americans had not surrendered (.)

II. Write *Yes* after the groups of words that are sentences and *No* after those that are not sentences. (Score: 3)
6. A friend Key's poem (No)
7. It was printed in a newspaper (Yes)
8. Many people read the beautiful poem (Yes)

III. Draw one line under the noun that the sentence is about. Draw two lines under the verb in each sentence. (Score: 6)
9. Key wrote the words to "The Star-Spangled Banner." (Key wrote the words to "The Star-Spangled Banner.")
10. Another composer wrote the music for the song. (Another composer wrote the music for the song.)
11. The song became America's national anthem. (The song became America's national anthem.)

Supplementary Activities

More Practice: Have the students make sentences out of the groups of words that are not sentences in part II of Lesson 44.

Instructional Variation: Divide the class into two groups. Have each student in one group write a noun on an index card and have each student in the other group write a verb on an index card. Next, have one student from the "noun" group and one student from the "verb" group stand so the rest of the class can see the word cards. Have several students in the class compare sentences using the noun and the verb.

Using Resources and Materials: Write the following questions on the chalkboard:
1. When was "The Star-Spangled Banner" written?
2. Where was Francis Scott Key during the battle?
3. What did he watch during the battle?
4. What did he do to express his thoughts and feelings?

Have the students outline and write the story of "The Star-Spangled Banner." Explain that they should answer the questions on the chalkboard and that they can find the necessary information in Lesson 44. Tell them to state the ideas in their own words.

Have the students read Key 47 before they write their stories. Remind them to proofread their writing, checking for sentences, paragraphing, and correct spelling, capitalization, and punctuation. Tell the students to draw one line under the noun that is the subject of each sentence and draw two lines under the verb in each sentence of their reports.

Lesson **45** (page 47)

Reviewing Capitalization and Punctuation
1, 2, 5, 6, 7, 8, 9, 10, 12

Key Objectives The student will be able to:
1. Identify words in sentences that should begin with a capital letter.
2. Place punctuation marks where they are needed in sentences.

Procedures

Broadcasting
What are the people pictured in Lesson 45 doing? In what parts of the country can people skate on frozen lakes? Name and describe several sports played on ice.

Explaining the Lesson
Briefly review Keys 1, 2, 5 to 10, and 12. Clarify points that the students ask about. Then make sure the children understand the directions for the exercises in Lesson 45. Let the students work independently.

In scoring this lesson, have the students deduct one point for every mistake from the perfect score 93. Because of the large number of points in this and other lessons, it would be difficult for the children to try to count the number of points they earned.

After answers to the exercises have been checked, ask one student to read the first sentence, telling why specific words were capitalized and where punctuation marks were used. Call on other students to follow the same procedure with the other sentences.

Supplementary Exercises
Rewrite the following sentences, using capital letters and punctuation marks where they are needed. (Score: 40)

1. miss jerue told fran ellie and me about famous skaters. (Miss Jerue told Fran, Ellie, and me about famous skaters.)

2. "have you ever heard of Peggy Fleming" she asked. ("Have you ever heard of Peggy Fleming?" she asked.)

3. On january 30 1976 I saw her at st. paul minnesota. (On January 30, 1976, I saw her at St. Paul, Minnesota.)

4. Miss Jerue explained she was the most graceful of American figure skaters. (Miss Jerue explained, "She was the most graceful of American figure skaters.")

5. Another famous skater came from connecticut said ellie. ("Another famous skater came from Connecticut," said Ellie.)

6. Fran asked isn't her name dorothy hamill (Fran asked, "Isn't her name Dorothy Hamill?")

7. Hasn't she performed throughout the united states asked Fran. ("Hasn't she performed throughout the United States?" asked Fran.)

8. She exclaimed what a wonderful skater she is (She exclaimed, "What a wonderful skater she is!")

Supplementary Activities

More Practice: Have the students write an imaginary dialogue between two persons. Ask the students to write ten sentences, checking for correct capitalization and punctuation.

Instructional Variation: After the students have completed writing sentences for the *More Practice* section, select several sentences and rewrite them on the chalkboard omitting the punctuation marks and not capitalizing letters. Then have students go to the chalkboard to add the correct punctuation marks and indicate which words should be capitalized in the sentences.

Using Resources and Materials: Have the students write about three kinds of ice skates. Explain that they should tell how the skates are alike, how they are different, and what each kind is used for. The students may use the information in Lesson 45, but they should state the ideas in their own words. Encourage them to consult encyclopedias and other resource material to find more information about the skates.

Have the students review Keys 43 to 45 before they write their compositions. Remind them to proofread their writing, checking for paragraphing, complete sentences, and correct spelling, capitalization, and punctuation.

Lesson **46** (page 48)

Reviewing Proper Word Forms
18, 20, 21, 25, 26, 27, 28, 29, 30

Key Objective The student will be able to select the proper word form to complete sentences.

Procedures
Review the information and examples in Keys 18, 20, 21, and 25 to 30. Answer the students' questions about this information. Then let them work the exercises in Lesson 46 independently.

To check the answers to the exercises, let several students read them aloud. Have individual students read the sentences, using the underlined word forms, and have them explain why they made that choice. If other students disagree with the answer, let them explain the reasons for their objections. If the students do not come to a quick agreement about the correct answer, have them refer to the appropriate key.

Supplementary Exercises
Choose the proper word form in parentheses to write in the blank. (Score 12)

1. (laid, lain) Tom _____ two iron nails on the table. (laid)

2. (was, were) One nail _____ covered with paint. (was)

3. (sat, set) Then Tom _____ both nails in a jar. (set)

4. (a, an) About _____ inch of water was put into the jar. (an)

5. (saw, seen) A few days later we _____ what had happened. (saw)

6. (did, done) "Look what water and air _____ to this," he said. (did)

7. (set, sat) We _____ down and looked at the unpainted nail. (sat)

8. (doesn't, don't) "This nail _____ look like iron," said Tom. (doesn't)

9. (knew, known) Susan _____ why the painted nail had not rusted. (knew)

10. (may, can) Paint _____ keep air away from the iron. (can)

11. (isn't, aren't) The painted nail _____ covered with rust. (isn't)

12. (is, are) There _____ no rust because no air reached the iron. (is)

Supplementary Activities

More Practice Have each student write ten sentences. Tell the students to use each of the following words in a sentence:

1. teach, learn
2. a, an
3. may, can
4. doesn't, don't
5. is, are

Suggest that the sentences tell about science experiments or something the students have studied in their science classes.

Instructional Variation: Divide the class into two teams. Ask the first student in a team to give the second and third principal parts of one of the verbs listed in Key 21 and to tell which verb needs a helping word. When students do not know the answer, they must leave the game, and the first member of the opposing team then has an opportunity to answer. Continue until each player has had a chance to give the principal parts of one of the verbs listed in the key. The team with the most players left at the end of the period wins the game.

Using Resources and Materials: Have the students perform the experiment described in Lesson 46. You will need iron filings, powdered sulphur, a magnet, a jar, and a hot plate. Perhaps the science teacher can help gather the materials and supervise the experiment. Then have the students write several sentences about the experiment using some of the word forms discussed in Lesson 46.

Lesson **47** (page 49)

Reviewing Study of Words
 14, 15, 16, 17, 19, 22, 37

Key Objectives   The student will be able to:
1. Write the plural forms of given nouns.
2. Write the possessive forms of given nouns.
3. Choose correct homophones to complete sentences.
4. Identify nouns, verbs, and pronouns in sentences.
5. Write contractions of given words.

Procedures

Tell the students that they will review the study of words in this lesson. Ask them to recall the word studies in previous lessons. They should emphasize the importance of the functions of words. Use the following questions and comments to stimulate discussion: What is a noun? How do you form plurals of nouns? How do you form possessives of nouns? What is a pronoun? What is a verb? What is a contraction? How do contractions affect writ-

ing? Name some contractions and tell what words they stand for. What are homophones? Name some pairs of homophones and tell their meanings.

Have the students study Keys 14 to 17, 19, 22, and 37 before they work the exercises in Lesson 47. After answers to the exercises have been checked, have the students correct their mistakes.

Supplementary Exercises

I. Write the plural forms of the following words. (Score: 6)
1. baby (babies)   4. fox (foxes)
2. child (children) 5. piece (pieces)
3. knife (knives)   6. girl (girls)

II. Write the possessive forms of the words below. (Score: 4)
7. Charles (Charles's)   9. dogs (dogs')
8. child (child's)   10. men (men's)

III. Choose the correct homophone in parentheses to write in each blank. (Score: 3)
11. (buy, by) The portrait of Washington was painted _____ Gilbert Stuart. (by)
12. (It's, Its) _____ a very famous painting. (It's)
13. (see, sea) You can _____ copies of the painting in many schools. (see)

IV. In the following sentences draw one line under each noun, two lines under each pronoun, and a circle around each verb. (Score: 12)
14. Tom saw a picture of George Washington. (Tom (saw) a picture of George Washington.)
15. It was in his room. (It (was) in his room.)
16. Perhaps you know the picture, too. (Perhaps you (know) the picture, too.)

V. Write the contractions of the words below. (Score: 2)
18. cannot (can't)
19. she will (she'll)

Supplementary Activities

Instructional Variation: On individual index cards have the students write the following homophones: *know, no, hole, whole, not, knot, new, knew, too, to.* Say sentences requiring one of the homophones in each sentence, but omit the homophone when saying the sentence. Tell the students to hold up the correct homophone to complete each sentence.

Using Resources and Materials: Write the following questions on the chalkboard:
1. Why were the people of Washington, D.C., hurrying to leave the city?
2. What did Dolley Madison do before leaving?
3. What did the British soldiers do?

4. What happened to the painting of George Washington?

Tell the students to outline and write a story about Dolley Madison's rescue of a famous painting. Explain that they should answer the questions on the chalkboard and that they can find the necessary information in Lesson 47. Tell the students that they may also use pertinent information from encyclopedias or social studies books. Have the students state the ideas in their own words and suggest that they use different kinds of sentences and some direct quotations.

Have the students read Key 47 before they write their stories. Remind them to proofread their writing, checking for complete sentences, paragraphing, and correct spelling, capitalization, and punctuation.

Lesson 48 (page 50)

Reviewing the Paragraph
 3, 43, 44

Key Objectives The student will be able to:
1. Write an outline for two paragraphs using given information.
2. Write two paragraphs from the outline.

Procedures

Ask the students what they remember about writing paragraphs. You may use the following questions: How does outlining help you write better paragraphs? How many subjects should a paragraph tell about? Should each sentence tell about a different subject? Which sentence should introduce the subject? Should the title tell anything about the subject of the paragraph? Quickly review Keys 3, 43, and 44 to confirm or correct the students' comments.

Ask the students to turn to Lesson 48; read the directions for the exercises with them. Tell the students that they should capitalize both words of the compound *trap-door* if they use the expression *trap-door spider* in their titles. Answer any questions about procedure; then let the students work independently. After answers have been checked and scores recorded, let several students read their paragraphs aloud or write them on the chalkboard. Tell the rest of the class to pay careful attention to each report. Have each student choose one sentence from the report that is effectively written. After each report is given, let the students tell which sentences they chose and the reasons for their choices.

Supplementary Exercises

Below are some facts about the saluki dog. Use the facts given to make an outline about this animal. Then write a paragraph from the outline. (Score: 20)

lives in Arabia	often has black fur
helps hunters	ears are long and silky
is very swift runner	looks something like a greyhound

NOTE: Answers will vary.

Supplementary Activities

More Practice: Have the students find a magazine picture that suggests a story. Then ask them to write an outline and then a paragraph telling the story. Let the students paste the picture on a sheet of paper and write the paragraph below it. Display the pictures and paragraphs in the classroom.

Instructional Variation: Write six facts on sentence strips about an interesting animal and place the strips in random order on the bulletin board. Have several students volunteer to arrange the strips in an outline form for two paragraphs. Then on a separate piece of paper, have the students use the outline to write two paragraphs about the animal.

Using Resources and Materials: Let students who are ready for extra work find out all they can about some unusual animal. They may use encyclopedias or other resource materials to find information. After they have gathered their information, study Keys 45 and 52a with them and help them organize their materials. Then let the students give oral reports to the class.

Read and discuss Key 52c with the class before the reports suggested above are given. Help the students state questions they want to have answered in the reports. After the oral reports have been given, let the listeners tell what they learned.

Lesson 49 (page 51)

Remembering What We Have Learned

Key Objectives The student will be able to apply the skills taught in Unit III.

Procedures

Explain that the exercises in Lesson 49 will help the students remember what they learned in Unit III and prepare for the post test that follows. Point out that no score or grade will be recorded for this lesson. Make sure that the students understand the directions for the exercises and tell them that they should find the keys and review the information.

Have several students read their answers to the exercises and correct the mistakes they make. Then direct a discussion of the following items that are being reviewed:
1. Titles
2. Outlining
3. The paragraph—its form and topic
4. Capitalization and punctuation of direct quotations
5. Alphabetical order of words
6. Use of the dictionary
7. Dividing words into syllables
8. Homophones
9. Proper use of *blew, blown, flew, flown, grew, grown, knew, known, threw,* and *thrown*

To check on oral language skills let several students tell stories they have read recently.

Post Test—Unit III

At the conclusion of Unit III, administer the post test for this unit. Post tests for all units are at the back of the Teacher's Edition. The results of the post test should indicate which students have mastered the concepts and skills in the unit. Instructions for administration of post tests appear in the introduction to the Teacher's Edition.

Pretest—Unit IV

Before beginning Unit IV, administer the pretest for this unit. Pretests for all units are at the back of the Teacher's Edition. The results should indicate the students' preliminary competency levels for concepts and skills presented in the unit. Instructions for administration and ways to use the pretests appear in the introduction to the Teacher's Edition.

Lesson **50** (page 70)

Writing Quotations
 42

Key Objectives The student will be able to:
1. Transform indirect quotations into direct quotations.
2. Transform direct quotations into indirect quotations.
3. Write a direct quotation.

Procedures

On the chalkboard write the following:

Everyone agreed that the play had been a success. John said that the audience seemed to enjoy

every moment of it. Marie laughed and said that no one seemed to mind when Ralph tripped. Ralph said that he believed that people in the audience thought that he was supposed to fall. John said that Ralph's falling made the play even funnier. Ralph said that it didn't seem very funny at the time.

Everyone agreed that the play had been a success.

John said, "The audience seemed to enjoy every moment of it."

"No one seemed to mind when Ralph tripped," Marie laughed.

"I believe the people in the audience thought that I was supposed to fall," Ralph replied.

"Your falling made the play even funnier," John said.

"It didn't seem very funny at the time!" Ralph exclaimed.

Briefly review direct and indirect quotations. Ask a student to tell what an indirect quotation is. Ask another student to write a sentence on the chalkboard that illustrates an indirect quotation. Then ask someone to tell what a direct quotation is. Have several students tell how direct quotations are punctuated. Be sure they list (1) beginning the first word of a direct quotation with a capital letter, (2) placing quotation marks at the beginning and end of a direct quotation, and (3) using a comma to separate a direct quotation from the words that tell who said it, unless the quotation is a question or exclamation that comes before the words that tell who said it. Let volunteers write sentences on the chalkboard that illustrate direct quotations.

Call the students' attention to the two compositions written on the chalkboard. Read the first and ask the students whether direct or indirect quotations are used. Then read the second and ask what kinds of quotations are used. Ask the students to tell which of the two compositions seems more interesting and why. Help the students see that the use of too many indirect quotations in the first composition makes it seem awkward, uninteresting, and full of *that*s.

Explain that questions and exclamations are usually more effective written as direct quotations. Use the following sentences to illustrate:
1. Miss Jones asked whether we had read the chapter.
2. "Have you read the chapter?" Miss Jones asked.
3. Dad said that I had done a good job.
4. "What a good job you did!" Dad exclaimed.

Before they begin the exercises in Lesson 50, remind the students that they may refer to the key section for information about direct and indirect quotations. Then let them work independently. After answers are checked and scores recorded, let several students read their answers and tell how the sentences are punctuated.

Supplementary Exercises

Dictate the following sentences and have the students write and punctuate each sentence.

1. Alex said that many rocks have beautiful colors in them.
2. Bette said, ''Many people enjoy hunting for interesting rocks.''
3. ''In the library there is a book about rocks,'' Renaldo told them.
4. Alex said that he would like to read that book.

After the students have written the dictated sentences, ask them to rewrite each one, changing direct quotations to indirect quotations and indirect quotations to direct quotations.

Supplementary Activities

More Practice: Have the students find examples of direct and indirect quotations in their reading books. Let several students read aloud the examples they find and have the rest of the class determine whether they are direct or indirect quotations. Let volunteers reword the direct quotations to form indirect quotations and the indirect quotations to form direct quotations. Discuss the effectiveness of both forms.

Instructional Variation: Suggest that each student write an imaginary conversation held among several friends. Tell the students they may discuss one of the following imaginary situations:

1. A party they have attended or plan to attend
2. Whether or not a player in a baseball game is out
3. A study assignment the teacher has given
4. Plans for starting a new club
5. A book, concert, movie, or television program they have enjoyed

Tell the students to use different kinds of sentences and direct and indirect quotations. Remind them to proofread their work, checking for complete sentences and correct punctuation, capitalization, and spelling.

Lesson **51** (page 71)

Using Periods in Writing Abbreviations
🗝 1c, 1f, 1g, 7c, 7d, 7e, 7f, 7g

Key Objective The student will be able to write and punctuate abbreviations for titles of courtesy,

directions, and street names, and for the names of days, months, and states.

Procedures

Read and discuss Keys 1c, 1f, 1g, and 7c, 7d, 7e, 7f, 7g with the students. Point out that abbreviations other than *Mr., Mrs., Ms.,* and *Dr.* are not usually used in letters or other writing that someone other than the writer will read. However, abbreviations are helpful in making lists and notes for personal use. Have the students pay particular attention to the examples in the keys, since most of the exercise items are listed there. Mention that there are two ways of writing the abbreviations of states and that this lesson requires the form used for lists and maps. Make the students aware that the two-letter, postal form presented in Key 7f is used only to address letters and envelopes.

Be sure everyone understands the directions before working the exercises in Lesson 51. If the students cannot recall the correct abbreviation for a word, they may refer to a dictionary or to the appropriate key. Let the students check their own work as several students give the correct answers.

Supplementary Exercises

Write the abbreviations of the words below. (Score: 16)

1. Tuesday (Tues.)	9. Mister (Mr.)
2. Friday (Fri.)	10. Colonel (Col.)
3. January (Jan.)	11. Governor (Gov.)
4. August (Aug.)	12. Avenue (Ave.)
5. October (Oct.)	13. Boulevard (Blvd.)
6. East (E.)	14. Oklahoma (Okla.)
7. Southwest (S.W.)	15. New York (N.Y.)
8. Northeast (N.E.)	16. Mississippi (Miss.)

Supplementary Activities

More Practice: Write the following paragraph on the chalkboard. Have the students rewrite the paragraph using abbreviations in place of the underlined words.

Doctor Logan lives at 26 Diamond Avenue in Seattle, Washington. Last Tuesday, February 10, Doctor Logan went to visit her parents, General and Mistress Logan, who live in Danbury, Connecticut. General and Mistress Logan live at 49 Walsh Boulevard in Danbury.

(Dr. Logan lives at 26 Diamond Ave. in Seattle, Wash. Last Tues., Feb. 10, Dr. Logan went to visit her parents, Gen. and Mrs. Logan, who live in Danbury, Conn. Gen. and Mrs. Logan live at 49 Walsh Blvd. in Danbury.)

Instructional Variation: On index cards write the words for titles of courtesy, directions, and street names, and for the names of days, months, and states. Then write the abbreviations for those words on another set of index cards. Place the word cards in various places in the classroom so they can be seen by the students. Distribute the abbreviation cards to the class and have them find the word card that matches their abbreviation card.

Using Resources and Materials: Have the students bring in samples of real want ads. What words are abbreviated? What do the abbreviations mean? Why do we see abbreviations in want ads that we don't see other places? Have the students decipher each abbreviation and write out the ads in full.

Lesson **52** (page 72)

Writing Titles of Courtesy
 1b, 7c

Key Objectives The student will be able to:
1. Write the titles of courtesy for given occupations.
2. Abbreviate titles of courtesy.

Procedures

Explain that titles of courtesy are words used with names for politeness, as *Mrs.* Smith, *Mr.* Roberts, and *Dr.* Jones. Ask such questions as: What title of courtesy would you use for a man? A woman? A judge? A physician?

Read and discuss Keys 1b and 7c with the students. Make sure they understand that *Miss* is not an abbreviation and should not be followed by a period and that *Judge* should never be abbreviated. Help them recognize the need for titles of courtesy in addressing envelopes and in writing letters, lists, notes, and reports.

As soon as the students understand the directions for the exercises in Lesson 52, let them work independently. After answers to exercises have been checked and scores recorded, let several students read aloud their answers to part II.

NOTE: Since some children's dictionaries do not list the abbreviation for *Senator,* you may need to tell the class that the correct abbreviation is *Sen.*

NOTE: In each of the exercises a title of courtesy should be correctly used. It should be abbreviated whenever possible. Names, abbreviations, and initials should be capitalized; abbreviations and initials should be followed by a period.

Supplementary Exercises

Rewrite the following names, using correct titles of courtesy, capital letters, and periods. Use abbreviations for those titles that can be abbreviated. (Score: 55)

1. a lincoln (president) (Pres. A. Lincoln)
2. margaret chase smith (senator) (Sen. Margaret Chase Smith)
3. u s grant (general) (Gen. U. S. Grant)
4. beverly cleary (author) (Ms. Beverly Cleary)
5. martin l. king jr. (minister) (Rev. Martin L. King, Jr.)
6. robert lawson (author) (Mr. Robert Lawson)
7. g b stone (professor) (Prof. G. B. Stone)
8. john paul jones (captain) (Capt. John Paul Jones)
9. thomas w. hill (physician) (Dr. Thomas W. Hill)
10. n h rogers (colonel) (Col. N. H. Rogers)

Supplementary Activities

More Practice: Have the students write the names of ten people in the community. Have them write a title of courtesy for each name. Suggest to the students that their lists include names of physicians, ministers, and others whose titles of courtesy are not Mr., Miss, Ms., or Mrs.

Instructional Variation: Have the students play a "title of courtesy" concentration game. On individual index cards write the names of real or fictitious characters. Next to each name write the character's profession in parentheses. On another set of index cards write the same names used above, but write the correct title of courtesy in front of each name and omit the profession. Place the cards face down on a table and have several students alternate turning over two cards trying to match the title of courtesy card with its corresponding profession card. For example, the *Paul R. Cruz* (a physician) card will match the *Dr. Paul R. Cruz* card.

Using Resources and Materials: Have the students choose a well-known person to write a report about. Tell the students that a title of courtesy needs to be part of the person's name. Have them use resource materials from the library to help them in writing their reports. Suggest that the students read Key 45 before writing their reports.

Lesson **53** (page 73)

Parts of a Friendly Letter
 50a

Key Objectives The student will be able to:

1. Write the names and functions of the five parts of a friendly letter.
2. Label the five parts of a friendly letter.

Procedures

Read and discuss Key 50a with the students. Make sure they understand the function of each part of a friendly letter. Then have them read directions for the exercises in Lesson 53 and let them work independently.

After answers to the exercises have been checked and scores recorded, direct the attention of the group to the letter in part II. Ask one student to find the heading, read it, explain what information it gives, and tell where capital letters and punctuation marks are used. Make it clear that all words in the heading should be capitalized and that commas should be used between the names of the city and the state as well as between the day of the month and the year. Let someone else find the greeting, explain its use, and tell what capitalization and punctuation are used. Have other students read the other parts of the letter and give similar information. Be sure to discuss the merits of the paragraphs in the body by using such questions as the following: How many paragraphs are there in the letter? What is the subject of each? Do all sentences tell about the subject? Are the first lines of the paragraphs indented? Do you think these are good paragraphs for a letter? Would you like to receive a letter like this? In discussing the complimentary close, make a point of the fact that the second word is not capitalized.

Assign the activity suggested in Other Things to Do at the bottom of Lesson 53.

Supplementary Exercises

In column A below are listed the parts of a friendly letter. The definitions of the parts are listed in column B. After each word in column A write the number of its definition. (Score: 5)

A	B
1. Heading (4)	1. Tells to whom the letter is written
2. Body (3)	2. Says good-by to the reader
3. Signature (5)	3. Gives the writer's message
4. Greeting (1)	4. Tells where and when the letter was written
5. Complimentary close (2)	5. Tells who wrote the letter

Supplementary Activities

More Practice: Let the students write letters to one another, telling about something they have learned recently. After the letters are written, let them deliver the letters. Individuals who think the letters they receive are especially interesting may read them aloud to the class.

Instructional Variation: Point out that the telephone is often used for the same purpose as a letter. Review with the students the rules for courteous use of the telephone. Then let pairs of students practice giving and receiving imaginary invitations on the telephone. Remind each student who is to give the invitation to tell for what event the invitation is being given, when the event is to be, and where it is to be. Suggest that each student who is to receive an invitation write the information on a piece of paper instead of trying to remember it. Remind the students that they can use abbreviations. Have the class listen to determine whether the person giving the invitation includes all the necessary information. Then have the person who received the invitation read aloud the information that was written down and have the class verify the accuracy of the information.

Using Resources and Materials: Have interested students read *Daddy Long-Legs* by Jean Webster. Then have the students tell what they know about Judy from reading the letters she writes to Mr. Smith.

Lesson **54** (page 74)

Writing a Friendly Letter
🔑 48, 50b, c

Key Objectives   The student will be able to:
1. Punctuate and indicate words which should be capitalized in a friendly letter.
2. Write a friendly letter.

Procedures

Ask several students to write on the chalkboard their addresses and today's date in the form of a heading in a letter. Have the class check each heading for capitalization and punctuation.

Let someone name the other four parts of a friendly letter. Ask students to tell what information is given in each part and how each part is punctuated. Then tell the class to check the accuracy of the answers by reading Key 50.

Have the students tell about gifts and invitations they have received and about ways in which people have entertained or helped them. Lead the discussion to a consideration of ways the students can show appreciation for such kindness. Be sure that thank-you letters are mentioned.

Ask the students to open their books to Lesson 54 and to look at the letter in part I. Show the students that this letter is written in block form. Explain what indented form is and tell the pupils that letters may also be written in this form. Point out that block form is more commonly used. Have the students notice that in the letter in Lesson 54 the heading, complimentary close, and signature are aligned. Explain that in the case of a long name or address such alignment might be difficult and is unnecessary. Tell the students that they should place these parts in such a way as to achieve a neat, attractive letter.

Be sure the students understand the directions for the exercises. Then let them work independently. After answers have been checked and scores recorded, assign the activity suggested in Other Things to Do. Let several students read aloud the letters they wrote for this assignment or the letters they wrote as answers to part II of the exercises.

Supplementary Exercises

Rewrite the following friendly letter, putting each part in its correct place. Use capital letters and punctuation marks where they are needed. (Score: 34—1 point for each capital letter or punctuation mark correctly used, and 2 points for each part correctly placed)

601 west oak street boston massachusetts april 2 1983 dear bill in school today we were studying about television i know you would have enjoyed it next week we shall study aviation could you visit our school one day i wish you would come your friend jack

(601 West Oak Street
Boston, Massachusetts 02111
April 2, 1983

Dear Bill,

In school today we were studying about television. I know you would have enjoyed it. Next week we shall study aviation. Could you visit our school one day? I wish you would come.
                              Your friend,
                              Jack)

Supplementary Activities

More Practice: Have the students write thank-you letters to their parents, friends or relatives who have been helpful in some way. Encourage the students to write about situations in which they sincerely felt gratitude. Explain that they need not mail the letters if they prefer not to.

Instructional Variation: Point out that there are ways other than writing thank-you letters to show courtesy. Set up hypothetical situations in which such expressions as *I beg your pardon, excuse me, I'm sorry, please,* and *thank you* are appropriate. Let the students practice using these words by dramatizing the situations. Then let them practice making proper introductions according to the following rules, which you may write on the chalkboard:
1. When you introduce a young person to an older person, speak the older person's name first.
2. When you introduce yourself, speak your own name. You may tell something else to explain who you are.
3. When you introduce a speaker to an audience, tell who the speaker is and what the topic of the speech is.

Using Resources and Materials: Write to a Pen Pal organization and request a list of names and addresses of children living in other parts of the United States. Some of the students may wish to correspond with one of the children on the list. Be sure the students check their letters for capitalization and punctuation.

Lesson **55** (page 75)

Parts of a Business Letter
🗝 48, 51

Key Objectives   The student will be able to:
1. Write the six parts of a business letter in their proper places.
2. Capitalize and punctuate the parts of a business letter.

Procedures

Read and discuss Keys 48 and 51 with the students. Point out that the business letter has six parts. Ask someone to tell what part a business letter has that a friendly letter does not have and to explain what the inside address tells. Have the students pay particular attention to the example, noting the use of the colon after the greeting.

Be sure the students understand the directions in Lesson 55. Explain that the parts of the letter are listed in correct order but that the students need to place the parts where they should be and to use captial letters and punctuation marks where they are needed. Let them work independently as they write the letter. After answers to the exercises have been checked and scores recorded, have the students correct their mistakes.

Supplementary Exercises

I. The parts of a business letter are listed in column A below. Their definitions are listed in column B. Write the number of the correct definition after each part. (Score: 6)

A	B
1. Greeting (5)	1. Gives the writer's message
2. Inside address (4)	2. Tells where and when the letter was written
3. Body (1)	3. Expresses courtesy in ending a letter
4. Heading (2)	4. Tells the title of respect and the name and address of the person to whom the letter is written
5. Signature (6)	5. Greets the person to whom the letter is written
6. Complimentary close (3)	6. Tells who wrote the letter

Supplementary Activities

More Practice: Write correctly the following headings for business letters. (Score: 15)

1. rural route 7 denver colorado 80227 april 7 1985
   (Rural Route 7
   Denver, Colorado 80227
   April 7, 1985
2. newman california 95360 august 11 1985
   (Newman, California 95360
   August 11, 1985)

Write the following inside addresses correctly. (Score: 15)

1. somnac kite company 111 east river street brownwood texas 76801
   (Somnac Kite Company
   111 East River Street
   Brownwood, Texas 76801)
2. smith dog kennels alpine kentucky 42512
   (Smith Dog Kennels
   Alpine, Kentucky 42512)

Using Resources and Materials: Appoint a committee to find out the name of the agency to which students may write to ask for information about their state's park, camping, and recreational facilities. Let another group find out the name of the agency that can supply information about the state's soil and water conservation program. Let still another group find out the name of the agency that can supply information about fish and wildlife preservation in the state. Suggest that the students may obtain the proper addresses from the local li-brary, the chamber of commerce, or the newspaper office.

After the addresses have been obtained, let the class compose a letter asking for information about state parks, camping, and recreation. Write the letter on the chalkboard and let a student copy it on school stationery and mail it. Follow the same procedure to write a letter asking about conservation and a letter asking about wildlife preservation.

Lesson **56** (page 76)

Writing a Business Letter
🔑 48, 51

Key Objective The student will be able to correctly write a business letter.

Procedures

Review the information presented in Lesson 55 by asking questions such as the following: How many parts are there in a business letter? What are the parts and what does each tell? What part does a business letter have that a friendly letter does not? What mark of punctuation is used after the greeting of a business letter? Have the students verify their answers by reading Keys 48 and 51.

Be sure the students understand directions for the activity suggested in Lesson 56. Explain that they may answer the advertisement that is more interesting to them. Make it clear that these advertisements are not real and that the companies are imaginary, so that the students will not make the mistake of mailing their letters.

After the exercises have been checked and scores recorded, let several students read their letters aloud.

Supplementary Exercises

On a separate piece of paper write a letter to answer the following advertisements. Use your address and today's date in the heading.

Make writing fun! Order your own set of personalized pencils. For three dollars you will receive 15 pencils with your name printed on each pencil. Send three dollars and the name you want printed on the pencils, to: Webster's Pen and Pencil Corporation, 1315 Atlas Road, Dover, Maryland 21225.

Supplementary Activities

More Practice: Have the students find real advertisements in magazines or newspapers and answer them. Suggest that the students mail the letters after you have checked them.

Instructional Variation: Suggest that the class might enjoy corresponding with a class of school children in another country. Have the class ask for information about such correspondence by writing a letter to the American Junior Red Cross, Washington, D.C. Let members of the class offer suggestions for writing the letter. When a satisfactory one has been written on the chalkboard, let someone copy it and mail it.

Using Resources and Materials: Let students who are especially interested in some city write the chamber of commerce of that city. Tell them to ask for folders or pamphlets that give information about the city. Be sure to check each student's letter before it is mailed. Have a student obtain the address of a travel bureau. Then let the class write a letter requesting folders that give information and show pictures of a country that the students are studying in social studies.

Lesson 57 (page 77)

Addressing Envelopes
 48, 49

Key Objective The student will be able to correctly address envelopes.

Procedures

Direct discussion about envelope addresses by asking questions similar to the following: Have you ever looked at an envelope that a letter came in? What was written on it? Was it easy to read? Point out that correct addresses and legible writing are a courtesy to postal workers, who must sort thousands of envelopes. Stress the fact that addressing envelopes correctly and writing legibly help a letter reach its destination quickly.

Read and discuss Keys 48 and 49 with the students. Then let them work the exercises in Lesson 57 independently. After answers to the exercises are checked, have the students correct their mistakes.

Have the students find out the ZIP code of their neighborhood. Encourage the students to use their ZIP codes in headings and return addresses of the letters they write.

NOTE: Students may substitute the two-letter, postal form abbreviation for the name of the state. See Key 7f to verify answers.

Supplementary Exercises

Address an envelope to Ms. Rebecca Campbell, 227 Firestone Boulevard, Akron, Ohio 44301. Use your own return address.

Supplementary Activities

More Practice: Have each student write a brief letter to a classmate who is ill. Next, have each student address an envelope for the letter. Check the letter and the envelope, and let the students mail their letters if they wish.

Instructional Variation: Have the class make a ZIP code map of the surrounding area.

Using Resources and Materials: Visit the local post office and see how the mail is processed. Do the people who sort the mail read the address or the ZIP code? How are the stamps canceled? How long does it take a letter to move through a post office?

Lesson 58 (page 78)

Capitalization and Punctuation
 1, 3, 5, 6, 7, 8, 9, 10, 12

Key Objectives The student will be able to:
1. Identify words in sentences that should be capitalized.
2. Place correct punctuation marks where they are needed in sentences.

Procedures

Broadcasting

How is the ship pictured in Lesson 58 different from a modern ship? Why do you think early ships had so many sails? Tell about the size and kind of boats you have seen.

Explaining the Lesson

Read and discuss Keys 1, 3, 5 to 10, and 12 with the students. Point out that capital letters and punctuation marks make writing easier to read and understand. Answer all questions and clarify points that cause confusion.

Be sure the students understand the directions in Lesson 58 before they work the exercises. Tell them to work carefully, not to guess, and to check their work after they have completed the exercises. In figuring scores, count off 1 point for each capital letter or punctuation mark left out and 1 point for each one incorrectly used.

Let several students read the sentences aloud, tell what capital letters and punctuation marks they used, and explain why they used each one. Be sure that the students correct their errors after they have checked the appropriate keys to correct their mistakes.

Supplementary Exercises

Copy the following sentences, using capital letters and punctuation marks where they are needed. (Score: 20)

1. have you studied about the War of 1812 asked Bob. ("Have you studied about the War of 1812?" asked Bob.)
2. This war was declared on june 18 1812. (This war was declared on June 18, 1812.)
3. The *chesapeake* was an american ship of this war. (The *Chesapeake* was an American ship of this war.)
4. The commander of the *chesapeake* was james lawrence. (The commander of the *Chesapeake* was James Lawrence.)
5. It was this commander who said don't give up the ship. (It was this commander who said, "Don't give up the ship.")
6. The *chesapeake* the *constitution* and the *united states* were american ships. (The *Chesapeake*, the *Constitution*, and the *United States* were American ships.)

Supplementary Activities

More Practice: Write the following questions on the chalkboard:

1. In what war was the *Constitution* used?
2. Why was the ship called *Old Ironsides*?
3. Why wasn't *Old Ironsides* torn apart after the war?

Tell the students to write the story of the *Constitution*. Have them outline the story before they write it, and suggest that they answer the questions on the chalkboard. Explain that they may use the information given in Lesson 58. Remind them to proofread their stories, checking for paragraphing, complete sentences, and correct spelling, capitalization, and punctuation.

Instructional Variation: On individual index cards draw the following punctuation marks: period, comma, question mark, exclamation mark, and quotation marks. Also write the words "capital letter" on several cards.

Write a sentence on the chalkboard omitting the punctuation marks and using lowercase letters for words that should begin with a capital letter. Pick two teams and have each team determine which punctuation marks are needed in the sentence and how many words in the sentence should be capitalized. When one team thinks they have the correct number of punctuation and capital letter cards to complete a sentence correctly, have the team send a representative to the chalkboard and place the cards on the chalkboard ledge, indicating where the punctuation marks belong and which words should begin with a capital letter. Score five

points for the team that correctly completes the sentence and repeat the procedure.

Using Resources and Materials: Have the students use encyclopedias and other resource materials to find information on famous ships and boats. Then have the students write a report describing the events which made a particular ship famous. Tell the students to read and study Key 45 before writing their report. Have the students check their reports for punctuation and capitalization.

Lesson **59** (page 79)

Recognizing and Using Pronouns
  17, 18

Key Objectives   The student will be able to:

1. Identify the personal pronouns in sentences.
2. Properly complete sentences by selecting one of the following pronouns: *she* or *her*, *they* or *them*, *I* or *me*, *we* or *us*, *he* or *him*.

Procedures

Broadcasting

What kind of uniform is the man in the picture wearing? When do you think this man lived? Name three things that would look different if this were a picture of a modern soldier.

Explaining the Lesson

Read and discuss Keys 17 and 18. Use the key examples to help the students understand the need for personal pronouns and the functions and proper uses of such pronouns. To give the students practice in substituting personal pronouns for nouns, say the following sentences. Let several students restate each sentence, using pronouns instead of some of the nouns.

1. Sue took Sue's dog into Sue's house.
2. Jack gave the book to Mary.
3. Ann told Dave about the party.
4. Mike and Linda were late.
5. Sally's mother gave Sally and Jack some cookies.
6. It was Tom who found Bill's ball.

If a student says, "It was Tom who found his ball," or "It was he who found his ball," when restating the last sentence, point out that substituting *his* for *Bill's* changes the meaning of the sentence. Help the students see that the ball seems to belong to Tom when *Bill's* is changed to *his*. Say, "It was he who found Bill's ball," to illustrate pronoun substitution in which the meaning is clear. Point out that students should not use a pronoun in place of a noun if the substitution changes the meaning or makes the sentence hard to understand.

Be sure the students understand the directions for the exercises in Lesson 59; then let them work independently. After answers to the exercises have been checked, have the students record their scores and correct their mistakes. For practice in recognizing and using nouns and verbs, assign the activity suggested in Other Things to Do at the bottom of Lesson 59.

Supplementary Exercises

I. After each sentence below list the pronouns used in the sentence. (Score: 6)

1. I have read your book about Sam Houston. (I, your)
2. It told about his friends the Cherokee Indians. (It, his)
3. He had lived with them for many years. (He, them)

II. Choose the proper word form in parentheses to write in each blank. (Score: 4)

4. (Us, We) _____ learned that Houston talked to the Cherokees. (We)
5. (me, I) John told her and _____ that the Cherokees left Tennessee. (me)
6. (her, she) He and _____ asked where the Indians had moved. (she)
7. (him, he) John told _____ that they had moved to Oklahoma. (him)

Supplementary Activities

More Practice: Have the students write ten sentences. Tell them to use each of the following pronouns in a sentence:

1. he	6. her
2. me	7. him
3. she	8. they
4. we	9. us
5. I	10. them

Instructional Variation: Have the students write five sentences without using pronouns. The students then exchange papers and substitute as many pronouns for nouns as possible. Do all the new sentences make sense? Are any of them confusing? Can we use too many pronouns in one sentence?

Using Resources and Materials: On the chalkboard write the following subjects. Let each student choose one of the subjects and give an oral report about it.

1. The Battle of San Jacinto
2. The Cherokee Indians
3. General Santa Anna
4. The Alamo

Suggest that the students consult encyclopedias, social-studies books, and other reference books to find information for their reports. Remind the children to read Key 52a before giving their reports. Tell the students to underline each pronoun in their reports.

Lesson **60** (page 80)

Using *I* or *Me* with Other Nouns and Other Pronouns

 18a–d

Key Objectives   The student will be able to:
1. Select the pronoun and pronoun pair, or the noun and pronoun pair which properly completes sentences.
2. Select *I* or *me* to properly complete sentences.

Procedures

Write the following sentences on the chalkboard:
1. (Me and Bill, Bill and I) went for a hike.
2. Mr. Blair told (him and me, he and I) that we could walk in his field.
3. The hike was fun for (Bill and I, Bill and me, me and Bill).

Have the students read and discuss Key 18a to d. Then direct their attention to the sentences on the chalkboard. Ask someone to read sentence 1, using the proper expression in parentheses. Explain that using *I* or *me* and leaving out the other words in parentheses will help the student make the proper choice. Let other students follow a similar procedure with the other sentences.

Be sure the students understand the directions for the exercises in Lesson 60 before they work independently. After answers to the exercises have been checked and scores recorded, have everyone correct their mistakes.

Supplementary Exercises

Underline the proper words in parentheses. (Score: 13)

1. (I and Amy, Amy and I) wanted to learn more about the forests of Brazil. (Amy and I)
2. Tad told (her and me, she and I) that many valuable trees grow there. (her and me)
3. (Me and Amy, Amy and I) knew that rubber trees grow wild in these forests. (Amy and I)
4. Miss Smith explained to (her and me, me and her) how rubber is collected. (her and me)
5. (Amy and I, I and Amy) were interested in learning about the rubber trees. (Amy and I)

54

Supplementary Activities

More Practice: Have the students write four sentences using one of the following pairs of pronouns in each sentence.

1. She and I
2. Her and me
3. He and I
4. Him and me

Instructional Variation: On the chalkboard write several sentences which use pronouns, pronouns in pairs, or a noun and a pronoun. Omit the pronouns when writing the sentences on the chalkboard. Distribute index cards on which you have written the pronouns that complete the sentences on the chalkboard. Have the students match the correct pronoun cards to the sentences on the chalkboard.

Using Resources and Materials: Have the students go to the library to find more information on Brazil. Tell the students to write about Brazil as if they had visited the country. Explain that they will need to use the word forms *I* and *me* in their reports. Suggest that the students read and study Key 45 before writing their reports.

Lesson **61** (page 81)

Using *Them, These,* and *Those*

 33

Key Objective The student will be able to select the proper word form *them, these,* or *those* to complete sentences.

Procedures

Broadcasting

What is the name of the animal in the picture in Lesson 61? Why do you think this animal has such a long pointed nose? Where could you see an animal like this?

Explaining the Lesson

Write the following sentences on the chalkboard:
1. Put (these, them) books on the table.
2. Bring (them, those) books to me.
3. I want to read (them, these).

Have the students read the information in Key 33, the first two expressions, and the footnote in the key. Explain that the pronoun *them* cannot be used in place of *these* or *those* to refer to something. Illustrate by telling the students that they may say *these flowers* when speaking of flowers that are near, and they may say *those flowers* when speaking of flowers that are at a distance, but they should not say *them flowers*. Ask someone to read sentence 1 on the chalkboard, using the proper

word in parentheses. Have the student explain why that word was chosen. Let other students follow the same procedure with the other sentences on the chalkboard. Point out that in sentence 3 either word in parentheses can be used since the word is used to take the place of the noun *books*.

Have the students read the information and examples in Lesson 61. Tell them to underline the proper word form in parentheses. Explain that in some of the sentences either word is correct. Tell the children to underline *them* in sentences in which *them* can be properly used.

After the answers have been checked and scores recorded, have the students correct their mistakes.

Supplementary Exercises

Choose the proper word form in parentheses to write in the blank. (Score: 6)

1. (those, them) Where did you see _____ anteaters? (those)
2. (these, them) I saw _____ at the zoo. (them)
3. (these, them) But _____ pictures show an anteater with gray fur. (these)
4. (those, them) They don't look like _____ animals at the zoo. (those)
5. (Them, These) _____ pictures show an anteater from South America. (These)
6. (Those, Them) _____ anteaters at the zoo came from Africa. (Those)

Supplementary Activities

More Practice: Have the students write six sentences about an interesting animal they have read about or seen in the zoo. Tell them to use the word forms *them, these,* and *those* in the sentences.

Instructional Variation: Dictate a tape for a listening center activity. Say sentences that use *them, these,* and *those,* but omit these words when dictating the tape. On a separate piece of paper have the students write the proper word form that completes each sentence.

Using Resources and Materials: Have the students review Keys 43 and 44. Then tell them to outline and write two paragraphs about the anteater. Suggest that in one paragraph they write about what it looks like and in the other tell what it does. Explain that the students may use the information in Lesson 61 but that they should state the ideas in their own words. Remind them to proofread their writing, checking for paragraphing, complete sentences, and correct spelling, capitalization, and punctuation. Remind the students to use the word forms *them, these,* and *those* in their paragraphs.

55

Lesson **62** (page 82)

Troublesome Words
 20a, 27, 30, 37

Key Objective The student will be able to complete sentences by selecting correct homophones and by selecting proper verb forms.

Procedures

Write the following words on the chalkboard:

1. blew, blue	5. their, there
2. buy, by	6. to, too, two
3. its, it's	7. who's, whose
4. one, won	8. your, you're

Have the students read Keys 20a, 27, 30, and 37. After they have discussed agreement of subject and verb and the proper use of *may* and *can*, direct their attention to the words on the chalkboard. Ask someone to read the first pair of words and explain the meaning of each. Have other students read and define the other words.

After the students have worked the exercises in Lesson 62, checked their answers, and recorded their scores, have them correct their mistakes.

Supplementary Exercises

Choose the proper word form in parentheses to write in the blank. (Score: 5)

1. (to, too, two) Annie had _____ work very hard to learn braille at the Perkins school. (to)
2. (to, too, two) Did she have fun _____ ? (too)
3. (Have, Has) _____ you heard that Helen Keller went to Radcliffe College? (Have)
4. (Its, It's) _____ a college in Boston. (It's)
5. (You're, Your) _____ sure to find her adventures interesting. (You're)

Supplementary Activities

More Practice: Have the students write sentences using the homophones *their* and *there*; *your* and *you're*; *two, to,* and *too*; *buy* and *by*; *one* and *won*; *who's* and *whose*; *blue* and *blew*. Have the students also write sentences using the verb forms *doesn't, don't, has, have, may* and *can*.

Instructional Variation: Have the class think of riddles whose answers are homophones. For example: "What did the man with the basketball do?" Answer: "He threw through." Have the students tell the riddles to each other and guess the answers. (Key 37 contains a list of homophones.)

Using Resources and Materials: Have the students read biographies of well known people and write reports on the people they read about. Suggest they include some of the word forms discussed in Lesson 62 in their reports. Have the students read Key 45 before writing their reports.

Lesson **63** (page 83)

Uses of the Dictionary
 38

Key Objectives The student will be able to:
1. Alphabetize a list of words.
2. Write the page numbers on which certain words would appear in a dictionary, given the guide words.
3. Select the proper definition for given words.

Procedures

Review the use of the dictionary by asking questions similar to the following: What can you find out from a dictionary? How do you go about finding a word quickly in a dictionary? Have the students check their answers to these questions by reading Key 38.

Since the students have previously worked exercises similar to the ones in Lesson 63, they should be able to understand directions and work the exercises independently. After answers to the exercises have been checked and scores recorded, have the students correct their mistakes.

If dictionaries are available, follow this lesson with dictionary drill. Have the students practice opening the dictionary to various sections. For example, say the letter *p* and have the students try to open their dictionaries to the section containing words that begin with *p*. Then say various words and see how quickly the students can find them. Allow the student who finds the word first to read its definition. Finally list a few words, such as *throe, conspire, lade, puckish,* and *ware*, on the chalkboard and have the students find the words, determine their pronunciations, and write their definitions on paper. If there are not enough dictionaries in the classroom, try to borrow some from other classrooms and work with small groups of children in this activity.

Supplementary Exercises

I. The words below are arranged in alphabetical order according to the first letter only. Alphabetize the words according to the second letter. (Score: 12)

1. ancient	5. bay	9. gentle
2. artist	6. buffalo	10. hill
3. altitude	7. gun	11. herd
4. boundary	8. green	12. hot

(Answers:)

1. altitude	5. boundary	9. gun
2. ancient	6. buffalo	10. herd
3. artist	7. gentle	11. hill
4. bay	8. green	12. hot

II. Using the guide words and page numbers listed below, after each word write the page number on which it would be found. (Score: 16)

Page 5	Page 6	Page 7	Page 8
b—bar	barb—can	car—cheer	circle—dock

13. care (7)	19. dig (8)	25. bee (6)
14. big (6)	20. bark (6)	26. charge (7)
15. circus (8)	21. cat (7)	27. bad (5)
16. camp (6)	22. baby (5)	28. bag (5)
17. back (5)	23. barn (6)	
18. carry (7)	24. close (8)	

Supplementary Activities

More Practice: Have the students use dictionaries to find the following words: *miscellaneous, prominent, speculate, disclose, communication,* and *fortitude.* Have them write the definition of each word and use the word in a sentence. Also have them write the two guide words found at the top of the page on which each word is located.

Instructional Variation: Divide the class into teams of five or six students and give each team a dictionary. Read definitions of familiar words but do not say the word. For example, A piece of furniture consisting of a smooth flat slab fixed on legs. (table). Have the students decide what word is being defined and have them find that word in the dictionary. A team earns five points when it finds the word and can give the two guide words found at the top of the dictionary page.

Lesson **64** (page 84)

Dividing Words into Syllables
 38a, 39

Key Objectives The student will be able to:
1. Alphabetize given words.
2. Divide given words into syllables.
3. Place accent marks on accented syllables of given words.

Procedures

Read and discuss Keys 38a and 39 with the students. Give them practice in determining the number of syllables in words and identifying the accented syllable. Say a word and then ask the stu-

dents how many syllables were heard and which one was accented. If the class has difficulty in hearing the syllables and accents, tap a pencil on your desk as you say each syllable and tap harder for the accented syllable. Use such words as *baton, famous, democracy, education,* and *refrigerator.*

Be sure the students understand that they should write the words in Lesson 64 in alphabetical order in the first column of blank spaces. In the second column they should divide the words into syllables, placing hyphens after unaccented syllables (unless they come at ends of words) and accent marks after accented syllables. After the exercises have been worked, answers checked, and scores recorded, have the students correct their mistakes.

Before assigning the activity suggested in Other Things to Do, use a dictionary to explain the markings of vowels. Direct the students' attention to the key words in the dictionary and help the students interpret the sound of each vowel marking. You may need to help students who are trying to determine the pronunciation of unknown words.

Supplementary Exercises

Rewrite each of the following words, dividing it into syllables and marking the accented syllable. (Score: 10)
1. dinner (din'ner)
2. belong (be-long')
3. cabin (cab'in)
4. station (sta'tion)
5. hello (hel-lo')
6. remember (re-mem'ber)
7. different (dif'fer-ent)
8. untidy (un-ti'dy)
9. religion (re-li'gion)
10. nightingale (night'in-gale)

Supplementary Activities

More Practice: Have the students divide this week's spelling words into syllables and place accent marks after the accented syllables.

Instructional Variation: Have the class work through this oral exercise. The first student says, "I am thinking of a two-syllable word that means . . ." Each time the number of syllables in the word and its definition should be given.

Using Resources and Materials: Have the students write down the lyrics of popular songs. Have them divide each polysyllabic word into syllables. Then have them add accent marks after each word or syllable that gets a beat in the song. Does word stress help give songs rhythm?

Lesson 65 (page 85)

Choosing Proper Word Forms
 21, 37

Key Objective The student will be able to select past forms of verbs and select homophones to properly complete sentences.

Procedures

Write the following words on the chalkboard:

1. broke—broken
2. flew—flown
3. froze—frozen
4. knew—known
5. rode—ridden
6. took—taken
7. wrote—written

Ask a student to write two sentences on the chalkboard, one with *whose* and the other with *who's*. Tell the student to explain the meaning of the homophones. Have someone else write two sentences on the chalkboard, using *its* and *it's*. Then let another member of the class read the first two words on the chalkboard, explain their correct use, and use each of them in oral sentences. Ask several students to follow the same procedure with the other words on the chalkboard. If someone disagrees with an explanation or the use of a word, have the class find the word in Key 21 or 37 and determine its proper use.

After the exercises in Lesson 65 have been worked, answers checked, and scores recorded, have the students correct their mistakes.

Supplementary Exercises

Choose the proper word form in parentheses to write in the blank. (Score: 8)

1. (wrote, written) Stephen and Rosemary Benét have _____ many poems. (written)
2. (knew, known) Perhaps you have _____ their poem "Johnny Appleseed." (known)
3. (Its, It's) _____ a poem you would enjoy reading. (It's)
4. (rode, ridden) The poem tells how Johnny _____ from place to place. (rode)
5. (rode, ridden) During winter he had _____ far into the wilderness. (ridden)
6. (froze, frozen) The land was _____ and Johnny could plant no trees. (frozen)
7. (flew, flown) Snowflakes _____ through the cold air. (flew)
8. (took, taken) Friends _____ Johnny into their homes for the winter. (took)

Supplementary Activities

More Practice: Have the students write 12 sentences. Tell them to use the past forms of the verbs ride, fly, freeze, know, take, break, and write in their sentences.

Instructional Variation: Read and discuss Key 52b with the students. Tell them to become very familiar with the story in Lesson 65 so that they can tell it effectively. Suggest that they practice telling the story to someone at home. Then let several students tell the class the story of the first American astronaut. Tell the students to use the word forms mentioned in Lesson 65 in their stories.

Using Resources and Materials: Have the students use the encyclopedia, magazines, and other resource materials to learn about current space exploration and travel. Suggest that the students write an outline and then a report discussing the information they have learned. Have them read and study Keys 43 and 45 before writing their reports. Remind the students to use the word forms mentioned in Lesson 65 when writing their reports.

Lesson 66 (page 86)

Remembering What We Have Learned

Key Objectives The student will be able to apply the skills taught in Unit IV.

Procedures

Have the students open their books to Lesson 66 and read the title of the lesson. Ask someone to explain the object of this lesson. The student should tell that it will help the class remember what they learned in Unit IV and prepare for the post test that follows. Make sure that everyone understands the directions for the exercises and explain that each person should find the keys and review the information for themselves.

Since the exercises are subjective, let several students read their answers aloud. Then direct a discussion of the material being reviewed, covering the following:

1. Friendly letters—their form, parts, capitalization, and punctuation
2. Business letters—their form, parts, capitalization, and punctuation
3. Envelopes and addresses
4. Abbreviations
5. Dictionary study, including alphabetical order, guide words, syllabication, accent, and word definitions
6. Homophones
7. Proper use of the second and third principal parts of verbs, of pronouns, and of *doesn't, don't, has, have, may,* and *can.*

Post Test—Unit IV

At the conclusion of Unit IV, administer the post test for this unit. Post tests for all units are at the back of the Teacher's Edition. The results of the post test should indicate which students have mastered the concepts and skills in the unit. Instructions for administration of post tests appear on page 3 in the introduction to the Teacher's Edition.

Pretest—Unit V

Before beginning Unit V, administer the pretest for this unit. Pretests for all units are at the back of the Teacher's Edition. The results should indicate the students' preliminary competency levels for concepts and skills presented in the unit. Instructions for administration and ways to use the pretests appear in the introduction to the Teacher's Edition.

Lesson 67 (page 87)

Adjectives

 23a

Key Objectives The student will be able to:
1. Identify adjectives used in sentences.
2. Select adjectives from a list that describe given nouns.

Procedures

Broadcasting

Where can you find shells similar to those pictured in Lesson 67? What kinds of animals live in shells? How does a shell help an animal survive? Describe how certain shells look and feel. (Each time a student uses an adjective, write it on the chalkboard.)

Explaining the Lesson

Let several students tell about objects they collect or things they make. Encourage them to use sensory impressions in describing what they work with or collect. Stimulate discussion by asking questions similar to the following: How does it look? What is its shape? What is its color? What does it feel like? Is it soft or hard, rough or smooth? Can you tell about the sound it makes? What does it smell like? Is the odor pleasant? What does it taste like? Each time a student uses an adjective write it on the chalkboard. At the conclusion of the discussion direct the attention of the class to the words you have written on the chalkboard and explain that the students have been using adjectives to tell how things look, feel, smell, taste, and sound.

Read Key 23a with the students. Discuss the five senses and give examples of adjectives. Then ex-plain the exercises in Lesson 67 and let the students work independently.

NOTE: At this grade level an adjective is considered one that tells about appearance, feeling, taste, sound, or odor. Students should not be expected to underline articles, *these* in exercise 3, or *this* in exercises 7 and 10.

Supplementary Exercises

After each sentence below write the adjectives that are used in the sentence. (Score: 10)
1. The starling is a beautiful bird of Europe. (beautiful)
2. Its brown plumage has yellow spots. (brown, yellow)
3. It has green feathers, too. (green)
4. Enormous flocks of starlings roost on large buildings in big cities. (Enormous, large, big)
5. The starling can mimic human sounds. (human)
6. The female lays blue eggs. (blue)
7. In 1890 the noisy starling was brought to New York City. (noisy)

Supplementary Activities

More Practice: Have the students write five sentences, one describing each of the following: thunder, rain, a forest fire, clay, and a mountain stream.

Instructional Variation: Have the students take turns describing animals while the other members of the class try to guess what is being described. For example, someone may say, "I am thinking of an animal that has white fur with black stripes." If the other students do not guess that a zebra is being described, they may be given a further description. The student who guesses the answer may give the next description.

Using Resources and Materials: Have the students think of an animal or an object and find its description in a dictionary or encyclopedia. Then tell the students to use a separate piece of paper to write the adjectives used to describe the animal or object. Collect the papers and read aloud a description, but do not say what is being described. Have the students guess what animal or object is being described.

Lesson 68 (page 88)

Using Conjunctions

 24

Key Objective The student will be able to use conjunctions to combine two short, choppy sentences into one more effective sentence.

Procedures

Read and study Key 24 with the students. Explain that conjunctions are words used to join other words or ideas. Use the following as examples: "Jack *and* I," "walk *or* run," "you sing *while* I play," and "Bill plays, *but* Barbara works." Then let the students practice using conjunctions. Say short sentences and let several students combine them by using conjunctions. Use sentences similar to the following: "Jane likes chocolate cookies. Jack likes chocolate cookies." "Ice-skating is fun. The ice must be thick before you skate on it." "When I was young, I liked to climb trees."

Before the students work the exercises in Lesson 68, explain that there is no particular conjunction that should be used in each sentence and that they may use the conjunction that seems to make the best sentence. Tell them to use as many different conjunctions as possible and to try to use a different one in each sentence. After the exercises have been worked, let several students read their sentences aloud.

Supplementary Exercises

Use one of the conjunctions below to combine the short sentences that follow. (Score: 3 for each sentence) Answers will vary.

and	if	while	although	for	where
but	as	when	because	after	that

1. I read about grass in the encyclopedia. I learned about different kinds of grass. (I learned about different kinds of grass when I read the encyclopedia.)
2. Grass grows in cold regions. Grass grows in tropical areas. (Grass grows in cold regions and in tropical areas.)
3. We eat cereal grasses. Wheat, oats, barley, and corn are cereal grasses. (Wheat, oats, barley, and corn are cereal grasses that we eat.)
4. Grass helps in conservation. It saves the topsoil from washing away. (Grass helps in conservation because it saves the topsoil from washing away.)
5. Some kinds of grass die at the end of a growing season. Other kinds of grass grow every year. (Some kinds of grass die at the end of a growing season but other kinds of grass grow every year.)

Supplementary Activities

More Practice: Have the students use their readers to find sentences containing conjunctions. Let several students read the sentences aloud. Then have them give the same information in two sentences without conjunctions. Ask other students to comment on the effectiveness of the two ways of saying the same thing.

Instructional Variation: Let the class play the conjunction game described in Lesson 68. Have one student make a statement and add a conjunction. Then have the next student complete the sentence.

Using Resources and Materials: Read and discuss Key 47 with the students. Tell them to make up stories about observing alligators in the saw grass. They may use the information in Lesson 68, but they should think of an original problem or exciting situation for their stories. Tell them to use conjunctions wherever possible. Remind them to proofread their stories.

Lesson **69** (page 89)

Combining Sentences
 24

Key Objective The student will be able to combine sentences by using conjunctions.

Procedures

Tell the students that you will read two paragraphs that tell the same thing in different ways. Instruct them to listen carefully and decide which paragraph sounds better. Then read the following paragraphs aloud:

There is an interesting bird. It is an ostrich. It is large. It is the largest of all birds. It can be eight feet tall. The ostrich has wings. It has feathers. It can't fly. But it has long legs. They are thin It can run. It can run faster than a horse. The ostrich can also kick. It can kick hard enough to hurt a person very badly. It can hurt a large animal very badly.

What an interesting bird an ostrich is! It is the largest of all birds and can be as much as eight feet tall. Although the ostrich has wings and feathers, it can't fly at all. Its long, thin legs make up for this lack. It can run faster than a horse. The ostrich can also kick hard enough to hurt a person or a large animal very badly.

After the students have expressed their opinions about the sentences, explain that the first paragraph is full of short, choppy sentences and needless repetition while the second has longer, more interesting sentences. Then tell them that in this lesson they will practice using conjunctions to combine short sentences into longer ones.

Have the students study Key 24 before they work the exercises in Lesson 69. After answers to the exercises have been checked and scores recorded, let several students read their sentences aloud.

Supplementary Exercises

Use one of the conjunctions listed below to combine the short sentences. (Score: 6)

and	if	while	although	for	where
but	as	when	because	after	since

1. Many people visit Virginia. They see Lee's home. (Many people visit Virginia, where they see Lee's home.)
2. People admire Lee. He was brave and honest. (People admire Lee because he was brave and honest.)
3. The Civil War ended. Lee became president of a college. (After the Civil War ended, Lee became president of a college.)
4. He returned to his home. He had been gone for many years. (He returned to his home after he had been gone for many years.)
5. Lee had fought bravely. He was glad when peace came. (Although Lee had fought bravely, he was glad when peace came.)
6. He wanted peace with the North. He wanted a strong nation. (He wanted peace with the North because he wanted a strong nation.)

NOTE: Answers will vary.

Supplementary Activities

Instructional Variation: Have the students hold conversations with each other omitting conjunctions from their speech. Have the students comment on how their conversations sound when they don't use conjunctions.

Have the students record ordinary conversations. Then have them listen to the conversations and count the conjunctions. How many conjunctions were recorded? Do people sometimes interrupt each other just after a conjunction is spoken? Why?

Lesson **70** (page 90)

Separating Sentences
 5, 7a, 24c

Key Objectives The student will be able to rewrite paragraphs, separating run-on sentences with punctuation marks and capital letters.

Procedures

Broadcasting

Where do whales live? Have you ever heard the expression, "A whale of an appetite?" What do you think that expression means? Have you ever seen a whale perform tricks at an amusement park? What kinds of tricks have you seen performed? What facts do you know about whales?

Explaining the Lesson

Read and discuss Keys 5, 7a, and 24c with the students. Point out that sometimes students run two or more sentences together by leaving out capital letters and punctuation marks and that this practice makes reading difficult.

Be sure the students understand the directions before they work the exercises in Lesson 70. After answers to the exercises have been checked and scores recorded, have the students correct their mistakes. Then ask someone to read the first paragraph as it appears in type and then read the corrected paragraph. Ask the student to explain which paragraph is easier to read and understand. Let someone else follow the same procedure with the second paragraph.

Supplementary Exercises

Rewrite the paragraph below, separating the sentences by using punctuation marks and capital letters. (Score: 20—2 for each sentence)

Florence Nightingale was born in Italy she lived in England one day when she was driving she met a shepherd. The shepherd's dog had been hurt Florence took the dog home and nursed it when she grew up, she studied nursing. A war broke out and she went to the Crimea she nursed the soldiers at night she carried a lamp the soldiers called her "the lady with the lamp."

(Florence Nightingale was born in Italy. She lived in England. One day when she was driving she met a shepherd. The shepherd's dog had been hurt. Florence took the dog home and nursed it. When she grew up, she studied nursing. A war broke out and she went to the Crimea. She nursed the soldiers. At night she carried a lamp. The soldiers called her "the lady with the lamp.")

Supplementary Activities

More Practice: Rewrite the three paragraphs below, separating the sentences by using punctuation marks and capital letters.

Every afternoon Rose Quickbear works on her book about American Indians. She goes to the local library there she finds history books that contain information she needs.

At the library Rose met Ruth Tewa Ruth writes for the daily newspaper. Ruth, a Hopi Indian, gave Rose several stories about Hopis in Arizona and New Mexico.

Rose's book is now over two hundred pages long she wants to illustrate it herself she will also use the photographs that Ruth Tewa gave her.

(Every afternoon Rose Quickbear works on her book about American Indians. She goes to the local library. There she finds history books that contain the information she needs.

At the library Rose met Ruth Tewa. Ruth writes for the daily newspaper. Ruth, a Hopi Indian, gave Rose several stories about Hopis in Arizona and New Mexico.

Rose's book is now over two hundred pages long. She wants to illustrate it herself. She will also use the photographs that Ruth Tewa gave her.)

Using Resources and Materials: Have the students read stories in magazines and newspapers. Then tell them to choose a story and rewrite it, omitting capital letters and punctuation marks at the ends of sentences. Have the students exchange articles and correctly punctuate and capitalize the article they receive. Discuss with the students how a story can have a different meaning when it is not punctuated correctly.

Lesson **71** (page 91)

Avoiding Too Many *Ands*
🔑 24a, 24c

Key Objective The student will be able to rewrite paragraphs, making shorter, clearer sentences by eliminating unnecessary *and*s.

Procedures

Read and discuss Key 24a and 24c with the students. Point out that many people use *and* and *and then* to string several sentences together. Tell the students that this practice not only makes reading boring but also makes the ideas difficult to understand. Use an example by obviously linking a series of sentences with *and:* "Yesterday we went to town *and* we bought some skates *and* then we went to the park *and* we skated until we were exhausted."

If the students think Lesson 71 seems contradictory in content to Lessons 68 and 69, point out that effective writing contains neither all short sentences nor all long sentences but rather has a variety of each.

Be sure the students understand the directions before they work the exercises in Lesson 71. Re-

mind them to proofread their paragraphs after they have written them.

Supplementary Exercises

Rewrite the following paragraph, leaving out the unnecessary *and*s. (Score: 5)

I have the cutest little puppy and his name is Spot and he is white with a tiny black spot in the middle of his back and he knows his name and when I call him, he comes rushing to me.

(I have the cutest little puppy. His name is Spot. He is white with a tiny black spot in the middle of his back. He knows his name. When I call him, he comes rushing to me.)

Supplementary Activities

More Practice: Rewrite the following paragraph, leaving out the unnecessary *and*s.

High on a plateau in India live four tribes of people and their names are the Todas, Kotas, Kurumbas, and Badagas and they lived peacefully there and worked together until the early 1800s and then the British built roads into their territory and now they no longer work together or trade with each other and some have fought against the changes brought by outside society and some have welcomed them and the tribes are slowly losing their identities.

(High on a plateau in India live four tribes of people. Their names are the Todas, Kotas, Kurumbas, and Badagas. They lived peacefully there and worked together until the early 1800s. Then the British built roads into their territory. Now they no longer work together or trade with each other. Some have fought against the changes brought by outside society and some have welcomed them. The tribes are slowly losing their identities.)

Using Resources and Materials: Have each student write a paragraph about an interesting or unusual kind of tree. Tell the students that they may choose one of the following trees to write about: the baobab tree, the sequoia tree, the soapberry tree, the manchineel tree, or the palm tree. Suggest that they consult encyclopedias or other reference books in the library about the subject chosen. Remind the students to use conjunctions to avoid having short, choppy sentences, but caution them not to use *and* or *and then* to string several sentences together. Point out that using a variety of sentences will help them achieve writing that is easy to understand, effective, and interesting. Have the students read Keys 44 and 45 before writing their paragraphs. Remind them to proofread their work.

Capitalization and Punctuation

 1, 2, 3, 5, 6, 7a, 7b, 7c, 8, 9, 10, 11, 12

Key Objectives   The student will be able to:
1. Identify words in sentences that should begin with a capital letter.
2. Punctuate sentences correctly.

Procedures

Briefly review possessives and contractions by asking the following questions: What two uses for the apostrophe do you know? What is a possessive noun? What is a contraction? What does the apostrophe show in a possessive word? What does the apostrophe stand for in a contraction? Point out that some possessives and contractions are included in Lesson 72 and that the students will need to add apostrophes where they are needed.

Read and discuss Keys 1, 2, 3, 5, 6, 7a, 7b, 7c, 8, 9, 10, 11, 12 with the students. Point out that capital letters and punctuation marks make writing easier to read and understand. Answer all questions and clarify points that cause confusion.

Be sure the students understand the directions in Lesson 72 before they work the exercises. Tell them to work carefully—not to guess—and to check their work after they have completed the exercises. Subtract 1 point for each capital letter or punctuation mark left out and 1 point for each one incorrectly used.

Let several students read the sentences aloud, tell what capital letters and punctuation marks they used, and explain why they used each one. Be sure that the students correct their errors after they have checked the appropriate keys.

Supplementary Exercises

Rewrite the following sentences, using capital letters and punctuation marks where they are needed. (Score: 23)
1. Sally deborah and nannie lived in massachusetts. (Sally, Deborah, and Nannie lived in Massachusetts.)
2. didnt they move to maine (Didn't they move to Maine?)
3. Sally reached her new home in maine in march or april. (Sally reached her new home in Maine in March or April.)
4. Didnt she meet andrew, from philadelphia pennsylvania? (Didn't she meet Andrew, from Philadelphia, Pennsylvania?)
5. Andrew and i shall be good friends Sally said.

("Andrew and I shall be good friends," Sally said.)
6. Sally i want you to meet Franz, a german friend of mine said Andrew. ("Sally, I want you to meet Franz, a German friend of mine," said Andrew.)

Supplementary Activities

More Practice: Rewrite sentences from the students' reading books omitting punctuation marks and changing capital letters to lowercase letters. Then have the students write the sentences correctly by adding punctuation marks and indicating which words should begin with a capital letter.

Instructional Variation: Make game cards similar to bingo cards, with 36 blank squares drawn on each. Write one of the following punctuation marks in each of the blank squares: period, question mark, comma, apostrophe, and quotation marks. Also write the words "capital letter" in several of the blank squares.

Write a sentence on the chalkboard leaving out punctuation marks and not capitalizing letters. After the students have read the sentence have them decide what letters should be capitalized and what punctuation marks are missing in the sentence. Then have the students cover the necessary squares on their game cards. Repeat this procedure until one student has all the squares on a game card covered.

Using Resources and Materials: Have the students write short reports of library books they have read. Suggest that they write two paragraphs. In the first paragraph they may tell the name of the book, the author, and the subject of the book. In the second paragraph they may tell an interesting incident from the book.

Lesson **73** (page 93)

Writing Descriptions

 23

Key Objectives   The student will be able to:
1. Write a descriptive sentence about a given subject.
2. Write a paragraph describing a sensory experience.

Procedures

On the chalkboard write the following words:
1. fur
2. house
3. kitten
4. cooky
5. bell
6. campfire

Read and discuss Key 23 with the students. Remind them that they have used adjectives to tell how things look, feel, sound, taste, or smell. Let several students give several adjectives that describe each of the words on the chalkboard.

Have the students open their books to Lesson 73. Read the information and examples with them. Ask the students to compare the three example sentences. Through discussion help them see that the last sentence gives the most effective description. Point out that the first sentence tells so little that the reader is given hardly any picture. The second sentence provides a better description, but the reader still is not given a very accurate picture of the table and pans; telling that the table is painted blue is unnecessary and even misleading, since it actually makes the table seem rather attractive. Only in the last sentence is each word carefully chosen to describe accurately the table and pans and their relation to each other.

Have the students read the directions for the exercises. Tell them to choose their words carefully to convey accurately sensations of sight, touch, sound, taste, and smell. Point out that some of the synonyms listed in Key 35 and some of the antonyms listed in Key 36 are good describing words. Suggest that the students consult these keys if they have trouble thinking of such words. Be sure the students understand the directions. Then let them work independently.

After the exercises are checked and scores recorded, read aloud several students' answers that are particularly apt descriptions.

Supplementary Exercises

Have the students write a descriptive sentence about each subject listed below. (Score: 15—5 for each sentence) (Answers will vary.)
1. A bumpy ride in a car
2. Eating spaghetti
3. Diving into a swimming pool on a hot summer's day

Supplementary Activities

More Practice: Have the students write a paragraph describing what they see, hear, and smell when they visit a gas station.

Instructional Variation: Put several objects such as a pencil, a piece of paper, and a roll of tape in a bag. Have the students reach inside the bag with one hand, but tell them not to look inside the bag. Have the students describe one of the objects they touch and then say what they think that object is. For example, a student might say, "I feel something that is long, hard, and smooth. It is sharp at one end and soft at the other end. I think it is a pencil." You may vary this activity by having students smell and describe the aroma of spices and herbs. You may also wish to tape-record familiar sounds such as a car accelerating or a door closing, and then have the students describe the sounds they hear.

Using Resources and Materials: Let the students write cinquains. Tell the students that a cinquain is a five-line poem that briefly expresses an idea. Explain that each line of the poem should make the idea grow and expand in the reader's mind. The book *Verse,* by Adelaide Crapsey, contains excellent examples of this form of poetry, which may be read to the class. Although a cinquain does not have to follow a set pattern, the students will probably find it easier to write one if they follow this pattern: the first line should give the title or subject; the second line should have two words describing the subject; the third line should contain three words expressing action related to the subject; the fourth line should have four words that continue and expand the idea of the poem; and the fifth line should be another word for the title or subject. Point out that words in a cinquain do not have to rhyme. Write the following cinquain on the chalkboard to illustrate:

Rain
Silver needles
Falling, striking, piercing
The earth's dry surface
Life

Write a cinquain on the chalkboard, using the best suggestions of the class. Then let the students write their own. Suggest that the students may wish to illustrate their cinquains. Make a booklet of the poems or display them.

Lesson **74** (page 94)

Using Antonyms
 36

Key Objective The student will be able to write antonyms for given words.

Procedures

Write the following sentences on the chalkboard:
1. We walked along a (narrow, wide) path.
2. All at once we saw a (huge, tiny) animal in the path.

Say several words, such as *up, open,* and *big,* and have the students name words with opposite meanings. Have a student read sentence 1 on the chalkboard, using first *narrow* and then *wide.* Point out the difference in meaning that is determined by the choice of words. Explain the value of word opposites in making vivid contrasts. Let another student read sentence 2 and comment on the difference in meaning determined by the choice of words in parentheses. Explain that words with opposite meanings are called *antonyms*.

Read and discuss Key 36 with the students. Ask students to think of other examples of antonyms not listed in the key.

Have the students fill the blanks in the exercises with the antonyms listed in Key 36 or with other antonyms. Encourage the students to think of antonyms other than those listed in the key, but suggest that they use a dictionary to check meanings to be sure the words are antonyms of the words in the exercises.

After the exercises have been worked, answers checked, and scores recorded, have the students correct their mistakes.

Supplementary Exercises

Beside each word below write its antonym. (Score: 12)
1. add (subtract)
2. ancient (new or young)
3. artificial (real)
4. buy (sell)
5. clumsy (graceful)
6. correct (incorrect or wrong)
7. ending (beginning or starting)
8. expensive (cheap or inexpensive)
9. fresh (stale)
10. harsh (mild)
11. imaginary (real)
12. seldom (often)
    NOTE: Answers will vary.

Supplementary Activities

Instructional Variation: Divide the class into two teams. Say a word and let the first player on one team give an antonym for the word. Say another word and let the first player on the other team give an antonym. Continue until each player has had an opportunity to give an antonym. A player who misses a word must leave the game. The team with the most players at the end of a designated period wins the game. You may use the following words:

1. quiet (noisy)	11. love (hate)
2. awake (asleep)	12. empty (full)
3. push (pull)	13. lost (found)
4. early (late)	14. tame (wild)
5. summer (winter)	15. outside (inside)
6. laugh (cry)	16. smile (frown)
7. deep (shallow)	17. far (near)
8. fast (slow)	18. wide (narrow)
9. top (bottom)	19. front (back)
10. scold (praise)	20. rough (smooth)

Using Resources and Materials: Have each student choose a pair of antonyms and draw pictures to illustrate their meanings. Tell the student to write two sentences that use the antonyms and explain the pictures. For example, a student may choose the antonyms *thin* and *fat,* draw pictures of a thin person and of a fat person, and write, ''The person is *thin,*'' and ''The person is *fat.*'' Cartoons or stick drawings are appropriate for this activity.

Lesson **75** (page 95)

Using Synonyms
🔑 35

Key Objective The student will be able to write synonyms for given words.

Procedures

Write the following sentences on the chalkboard:
1. The player will _____ the baseball.
2. Another player _____ toward home plate.

Ask the students to name words that mean almost the same thing as *throw*. After they have named such words as *toss, pitch,* and *fling,* direct their attention to sentence 1 on the chalkboard. Ask someone to fill the blank with one of the words named previously and tell the student to use the word that fits the meaning best. The student should write *pitch* in the blank. Next ask the students to name words that mean almost the same thing as *ran,* such as *raced, loped,* and *trotted.* Then have someone fill the blank in sentence 2 with the most appropriate word.

Ask what name is given to words that mean the same or almost the same thing. Then have the students read Key 35 to find out that such words are called *synonyms*. Discuss each example, since each pair of synonyms in the exercise is listed in the key.

Be sure that everyone understands the directions before working the exercises in Lesson 75. If the students do not know which word to use in an exercise, refer them to the key or to a dictionary. After answers to the exercises have been checked and scores recorded, have several students read the sentences in part II, first with the words in parentheses and then with the words that fill the blanks. Call attention to the different ways of saying the same thing.

Supplementary Exercises

After each word below write a synonym for it. (Score: 12)

1. brief (short)
2. flabby (soft)
3. genuine (real)
4. ran (raced)
5. raised (lifted)
6. grateful (thankful)
7. leaped (jumped)
8. strike (hit)
9. above (over)
10. put (place, set, or lay)
11. only (just)
12. injure (hurt)

NOTE: Answers will vary.

Supplementary Activities

More Practice: Point out that using a variety of synonyms can make writing more interesting and exact. For example, ask the students to compare the phrases *a lovely piece of lace* and *a delicate piece of lace.* They should see that *delicate* gives a more definite description than *lovely.* Have the students consult Key 35 or a dictionary to find a more descriptive or exact synonym for each adjective in the following phrases:

1. a flying bird (soaring)
2. a small speck of dust (tiny)
3. the old ruins (ancient)
4. the fast deer (fleet)
5. a good report (excellent)

Then have each student write five sentences, using each of the better phrases.

Instructional Variation: Divide the class into two teams. Say a word and let the first player on one team give a synonym for the word. Say another word and let the first player on the other team give a synonym. Continue until each player has had an opportunity to give a synonym. A player who misses a word must leave the game. The team with the most players at the end of a designated period wins the game. You may use the list of synonyms in Key 35 for the game.

Using Resources and Materials: Have the students find in a dictionary at least two synonyms for each of the following words:

1. high
2. enormous
3. new
4. dark
5. discover
6. make
7. fear
8. plan

After the students have written the synonyms, have each one write eight sentences; each sentence should contain one of the synonyms found.

Lesson 76 (page 96)

Plurals, Possessives, and Contractions

🔑 15, 16, 22

Key Objectives The student will be able to:
1. Write the plural forms of given words.

2. Write the possessive forms of given words.
3. Write the contractions of given words.

Procedures

Help the students recall information about plurals, possessives, and contractions by asking the following questions: What is a noun? How do you form the plurals of most nouns? How do you form the plural of a noun ending in *ch, sh, s, x,* or *z*? How do you usually form the plural of a noun ending in *f* or *fe*? How do you form the plural of a noun ending in *y* with a consonant before it? What other ways do you know to form plurals of nouns? How do you form the possessive of a singular noun? How do you form the possessive of a plural noun that ends in *s*? How do you form the possessive of a plural noun that does not end in *s*? What is a contraction? What does the apostrophe in a contraction stand for? How do contractions affect writing? Have the students give examples of plurals, possessives, and contractions. Then let them check the accuracy of their answers and examples by reading Keys 15, 16, and 22.

Be sure the students understand directions for the exercises in Lesson 76 before they work independently. After answers have been checked and scores recorded, have the students correct their mistakes.

Supplementary Exercises

I. Write the plural form of each noun below. (Score: 12)

1. rocket (rockets)
2. candle (candles)
3. monkey (monkeys)
4. bunch (bunches)
5. brush (brushes)
6. glass (glasses)
7. wife (wives)
8. loaf (loaves)
9. calf (calves)
10. baby (babies)
11. berry (berries)
12. child (children)

II. Write the possessive form of each noun below. (Score: 8)

13. Ross (Ross's)
14. James (James's)
15. lady (lady's)
16. planets (planets')
17. tales (tales')
18. grass (grass's)
19. brush (brush's)
20. boats (boats')

III. Write the contractions after each word below. (Score: 10)

21. will not (won't)
22. we are (we're)
23. are not (aren't)
24. who is (who's)
25. cannot (can't)
26. should not (shouldn't)
27. they are (they're)
28. I will (I'll)
29. have not (haven't)
30. was not (wasn't)

Supplementary Activities

More Practice: Have the students choose ten nouns from their spelling lists and write the plural forms of those nouns. Tell the students to use the nouns in sentences. Next, have the students write the possessive forms of the names of ten of their classmates and write sentences using those names.

Instructional Variation: Have each student list three things in the plural. Then have the students exchange papers and make up names for three people who own these things. Ask them to exchange papers again and to write stories about the people and the things they own.

Lesson 77 (page 97)

Choosing Homophones
 37

Key Objective The student will be able to choose the correct homophone to complete sentences.

Procedures

Broadcasting

What kind of aircraft is pictured in Lesson 77? Imagine that you are traveling through space. Describe your feelings. Describe how outer space might look through the window of a spacecraft.

Explaining the Lesson

Ask a student what homophones are. The student should explain that they are words that sound alike but have different spellings and meanings. Ask another student to write *tail* and its homophone on the chalkboard. Then ask the student to write sentences containing each word in order to show its meaning. Let several students name other homophones and use them in sentences. To help the students understand the importance of using the correct homophone, write the following sentence on the chalkboard:

Della picked up the (cent, scent).

They should quickly see that the meaning of the sentence depends on the homophone used. Next read Key 37 with the students and discuss the examples, making sure that the meaning of each homophone is clear.

After the exercises in Lesson 77 have been worked, answers checked, and scores recorded, have the students correct their mistakes.

Supplementary Exercises

Underline the correct homophone in parentheses. (Score: 10)

1. The Greeks and the Trojans fought nearly (ate, eight) years. (eight)

2. They lived near a (see, sea) called the Mediterranean. (sea)
3. There were many (grate, great) heroes on both sides. (great)
4. The Greeks wanted (to, too, two) capture Troy. (to)
5. They built a (grate, great) wooden horse on the (beech, beach). (great, beach)
6. But they pulled the horse (through, threw) the gate. (through)
7. At night the Greeks crawled out of (there, their) horse. (their)
8. They opened the gates to the (beach, beech). (beach)
9. The (whole, hole) Greek army rushed into Troy. (whole)

Supplementary Activities

More Practice: Have the students write twenty sentences using one of the following homophones in each sentence: no, know; sum, some; won, one; new, knew; sent, cent; sea, see; tail, tale; son, sun; grate, great; not, knot.

Instructional Variation: Have the students play "homophone concentration." Make homophone cards by writing 30–40 homophones on separate index cards. Place the homophone cards face down on a table. Next, have several students alternately turn over two cards at a time until one player matches two homophones. (Example: tail and tale) Have the students continue playing the game until all homophone cards have been matched. The player with the most homophone cards at the end of the game, wins.

Using Resources and Materials: Have the students write two sentences using a pair of homophones. Then have the students draw or paint two pictures which illustrate the sentences. You may wish to display the pictures in the classroom.

Lesson 78 (page 98)

Unnecessary Words
 32

Key Objective The student will be able to delete unnecessary words from sentences.

Procedures

Write the following sentences on the chalkboard:

1. One day Sam he went and rode his bicycle to school.
2. One day Sam rode his bicycle to school.

Tell the students to read the sentences on the chalkboard. Then ask which is the better sentence. Point out that sentence 1 seems wordy because of its unnecessary words and that sentence 2 briefly and clearly tells the same thing.

Read Key 32 with the students and discuss the examples, being careful to point out that the first sentence in each example is written more clearly than the second sentence. Before the students work the exercises in Lesson 78, tell them that there is only one unnecessary expression in each sentence, although some expressions are made up of two words.

After answers to the exercises have been checked, have the students correct their mistakes. Then let several students read the sentences aloud and tell what unnecessary expression was marked out.

Supplementary Exercises

Draw lines through the unnecessary words in the sentences below. (Score: 8)
1. Aladdin he was a young boy. (he)
2. One day a magician went and said, "Aladdin, I am your uncle." (went and)
3. "Pick up some of these here sticks to make a fire," the man said. (here)
4. Aladdin he gathered the sticks to make a fire. (he)
5. Then the magician told Aladdin to go get a lamp. (go)
6. Aladdin took the lamp off of the shelf, but he did not give it to the man. (of)
7. He went and rubbed the lamp, and a great genie stood before him. (went and)
8. The genie he took Aladdin from the cave. (he)

Supplementary Activities

Instructional Variation: Have several students re-tell one of their favorite stories. Tape-record the stories. Have the class copy down the students' stories and cross out as many words as possible without changing the meaning. Then have the students reread the stories. Have they crossed out too many words? Is the action still clear?

Lesson **79** (page 99)

Double Negatives

 34

Key Objectives   The student will be able to:
1. Recognize that only one negative word should be used to tell about one thing.

2. Select proper negative word forms to complete sentences.

Procedures

Broadcasting

How does the animal pictured in Lesson 79 look like a prehistoric animal? The animal in the picture is an armadillo. Its shell is very hard. Name other animals whose hard shells or tough skins protect them. Tell why and how these animals need such protection.

Explaining the Lesson

Read and discuss Key 34 with the students. Be sure they understand that *no, not, nothing, none, never, hardly, scarcely,* and contractions made from *not* are considered negative words and that not more than one of these words should be used to tell about one thing. Let them practice using these words by answering each of the following questions negatively: Have you ever seen an armadillo? How many armadillos have you seen? Would you like an armadillo as a pet? Would an armadillo like to be walked on a leash? How much food does an armadillo eat?

After the students understand double negatives, have them work the exercises in Lesson 79. Let several students read the sentences aloud after answers have been checked, scores recorded, and errors corrected.

Supplementary Exercises

In each sentence below underline the proper word form in parentheses. (Score: 5)
1. Armadillos are hardly (ever, never) seen in zoos in the North. (ever)
2. The weather (is, isn't) not warm enough for them. (is)
3. They (wouldn't, would) hardly be able to survive. (would)
4. Don't (none, any) of them live in cold climates? (any)
5. There isn't (nothing, anything) the armadillo likes more than warm sun. (anything)

Supplementary Activities

More Practice: In the phrases below have the students choose the proper word form in parentheses. Then have the students write sentences by completing each phrase.
1. Haven't you (ever, never) _____
2. It couldn't (never, ever) _____
3. Don't (none, any) _____
4. You can hardly (ever, never) _____
5. There isn't (nothing, anything) _____

Using Resources and Materials: Write the following questions on the chalkboard:

1. How large is the armadillo, and what does it look like?
2. Where does it live?
3. How does it protect itself?

Read and discuss Keys 43 to 45 with the students. Tell them to outline a report about the armadillo. Then have them write the report. Explain that they should answer the questions on the chalkboard and that they may use the information in Lesson 79 or use resources from the library. Remind them to use only one negative word when telling about one thing. Have them proofread their writing, checking for paragraphing, complete sentences, and correct spelling, capitalization, and punctuation.

Lesson **80** (page 100)

Using Himself, Themselves, Their, and There
 18e, 37

Key Objective   The student will be able to select one of the following words to properly complete sentences: *himself, themselves, their,* and *there.*

Procedures

Write the following sentences on the chalkboard:
1. Jack went to Colorado by (himself, hisself).
2. Not many children his age travel by (themselves, theirselves).
3. (There, Their) are many children who travel with (there, their) parents.

Direct the attention of the students to the sentences on the chalkboard. Ask a student to read sentence 1 and draw a line under the word in parentheses that the student thinks is correct. Have other students follow the same procedure with sentences 2 and 3. Then have the class check the accuracy of the work by reading Keys 18e and 37 and example 25 in the latter key. If there are underlining mistakes on the chalkboard, have someone correct them.

After the students understand the proper use of the words in this lesson, let them work independently to complete the exercises in Lesson 80. Have them correct their mistakes after answers have been checked and scores recorded.

Supplementary Exercises

Underline the proper word form in parentheses to complete each of the following sentences. (Score: 5)

1. Some people enjoyed living by (theirselves, themselves) on ranches. (themselves)
2. (There, Their) were very few other people around. (There)
3. People had to take care of problems by (themselves, theirselves). (themselves)
4. Joe Downs might have built his house by (hisself, himself). (himself)
5. Some people were lonely, but others enjoyed (their, there) privacy. (their)

Supplementary Activities

More Practice: Have the students write four sentences about a cattle drive, using one of the following words in each sentence: *himself, themselves, their,* and *there.*

Instructional Variation: Give each student four index cards and have the students write one of the following words on each card: *himself, themselves, their,* and *there.* On the chalkboard write one of the sentences written by a student for the *More Practice* section, but omit the words *himself, themselves, their,* and *there.* Have the students hold up the word card that properly completes the sentence. Repeat this procedure using other sentences that require the students to show all of the word cards.

Using Resources and Materials: Have the students use the encyclopedia and other resource materials to learn about cattle trails other than the Chisholm Trail. Have them write a story or report about one of these trails. Have the students read and study Keys 45 and 47 before writing their story or report. Tell the students to use the words *himself, themselves, their,* and *there* in their stories or reports.

Lesson **81** (page 101)

Choosing Proper Word Forms
 18e, 21, 37

Key Objective   The student will be able to select the proper word forms, verb forms, and homophones to complete sentences.

Procedures

Broadcasting

What is the person pictured in Lesson 81 doing? Give several reasons why you think drawing birds would be difficult. Name several birds you have seen and describe their size, color, and where you have seen them.

Explaining the Lesson

Write the following words on the chalkboard:

1. became—become
2. drew—drawn
3. fell—fallen
4. himself—themselves
5. their—there
6. to—too—two
7. whose—who's
8. your—you're

Ask a student to read the first pair of words on the chalkboard, explain their proper use, and use each of them in sentences. If other students disagree with the student's explanation, have the class find the words in the appropriate key. Follow the same procedure with the other words on the chalkboard.

After the exercises on page 107 have been worked, answers checked, and scores recorded, have the students correct their mistakes.

Supplementary Exercises

Underline the proper word form in parentheses to complete each of the following sentences. (Score: 5)

1. The pictures that John Audubon (drew, drawn) hang in museums all over the world. (drew)

2. There are people (who's, whose) homes are decorated with paintings by John Audubon. (whose)

3. John Audubon published more than (to, two, too) books that contain his pictures. (two)

4. He drew all the pictures in the books by (himself, hisself). (himself)

5. Perhaps the library in (your, you're) school has a book of John Audubon's pictures. (your)

Supplementary Activities

More Practice: Have the students write 15 sentences about birds they have seen or read about. Tell the students to use each of the following words in their sentences: *became, become, drew, drawn, fell, fallen, their, there, to, two, too, whose, who's, your, you're.*

Using Resources and Materials: Have the students find information about the various kinds of birds that live in their area. They may use encyclopedias, bird books, and any other reference books available at home or school. They may also interview bird watchers. Tell the students to write poems, stories, or reports about birds, their appearance, their songs, or their way of life. Let them draw or paint pictures to illustrate their written work. Be sure the students use some of the word forms mentioned in Lesson 81 when writing their poems, stories, or reports. You may wish to display the students' work in the classroom.

Lesson **82** (page 102)

Remembering What We Have Learned

Key Objective   The student will be able to apply the skills taught in Unit V.

Procedures

Have the students open their books to Lesson 82 and read the title of the lesson. Ask someone to explain the object of this lesson. The student should tell that it will help the class remember what they learned in Unit V and prepare for the post test that follows. Make sure the students understand the directions for the exercises and tell them that they should find the keys and review the information for themselves.

Since the exercises are subjective, let several students read their answers aloud. Then direct a discussion of the material being reviewed, covering the following:

1. Using conjunctions to join sentences and avoiding too many *and*s
2. Adjectives
3. Antonyms and synonyms
4. Plurals, possessives, and contractions
5. Homophones
6. Unnecessary words
7. Double negatives
8. Capitalization and punctuation
9. Proper use of *became, become, drew, drawn, fell, fallen, himself, themselves, their, there, to, too, two, whose, who's, your,* and *you're*

Post Test—Unit V

At the conclusion of Unit V, administer the post test for this unit. Post tests for all units are at the back of the Teacher's Edition. The results of the post test should indicate which students have mastered the concepts and skills in the unit. Instructions for administration of post tests appear in the introduction to the Teacher's Edition.

Pretest—Unit VI

Before beginning Unit VI, administer the pretest for this unit. Pretests for all units are at the back of the Teacher's Edition. The results should indicate the students' preliminary competency levels for concepts and skills presented in the unit. Instructions for administration and ways to use the pretests appear in the introduction to the Teacher's Edition.

70

Lesson **83** (page 103)

Writing Stories
 47

Key Objectives   The student will be able to:
1. Plan and write a story.
2. Use direct quotations in a story.
3. Write a title for a story.

Procedures

Briefly review what the students have learned about writing paragraphs, quotations, descriptive sentences, and sentences with conjunctions. Ask questions similar to the following: How many subjects are told about in a paragraph? Where should the first line of a paragraph begin? What is a topic sentence? What is a direct quotation? How should a direct quotation be punctuated? Should you begin a new paragraph each time a different person's words are quoted directly? What kinds of words can be used to make writing more exact, varied, and interesting? What is a conjunction? What should you remember about using conjunctions? Point out that the practice students have had in writing paragraphs and quotations and in using adjectives and conjunctions will be helpful in writing stories.

Read and discuss Key 47 with the students. Then ask them to turn to Lesson 83 in their books. Read and discuss the directions for the exercise. Explain that an incident is something that happens during a specified period of time. Point out that students should include in their stories all the information that contributes to describing what happened. For example, a student telling about an unsuccessful attempt to cook dinner might tell why the dinner was being made, how the dinner was planned, what mistakes were made, and the results of those mistakes. Encourage the students to include information that is pertinent only to the incident they are describing. For example, in telling about the unsuccessful dinner, the student should not tell about making a cake, unless the cake was a part of the dinner.

Suggest that the students may find it helpful to write their story plans on separate paper. You may wish to check the plans and give needed assistance before the students write their stories in Lesson 83. Remind the students to proofread their stories, checking for complete sentences, paragraphing, and correct capitalization, punctuation, and spelling.

After the exercises are checked and scores recorded, let several students read their stories aloud.

Supplementary Exercises

Rewrite the paragraph below, putting the sentences in order so that they tell a story. Leave out any sentences that are not necessary to the story. (Score: 8)

Liza started to throw the boot away, but then she saw something that made her shout. Early on Saturday morning Liza hurried to the creek to try out her new fishing rod. I like to go fishing. Liza pulled and tugged until at last she could see that her catch was an old rubber boot. Again and again Liza cast her hook into the water, but nothing happened. This summer we are going to the lake to fish. Just as Liza was about to give up, she felt something heavy on her line. Inside the boot was a fine, big fish.

(Early on Saturday morning, Liza hurried to the creek to try out her new fishing rod. Again and again Liza cast her hook into the water, but nothing happened. Just as Liza was about to give up, she felt something heavy on her line. Liza pulled and tugged until at last she could see that her catch was an old rubber boot. Liza started to throw the boot away, but then she saw something that made her shout. Inside the boot was a fine, big fish.)

Supplementary Activities

More Practice: Let the students plan and write original stories. Have them study Key 47 before they write. Remind them to use adjectives, direct and indirect quotations, and a variety of sentences to make their writing more interesting. Tell the students that they may illustrate their stories if they wish to. You may wish to display the finished work.

Instructional Variation: Let the students prepare stories to tell the class. Have them study Key 52b and tell them to practice by telling the story to someone at home. After each story is told, let the students in the audience discuss whether or not the events of the story were told in their proper sequence.

Lesson **84** (page 104)

Outlining
 43

Key Objective   The student will be able to write an outline for a two paragraph story.

Procedures

Read and discuss Key 43 with the students, paying particular attention to the key example. Point

71

out that the title gives an idea of the subject of the report, and that each paragraph topic tells an important idea about the subject. Remind the students that an outline is a brief plan of the information to be included in a report or story and that this information will be presented more fully and interestingly in the report or story itself.

Be sure that the students understand the explanations and directions in Lesson 84 before they work the exercises. After they have properly outlined the information about Harriet Tubman, assign the activity suggested in Other Things to Do. Let someone explain what things the students should check when proofreading their reports.

Supplementary Exercises

Use the facts given below about Robert Louis Stevenson to make an outline for two paragraphs. (Score: 20)

Born in Edinburgh, Scotland
Often ill during childhood
Could not attend school regularly
Spent much of youth practicing writing
Spent twenty years of adulthood as an invalid
Went from place to place searching for health
In spite of illness, considered life an exciting adventure
Became famous after writing *Treasure Island*
Spent his last years on the beautiful island of Samoa
NOTE: Answers will vary. Check for correct arrangement, numbering, and capitalization.

Supplementary Activities

More Practice: Have the students outline a page from a science or social studies book. Does the author have one main idea for each paragraph? Does the outline help you remember what was said on the page?

Instructional Variation: Write the following statements on the chalkboard:
1. School should be held year round with vacations held at several times during the year rather than only in the summer.
2. Students should be paid for going to school.
3. Children's toys and games should not be advertised on television.
4. Students should be required to read at least two books a month outside of school.

Divide the class into groups. Tell the first group to write an outline for a speech giving arguments in favor of the first statement on the chalkboard. Tell the second group to write an outline for a speech giving arguments in opposition to the first statement. Follow the same procedure with the other groups, having each group take an affirmative or negative stand on each of the other statements.

When the outlines are completed, let each group choose a representative. Have the representative prepare a speech from the outline and give it before the class. Let the class vote on whether the affirmative or negative speech concerning each statement was more effective.

Using Resources and Materials: On the chalkboard write the following names of presidents:
1. Thomas Jefferson
2. Andrew Jackson
3. Grover Cleveland
4. Franklin Roosevelt
5. Dwight Eisenhower
6. Jimmy Carter
7. Ronald Reagan

Let each student choose one of the names listed and write an outline for a report about that president. Suggest that the outline include information about the president's early life, adulthood, and administration. Tell the students that they may consult encyclopedias and other reference books for information.

Lesson **85** (page 105)

Writing Reports
 43, 45

Key Objectives The student will be able to:
1. Select a subject for a report.
2. Write an outline for the report.
3. Write the report.

Procedures

Direct a discussion of paragraphs by asking questions similar to the following: How many subjects are told about in a paragraph? Can more than one paragraph be used to tell about one subject? How does outlining help in writing interesting paragraphs? After the students have discussed the pertinent information about paragraphs and outlines, ask them what a report is and whether or not paragraphs are used in a report. Suggest that they read Keys 43 and 45 and the first paragraph in Lesson 85 to find out about reports.

Emphasize the importance of limiting the subject. Give the children practice in selecting specific subjects rather than broad, general, or vague ones. Let them choose the better subject from each of the following pairs: "Safety" or "The Safe Way to Ride Bicycles," "Wildlife" or "How Giraffes Protect Themselves," "Games" or "How to Play Bingo."

Suggest that in planning a report the students should ask if each idea is important. After choosing the main ideas, the students should decide whether the ideas belong in one or more than one paragraph. Explain that it is very important to outline the report before writing it and to proofread it after writing it. Help the students recall the information about proofreading given in Key 47c.

After the students have written their reports in Lesson 85, encourage them to evaluate their own writing. Ask questions similar to the following: Did you use a good subject for your report? Is the subject too broad? Are all your sentences important? Have you told everything the reader needs to know about your subject? Will your first sentence make me want to read the whole report? Does your title tell something about your subject? After the students have looked at their reports critically, allow them to make changes.

Assign the activity suggested in Other Things to Do at the bottom of Lesson 85.

Supplementary Exercises

Choose one of the subjects listed below or think of your own subject. On another sheet of paper make an outline for a report about the subject you chose. Write the report on another sheet of paper. (Score: 50)

Playing a musical instrument
Mountain climbing
Constellations in the night sky
Monster movies

Supplementary Activities

More Practice: Tell the students that sentences can be written in different ways in order to emphasize different parts. Write the following sentences on the chalkboard and have the students discuss the difference in emphasis between the two sentences that say the same thing. Then have the students write similar sentences.

1. The magician pulled a white rabbit from his tall, black hat. From his tall, black hat the magician pulled a white rabbit.
2. A huge genie suddenly appeared. Suddenly a huge genie appeared.
3. Bob eagerly helped the crossing guard every day. Every day Bob eagerly helped the crossing guard.

Using Resources and Materials: Have the students read articles and reports in magazines and newspapers. Tell the students to note the subject of the report and underline the topic sentence in each paragraph. Next have the students outline at least two paragraphs of the report making sure that each paragraph tells about one main idea.

Lesson **86** (page 106)

Combining Sentences

 24, 41e

Key Objective The student will be able to use conjunctions to combine pairs of sentences.

Procedures

Broadcasting

What is the name of the animal pictured in Lesson 86? Why do you think this animal is called a sea horse? Where could you see sea horses?

Explaining the Lesson

Explain that people sometimes write short, choppy sentences that repeat words and ideas unnecessarily. Tell the students that they can often combine such sentences to make longer, more interesting ones. Ask them to listen carefully while you read the two paragraphs below.

Look at that animal. It is an interesting animal. Its head looks like a horse's head. It looks small. It can't run. Is it a sea horse?

Look at that interesting animal! It looks like a small horse, but it can't run. Is it a sea horse?

Let the students tell which paragraph they like better, being sure that they mention the short, choppy sentences in the first paragraph and the longer, more interesting ones in the second paragraph. Then have them read and discuss Keys 24 and 41e.

Have the students read the directions for the exercises in Lesson 86. Explain that they may use conjunctions other than those suggested. Tell the students that they may rearrange or change the wording of the sentences given in Lesson 86, but caution them to retain the meaning of the original sentences when writing sentences of their own. After answers have been checked and scores recorded, let several students read their sentences aloud.

Supplementary Exercises

Rewrite each pair of sentences below to make one better sentence. You may need to change the wording, and you may use conjunctions if you wish. (Score: 18—3 for each sentence correctly written) (Answers will vary)

1. The sea horse has a long pipe. The pipe is a mouth. (The sea horse has a long pipe for a mouth.)
2. It has eyes. The eyes stick out. (It has eyes that stick out.)

73

3. Its body has a cover. It has bony plates. (Its body has a cover of bony plates.)
4. The mother sea horse lays eggs. She does not care for them. (The mother sea horse lays eggs, but she does not care for them.)
5. The father sea horse carries the eggs. He carries them in a pouch on his stomach. (The father sea horse carries the eggs in a pouch on his stomach.)
6. He cares for the eggs. They hatch. (He cares for the eggs until they hatch.)

Supplementary Activities

More Practice: On the chalkboard write the following conjunctions:

1. when   5. while
2. or   6. as
3. if   7. although
4. after   8. for

Have the students write eight sentences using the conjunctions on the chalkboard. Tell them to use a different conjunction in each sentence.

Instructional Variation: Have each student write one short sentence about a sea animal. Display the sentences on a bulletin board or at a learning center. Tell the students to choose ten of the sentences and combine them to make five more effective sentences. Tell the students to write their five sentences on sentence strips and display the combined sentences in the classroom. Some students may wish to illustrate their sentences.

Using Resources and Materials: Ask the students to study Keys 43 and 45. Then have them outline and write reports about a plant or animal that lives in the sea. Tell the students that they may consult encyclopedias and other reference books for information, but caution them to write the reports in their own words. Suggest that they use conjunctions to avoid having short, choppy sentences. Remind them to proofread their work.

Lesson **87** (page 107)

Punctuation and Capitalization
🔑 1, 2, 3, 5, 6, 7, 8, 9, 10, 11, 12

Key Objectives The student will be able to:
1. Use capital letters correctly in sentences.
2. Use periods, question marks, exclamation points, commas, and quotation marks correctly in sentences.

Procedures

Broadcasting

The man pictured in Lesson 87 is an aircraft controller. Name several things an aircraft controller does. What do you think air traffic would be like if there were no aircraft controllers? Explain.

Explaining the Lesson

Read and discuss Keys 1 to 3 and 5 to 12 with the students. Clarify points that they ask about. Make sure they understand the directions for the exercises in Lesson 87. Then let them work independently.

After the students have completed the exercises, ask someone to read sentence 1, telling which words were capitalized and what punctuation marks were used. Have the student explain why capital letters and punctuation marks were used. Call on other students to follow the same procedure with the other sentences. Then have the students correct their mistakes.

Assign the activity suggested in Other Things to Do at the bottom of Lesson 87.

Supplementary Exercises

Rewrite the following sentences, using capital letters and punctuation marks where they are needed. (Score: 16)
1. Do you think you would like to be an aircraft controller (Do you think you would like to be an aircraft controller?)
2. aircraft controllers need to be alert intelligent and quick thinking. (Aircraft controllers need to be alert, intelligent, and quick thinking.)
3. How difficult their job must be (How difficult their job must be!)
4. Mr Walsh said perhaps an air traffic controller can come and speak to the class (Mr. Walsh said, "Perhaps an air traffic controller can come and speak to the class.")
5. there are many questions we could ask said Kim ("There are many questions we could ask," said Kim.)

Supplementary Activities

More Practice: Have the students copy a paragraph from one of their favorite stories, leaving out punctuation marks and not capitalizing letters. Have the students exchange paragraphs and correct the errors. Then have them check their work against the original.

Using Resources and Materials: Invite an air traffic controller to visit the class and tell the students about air traffic control. Later, have the students write a report about the visit. Remind the students to proofread their reports checking for correct capitalization and punctuation.

Lesson **88** (page 108)

Using *In, Into, Those,* and *Them*
 31, 33

Key Objective   The student will be able to select *in, into, those,* and *them* to properly complete sentences.

Procedures

Explain to the class the use of *in* and *into*. Tell the students that *into* is used to tell about movement from the outside to the inside of something. Tell the students to use *in* to refer only to the inside of something.

Demonstrate the meanings and uses of *in* and *into*. Place a piece of chalk inside a box and say, "I put the chalk *into* the box." "Now the chalk is *in* the box." Sit down and ask, "Where am I sitting?" Someone should answer, "You are sitting *in* the chair." Go out of the room and come back in, saying, "I come *into* the room." "Now I am *in* the room."

As soon as the students understand the use of *in* and *into*, review the use of *these, those,* and *them*. Be sure they understand that *these* points out persons or things that are near, that *those* points out persons or things that are farther away, and that *them* refers to two or more persons and does not point out things. Then have the students read Keys 31 and 33.

Let the students work independently to complete the exercises in Lesson 88. After the answers have been checked and scores recorded, have the students correct their mistakes. Then let several students read the sentences aloud, using the proper word forms in parentheses.

Supplementary Exercises

In each sentence below fill the blank with the proper word form in parentheses. (Score: 11)

1. (in, into) People are careful when they go _____ a swimming pool. (into)
2. (in, into) Do you go _____ a locker room for a shower? (into)
3. (These, Them) _____ showers keep the pool water clean. (These)
4. (in, into) Some people like to dive _____ the water. (into)
5. (into, in) Do they know how deep the water is _____ the pool? (in)

6. (These, Those) _____ people over there are having a race. (Those)
7. (them, these) They are swimming toward _____ markers near us. (these)
8. (into, in) It is fun to swim _____ the cool, clear water. (in)
9. (in, into) Let's go back _____ the house. (into)
10. (into, in) There is some food _____ the kitchen. (in)
11. (those, them) We ate none of _____ sandwiches before we went swimming. (those)

Supplementary Activities

More Practice: Have the students write ten original sentences which use the word forms: *in, into, these, those,* and *them*. Have the students write two sentences for each word form.

Using Resources and Materials: Let each student write a list of safety rules to be observed when swimming. Suggest that the students consult the American Red Cross, encyclopedias, or health books for information about swimming safety. Tell the students to use complete sentences, stated in their own words, when writing their lists of rules. Tell the students to use *in, into, these, those,* and *them* in their sentences.

Lesson **89** (page 109)

Using Proper Word Forms
 20, 21, 26, 27, 31, 37

Key Objective   The student will be able to complete sentences by selecting the proper word form.

Procedures
Write the following words on the chalkboard:

1. became—become
2. began—begun
3. broke—broken
4. drew—drawn
5. flew—flown
6. threw—thrown
7. wrote—written
8. hasn't—haven't
9. is—are
10. in—into
11. may—can
12. teach—learn
13. it's—its
14. their—there—they're
15. threw—through
16. to—too—two
17. who's—whose
18. your—you're

Ask someone to read the first two words on the chalkboard and explain their proper use. After the student has told that *became* does not need a helping verb and *become* needs a helping verb, have the student say two sentences using *became* and *become* properly. Let several students follow the same procedure in explaining and giving examples of the proper use of the other words on the

75

chalkboard. Then have the students check the accuracy of the explanations by reviewing Keys 20, 21, 26, 27, 31, and 37.

After the students work the exercises in Lesson 89 and check their answers, let several students read the sentences aloud, using the proper word form in parentheses. Have them correct their mistakes.

Supplementary Exercises

Choose the proper word form in parentheses to write in the blank. (Score: 9)

1. (you're, your) Wasn't _____ cousin in Alaska? (your)
2. (became, become) It was before Alaska _____ a state. (became)
3. (there, their) Many people in Alaska make _____ living by fishing. (their)
4. (in, into) There are many fish _____ the ocean near Alaska. (in)
5. (are, is) The northern lights _____ often seen here. (are)
6. (They're, Their) _____ seen flashing through the cold air. (They're)
7. (It's, Its) _____ very cold in parts of Alaska during the winter. (It's)
8. (began, begun) Many years ago people _____ to find gold in Alaska. (began)
9. (there, their) Some people still mine gold _____ . (there)

Supplementary Activities

More Practice: Have the students write ten sentences using each of the following word forms in a sentence: *became, become, broke, broken, flew, flown, hasn't, haven't, may, can.* You may wish to choose other word forms mentioned in Lesson 89 and have the students write sentences using those words.

Using Resources and Materials: Write the following questions on the chalkboard:

1. When are the northern lights seen?
2. Where are they seen?
3. What kind of sound is sometimes heard before the lights are seen?
4. Can a scientist produce lights similar to the northern lights?
5. How does he perform this experiment?

Ask the students to write two paragraphs about the northern lights. Explain that in their first paragraph they should tell what the northern lights are and answer questions 1, 2, and 3 above and that in their second paragraph they should answer questions 4 and 5. Encourage the students to use encyclopedias and other resource materials to answer the questions. Tell the students to be sure they use the word forms mentioned in Lesson 89 when writing their paragraphs.

Lesson **90** (page 110)

Reviewing Sentences
🔑 7a, 8a, 9a, 41a–41d

Key Objectives The student will be able to:
1. Distinguish between groups of words that are sentences and groups of words that are not sentences.
2. Place the correct punctuation mark at the ends of sentences.

Procedures

Broadcasting

What is the name of the large planet pictured in Lesson 90? What instrument do people use to observe the planets? Why are telescopes used? What kinds of information can be learned from studying the planets?

Explaining the Lesson

Review sentences by asking the following questions: What is a sentence? How can you tell whether or not a group of words is a sentence? What are three kinds of sentences? What punctuation mark belongs at the end of each kind of sentence? Have the students check their answers by reading and discussing Keys 41a to 41d, 7a, 8a, and 9a, in that order. Stress the fact that every sentence must express a complete thought.

After the students have worked the exercises in Lesson 90, checked their answers, and recorded their scores, have them correct their mistakes.

Supplementary Exercises

I. Write *Yes* before each group of words that is a sentence. Write *No* before each group of words that is not a sentence. (Score: 5)

(Yes) 1. Telescopes magnify objects that are seen at great distances

(No) 2. Opened new worlds in astronomy

(No) 3. Invented in 1608 by Lippershey

(Yes) 4. Scientists had experimented with telescopes since the 1200s

(Yes) 5. Galileo built a telescope in 1609

II. Put the correct punctuation mark at the end of each sentence. (Score: 5)

6. What a crude telescope Galileo built (!)

7. It magnified an object only 33 times larger than its original size (.)
8. Are telescopes built today more powerful (?)
9. Yes, telescopes can magnify an object thousands of times its original size (.)
10. Have you ever looked through a telescope (?)

Supplementary Activities

More Practice: Have the students make sentences of the sentence fragments in part I of Lesson 90.

Instructional Variation: Have the students write about an imaginary landing on one of the planets. Remind them to use sentences and to use the correct punctuation mark at the end of each sentence. Then, let several groups of students plan and present a dramatization of the imaginary landing. Have the students tell what they see and how they feel.

Using Resources and Materials: Have the students write reports about different planets. They may use encyclopedias and other resource material to find out what is known about each planet. Have the students study Key 45 before writing their reports. Remind the students to proofread their reports to make sure they have written sentences and punctuated them correctly.

Lesson **91** (page 111)

Reviewing Paragraphs
🔑 24, 41e, 44

Key Objectives The student will be able to:
1. Rewrite a paragraph to eliminate run-on sentences.
2. Rewrite a paragraph by combining short sentences into longer ones.

Procedures

Review paragraphs by asking the following questions: How many main ideas should be discussed in a paragraph? Which sentence in a paragraph should introduce the subject? Which line of a paragraph should be indented? Why are many short sentences undesirable in a paragraph? Why is it undesirable to have long sentences strung together by *and*s? Have the students check their answers by reading and discussing Keys 44, 24, and 41e, in that order. Stress the fact that all the sentences in a paragraph must tell about the same subject.

As soon as the students understand directions for the exercises in Lesson 91, let them work inde-

pendently. After answers have been checked and scores recorded, let several students read their paragraphs aloud.

Supplementary Exercises

Write *Yes* after each sentence that is true and *No* after each sentence that is not true. (Score: 6)
1. Several topics should be discussed in a paragraph. (No)
2. Usually the topic sentence introduces the subject of a paragraph. (Yes)
3. A paragraph must have six sentences. (No)
4. The first sentence of a paragraph should be especially interesting. (Yes)
5. The title of a paragraph tells what the paragraph is about. (Yes)
6. The first sentence of a paragraph is not indented. (No)

Supplementary Activities

More Practice: I. Rewrite the following run-on sentences to make four more effective sentences. Write the sentences in paragraph form. (Score 20–5 for each sentence)

The tree hyrax lives in East Africa and it is a tiny animal that looks like a cross between a puppy and a beaver and its shriek has frightened many jungle explorers and its nearest living relative, strangely, is the elephant!

(The tree hyrax lives in East Africa. It is a tiny animal that looks like a cross between a puppy and a beaver. Its shriek has frightened many jungle explorers. Its nearest living relative, strangely, is the elephant.)

II. Rewrite the following short, choppy sentences to make five longer, more interesting sentences. Use conjunctions where they are needed. Write the sentences in paragraph form. (Score: 25–5 for each sentence)

The pangolin is an East African animal. It looks like an armadillo. It has short, triangular scales. They act as its armor. The pangolin comes out at night. It goes to the lake. It eats water beetles. When frightened, the pangolin rolls up. It rolls up into a tight ball. Some live on land. Others live in trees.

(The pangolin is an East African animal which looks like an armadillo. It has short, triangular scales that act as its armor. The pangolin comes out at night and goes to the lake to eat water beetles. When frightened, the pangolin rolls up into a tight ball. Some live on land, and others live in trees.)

Using Resources and Materials: Let the students use encyclopedias and other resource material to help them write a story about exploring the ocean's surface or its depths. Suggest that the stories may be factual accounts of an actual exploration, such as Jacques Cousteau's Conshelf Saturation Dive Program, or they may be imaginary accounts. Tell the students to read Key 47 before they write their stories. Suggest that they use a variety of sentences, direct and indirect quotations, adjectives, and conjunctions to make their writing more interesting, exact, and easily read. Remind the students to proofread their stories.

Lesson 92 (page 112)

Capitalization and Punctuation

 1, 2, 3, 5, 6, 7, 8, 9, 10, 11, 12

Key Objectives The student will be able to:
1. Indicate words that should be capitalized in sentences.
2. Place periods, question marks, exclamation points, commas, and quotation marks where needed in sentences.

Procedures

Read and discuss the information about capitalization and punctuation in Keys 1 to 3 and 5 to 12. Be sure to consider the use of capital letters for the following:
1. Names of persons, pets, particular places and things, days, months, and holidays
2. Initials
3. Titles of courtesy
4. The word *I*
5. Titles of stories and books
6. Words made from the names of places
7. First words of sentences
8. First words of direct quotations

Also discuss the following uses of punctuation marks:
1. Periods at the ends of declarative sentences, direct quotations, abbreviations, and initials
2. Question marks at the ends of interrogative sentences and direct quotations
3. Exclamation points at the ends of exclamatory sentences and direct quotations
4. Commas around words of direct address; after *yes* or *no;* in dates, addresses, and series of words; and between direct quotations and the other words in sentences
5. Quotation marks around direct quotations and titles of books or stories
6. Apostrophes in contractions and possessive nouns

After the exercises in Lesson 92 have been completed, have several students read the sentences aloud and tell the reason for the use of each capital letter and punctuation mark.

Supplementary Exercises

Rewrite the sentences below, using capital letters and punctuation marks where they are needed. (Score: 46)
1. Do you enjoy reading about horses dogs and other animals (Do you enjoy reading about horses, dogs, and other animals?)
2. On tuesday july 17 1983 i read an interesting book said Paul. ("On Tuesday, July 17, 1983, I read an interesting book," said Paul.)
3. it was named wilderness champion (It was named Wilderness Champion.)
4. My cousin in hartford connecticut sent the book to me. (My cousin in Hartford, Connecticut, sent the book to me.)
5. The book was written by joseph w lippincott. (The book was written by Joseph W. Lippincott.)
6. It is about a dog named reddy and a wolf called king, said Paul. ("It is about a dog named Reddy and a wolf called King," said Paul.)
7. Does the book take place in the united states or in canada (Does the book take place in the United States or in Canada?)
8. Dont Reddy and King live in a forest asked Kay. ("Don't Reddy and King live in a forest?" asked Kay.)
9. Paul replied yes Kay Reddy was raised by the wolf. (Paul replied, "Yes, Kay, Reddy was raised by the wolf.")
10. Reddys owner finds the dog in the forest (Reddy's owner finds the dog in the forest.)

Supplementary Activities

More Practice: On a duplicating master, rewrite sentences from a reading book leaving out punctuation marks and not capitalizing letters. Distribute copies to the class. Have the students underline each word that should begin with a capital letter and place punctuation marks where they are needed.

Instructional Variation: Draw one of the following punctuation marks on individual index cards: periods, question marks, exclamation points, commas, apostrophes, and quotation marks. Also write the words "capital letter" on individual index cards. Divide the class into groups of five to six students and distribute several punctuation cards and several capital letter cards to each group.

Tell the students that each group is to write a sentence which uses the same punctuation marks that are shown on the group's punctuation cards. The capitalized words in the sentence must also correspond to the number of "capital letter" cards the group receives. For example, one group might receive the following cards: 1 period card, 1 question mark card, 2 comma cards, 2 quotation mark cards, and 2 capital letter cards. The group could then use their punctuation cards and capital letter cards to write a sentence similar to the following: "Have you seen the exhibit of glass, pottery, and china at the museum?" asked Evie. You may wish to repeat this procedure and give each group a different combination of cards.

Using Resources and Materials: Have the students choose books from the library about animals as pets. Have the students read the book they chose and write a report. Tell the students to read and study Key 45 before writing their reports. Remind the students to proofread their reports checking for capitalization and punctuation. Suggest that some students may wish to present their book reports to the class orally.

Lesson **93** (page 113)

Word-Study Review
 14, 15, 16, 17, 19, 22

Key Objectives The student will be able to:
1. Identify nouns, pronouns, and verbs in sentences.
2. Write the plural forms of given words in sentences.
3. Write the possessive forms of given words in sentences.
4. Write contractions of given words in sentences.

Procedures

Broadcasting

What is the name of the animal pictured in Lesson 93? Where could you see a koala? Koalas are not bears although they are sometimes called "teddy bears." Why do you think they are called by that name?

Explaining the Lesson

Begin the lesson by asking the following questions: What is a noun? How do you form plurals of nouns? How do you form possessives of nouns? What are pronouns? What are verbs? What are contractions? How do you form contractions? During this discussion try to impress upon the students

the importance of studying words, their functions, their meanings, and their proper use.

Read and discuss Keys 14 to 17, 19, and 22 with the students. Clarify any point that seems unclear to them. Be sure they understand directions before they work the exercises on page 119. After the answers have been checked and scores recorded, have the students correct their mistakes.

Supplementary Exercises

I. Write the plural forms of the words below. (Score: 4)
1. woman (women)
2. self (selves)
3. dog (dogs)
4. match (matches)

II. Write the possessive form of the following words. (Score: 4)
5. Jones (Jones's)
6. mouse (mouse's)
7. dogs (dogs')
8. people (people's)

III. Write contractions of the words below. (Score: 4)
9. should not (shouldn't)
10. will not (won't)
11. I am (I'm)
12. do not (don't)

IV. Read the sentences below. Make a list of the nouns, pronouns, and verbs in the sentences. (Score: 15)

I saw some koalas at the zoo. They were in a tall tree. Long claws grew from their feet. We watched them for an hour.
(Answers:)

Nouns		Pronouns		Verbs	
koalas	claws	I	we	saw	grew
zoo	feet	they	them	were	watched
tree	hour	their			

Supplementary Activities

More Practice: Have the students choose a paragraph from their reading books. After the students have read the paragraph, have them make separate lists of the nouns, pronouns, and verbs in the paragraph.

Instructional Variation: Have the students write a string of verbs that describe what an animal does. For example a series about a dog might be: *Barking. Barking. Sniff. Sniff. Scratch. Scratch.* Have the other students try to guess what animal is being described.

Using Resources and Materials: Have the students use the information in Lesson 93 or other resource materials to write a paragraph about koalas. Tell the students to use plural forms and possessive forms of nouns, and contractions wherever possible in the paragraph.

Lesson **94** (page 114)

Word-Study Review
🔑 35, 36, 37

Key Objectives The student will be able to:
1. Select the correct homophone to complete sentences.
2. Write synonyms of given words to complete sentences.
3. Write antonyms of given words to complete sentences.

Procedures

Begin the lesson by asking the following questions: What are homophones? Can you give examples of homophones? What are synonyms? Can you give examples? What are antonyms? Can you give examples? During this discussion try to get the students to see the importance of studying words, their meanings, and their proper use.

Read and discuss Keys 35 to 37 with the students. Clarify any point that seems unclear to them. Then have the students read the directions in Lesson 94. It might be well to have them draw a circle around the word *homophone* in the directions for part I, around *synonym* in part II, and around *antonym* in part III. This procedure may keep them from confusing one part of the lesson with another.

After the exercises have been worked, answers checked, and scores recorded, have the students correct their mistakes.

Supplementary Exercises

I. Write a synonym for each word below. (Score: 5)
1. funny (amusing)
2. start (begin)
3. short (brief)
4. sure (certain)
5. real (genuine)

II. Write an antonym for each word below. (Score: 5)
6. glad (sad)
7. last (first)
8. often (seldom)
9. old (young)
10. after (before)

III. Choose the correct homophone to write in each blank. (Score: 8)
11. (too, to) Railroads helped our country _____ grow. (to)
12. (sent, cent) Farmers _____ food to cities by the railroads. (sent)
13. (Their, There) _____ tools came to them by the railroads. (Their)
14. (great, grate) It was a _____ distance across the United States. (great)
15. (heard, herd) A passenger on the train would often see a _____ of buffalo. (herd)
16. (buy, by) But it was quicker to travel _____ train. (by)
17. (knew, new) People could move to _____ parts of the country. (new)
18. (you're, your) Doesn't _____ book tell about early railroads? (your)

Supplementary Activities

More Practice: Have the students choose a paragraph from their reading books. Then have the students rewrite the paragraph using synonyms of words in the paragraph. Have the students rewrite the paragraph a second time replacing certain words in the paragraph with antonyms. Ask the students to read their changed paragraphs and say how the meaning of their paragraph changed.

Instructional Variation: Divide the class into two teams. Say a word and ask the first member of one team to give a synonym, antonym, or homophone of the word. Then ask the student to use the word in a sentence and tell whether it is a synonym, homophone, or antonym of the other word. The student must leave the game if an incorrect answer is given, if the word is used incorrectly, or if no answer is given. Use the example words in Keys 35, 36, and 37 or other suitable words of your own choosing. The team having the most members left at the end of the game wins.

Using Resources and Materials: Have the students use encyclopedias and other resource materials to learn more information about trains. Then have each student write two paragraphs about a train. Suggest that the first paragraph should describe the train's appearance, sound, feel, and odor and that the second paragraph should tell about the student's feelings upon seeing a train, hearing a train, and riding in one. Tell the students to use at least one pair of homophones, one pair of synonyms, and one pair of antonyms in their paragraphs. After they have written the paragraphs, have them underline the homophones, synonyms, and antonyms they used. Remind the students to proofread their work.

Lesson **95** (page 115)

Reviewing the Use of Pronouns
 18, 33

Key Objective   The student will be able to select pronouns to properly complete sentences.

Procedures

Read and discuss Keys 18 and 33 with the students. Pay particular attention to the examples, which show the use of pronouns. Point out the pronouns that are used in pairs and the use of *I, he, she, we,* and *they* after *is* or *was.*

As soon as the students recall the key information about using pronouns, have them work the exercises in Lesson 95. After answers have been checked and scores recorded, have the students correct their mistakes.

Supplementary Exercises

Choose a pronoun in parentheses to write in each blank. (Score: 8)
1. (I, me) Sally told Tom and _____ that people breathe oxygen. (me)
2. (I, me) It was _____ who said that oxygen is in the air. (I)
3. (Us, We) _____ wondered how the astronauts breathe. (We)
4. (he, him) Sally told _____ and me that there is no oxygen in space. (him)
5. (those, them) Some of _____ students learned how astronauts breathe. (those)
6. (I, me) Tom and _____ told Sally about oxygen masks. (I)
7. (him, he) It was _____ who said that oxygen is put into a tank. (he)
8. (her, she) Tom told _____ and me that astronauts breathe this oxygen. (her)

Supplementary Activities

More Practice: In each sentence below underline the pronoun in parentheses that properly completes the sentence. (Score: 6)
1. Red Hanrahan's father told us that (he, him) and his family came to the U.S. from Ireland. (he)
2. (Fran and I, Fran and me) both have grandfathers from Sweden. (Fran and I)
3. (She, her) and (I, me) are half Swedish and half French. (She, I)
4. Tonio told (she and I, her and me) that his family is Italian and French. (her and me)
5. (Us, We) know that Rosa and Juan are from Mexico. (We)

Using Resources and Materials: On the chalkboard write the following questions:
1. What is oxygen and where is it found?
2. Is oxygen necessary for life?
3. What harmful effect does oxygen have on steel, and how can this be prevented?

Have the students outline and write sentences about oxygen. Suggest that the sentences answer the three questions written on the chalkboard. Tell the students that they may use the information in Lesson 95 or other resource materials, but they should state the ideas in their own words. Have the students write sentences similar to those used in Lesson 95. Tell them to use pronouns and pronouns in pairs in each sentence. Remind them to proofread their writing, checking for sentences, correct spelling, capitalization, and punctuation.

Lesson **96** (page 116)

Reviewing Proper Word Forms
 20, 21, 27, 28, 30, 33, 37

Key Objective   The student will be able to select the proper word form to complete sentences.

Procedures
Write the following on the chalkboard:

Group I
1. may—can
2. sit—set
3. there—their
4. these—those—them
5. to—too—two
6. who's—whose

Group II
1. began—begun
2. came—come
3. drank—drunk
4. fell—fallen
5. knew—known
6. ran—run
7. rode—ridden
8. saw—seen
9. took—taken

Group III
1. doesn't—don't
2. is—are
3. was—were

Remind the students that they have learned the proper use of many word forms this year. Direct their attention to the groups of words on the chalkboard, asking whether they notice a similarity among the words in each group. Help them see that the meaning would determine the proper word form from each pair in group I. As an example have a student make a sentence with one of the first two words. Then point out that the student had to decide whether to ask or give permission or to tell that someone is able to do something before knowing which word to use in the sentence. Have other students read the other pairs of words in group I, tell their meanings, and use them in sentences. If any word gives difficulty, clarify its use by referring the students to the key section.

If the students do not see a usage similarity among the word pairs in group II, tell them that they must decide which word of each pair needs a helping verb in order to know the proper word form to use. Ask a student to make a sentence with one of the first two words and explain how the decision was made to use that word. The student should explain that *began* does not need a helping verb but that *begun* does. Let several students read the other pairs of words in group II, tell which need helping verbs, and use them in sentences. Again refer the students to the key section when they indicate they are confused.

The students should see that, in order to choose the proper word form from each pair in group III, they need to find out whether it tells about one or more than one person or thing. In the discussion of these words care should be taken to point out exceptions involving the use of the words *you* and *I*. Let various students read the words in group III, explain their proper use, and use them in sentences.

As soon as all usage items have been discussed, have the students work independently to complete the exercises in Lesson 96.

Supplementary Exercises

Choose the proper word form in parentheses to write in the blank. (Score: 11)

1. (began, begun) In 1849 many people _____ to move to California. (began)
2. (to, too, two) People hoped _____ find gold in California. (to)
3. (there, their) Some people left _____ families at home. (their)
4. (saw, seen) Soon mining towns were _____ all over California. (seen)
5. (these, them) Many of _____ towns became large cities. (these)
6. (who's, whose) John Sutter is a man _____ famous for finding gold. (who's)
7. (saw, seen) It's interesting to read how he _____ the gold. (saw)
8. (were, was) Other people _____ eager to hunt for the metal. (were)
9. (came, come) Some settlers _____ to California for other reasons. (came)
10. (took, taken) They had _____ farming tools to their new homes. (taken)
11. (knew, known) These people _____ that there was rich farmland in California. (knew)

Supplementary Activities

More Practice: Have the students write ten sentences using each word of the following pairs of

words in a sentence: *may—can, who's—whose, fell—fallen, saw—seen,* and *doesn't—don't.*

Using Resources and Materials: Have the students use the encyclopedia and other resource materials to learn about deserts in other parts of the world. Have the students write sentences describing the desert and telling about the animal and plant life in the desert. Tell the students to use the word forms mentioned in Lesson 96 when writing their sentences. Some students may wish to illustrate their sentences.

Lesson **97** (page 117)

Reviewing Proper Word Forms
 18e, 20, 21, 28, 29, 31, 33, 37

Key Objective The student will be able to select the proper word form to complete sentences.

Procedures

Broadcasting

Where do you think the people pictured in Lesson 97 are? Describe how living and working in the South Pole would be different from living and working in a warmer climate.

Explaining the Lesson

Write the following on the chalkboard:

Group I

1. in—into   4. teach—learn
2. lie—lay   5. these—those—them
3. sit—set   6. they're—there

Group II

1. ate—eaten   7. froze—frozen
2. became—become   8. gave—given
3. blew—blown   9. grew—grown
4. broke—broken   10. went—gone
5. did—done   11. wrote—written
6. flew—flown

Group III

1. has—have
2. was—were

Group IV

1. a—an
2. himself—themselves

In working with the words on the chalkboard follow the procedure that was used in Lesson 96. Help the students understand that the meanings of the words in group I govern their use. The use of helping verbs determines the choice in group II. The choice of words in group III depends on the number of persons or things being told about. The use of *a* and *an* in group IV depends on the words that follow them, and *himself* and *themselves* replace *hisself* and *theirselves.*

Let the students work independently to complete the exercises in Lesson 97. After answers to the exercises have been checked, have the students correct their mistakes.

Supplementary Exercises

Choose the proper word form in parentheses to write in the blank. (Score: 10)

1. (went, gone) Many explorers have _____ to the North Pole. (gone)
2. (teach, learn) They are eager to _____ about this area. (learn)
3. (their, there) Several airfields have been built _____ . (there)
4. (ate, eaten) Food that is _____ in the North Pole comes from far away. (eaten)
5. (flew, flown) It is _____ to the North Pole in airplanes. (flown)
6. (froze, frozen) Sometimes the airplanes' engines have almost _____ . (frozen)
7. (laid, lain) The food is _____ in the storage houses. (laid)
8. (blew, blown) The swift wind _____ snow over the buildings. (blew)
9. (was, were) Often sleds _____ used by the explorers. (were)
10. (They're, There) _____ pulled by a team of large dogs. (They're)

Supplementary Activities

More Practice: Have the students use the following word forms in sentences: *in—into, sit—set, these—those—them, ate—eaten, did—done, gave—given, went—gone, has—have, himself—themselves.*

Using Resources and Materials: Have the students use the encyclopedia and other resource materials to learn more about polar expeditions. Have the students write sentences about an expedition and tell them to use several of the word forms mentioned in Lesson 97. Remind the students to proofread their work.

Lesson **98** (page 118)

Remembering What We Have Learned

Key Objective The student will be able to apply the skills taught in Units I–VI.

Procedures

Have the students read the title of Lesson 98. Explain that this lesson reviews not only Unit VI but also the entire book. Point out that key numbers are listed after the directions for each part of the lesson and that each person should read the keys and review the information. Call attention to the fact that this is a two-page lesson and be sure the students understand that they are to work all of the exercises in Lesson 98.

Let several students read their answers to the exercises and correct their mistakes. Then have the students open their books to the text section. Briefly consider the information in Keys 1 to 51, dwelling only on those points about which there are questions or apparent confusion.

NOTE: It might be best to use two periods on succeeding days for this lesson rather than one long period.

Post Test—Unit VI

At the conclusion of Unit VI, administer the post test for the entire book found in the back of the Teacher's Edition. The results should indicate which students have mastered the concepts and skills in the book. Instructions for administration of post tests appear in the introduction to the Teacher's Edition. Note: The post test for Units I–VI contains two pages.

Keys to Good Language

TEACHER'S EDITION

Phoenix Learning Resources, LLC.

Keys to Good Language

Phoenix Learning Resources, LLC.

Contents

Contents

The Text begins on page 52.

Effective Sentences

An effective sentence expresses a thought clearly. Faulty sentences leave the reader in doubt about what is being said.

I. Check the more effective sentence in each pair below. (Score: 24)

1. Sandy touched the bird's nest, which flew out chirping loudly. ____
   Sandy touched the nest, and the bird flew out chirping loudly. √

2. The story of Tom Sawyer has been enjoyed ever since it was written. √
   The story of Tom Sawyer has been enjoyed ever since he wrote it. ____

3. After Emily spoke to Miss O'Keefe, she disappeared. ____
   Emily spoke to Miss O'Keefe and then disappeared. √

4. She likes to paint more than her sister does. √
   Her sister does not like to paint as often as she does. ____

5. Open your book and turn to page 10. √
   Open your book and then you should turn to page 10. ____

6. Walking up the steps, the bell rang. ____
   The bell rang while I was walking up the steps. √

7. Our trip started by leaving early in the morning. ____
   We started our trip early in the morning. √

8. They enjoy the books they read so much that they are hard to put away. ____
   It is hard for them to put away books they enjoy reading. √

9. After Steve read the magazines, he gave them to a friend. √
   Steve gave magazines to a friend that he had read. ____

10. Rosa rushed to save the puppy not thinking of herself. ____
    Not thinking of herself, Rosa rushed to save the puppy. √

11. He put the glove on his hand, which had a hole in it. ____
    The glove had a hole in it, but he put it on his hand. √

12. The tree has only one branch left, caused by the hurricane. ____
    In the hurricane the tree lost all but one branch. √

II. Rewrite the sentences below to make them clear and effective. (Score: 10)

13. We have a tree house, which is an oak tree.

(Answers will vary.)

_____

14. Coming into the room, the desks should look neat.

(Answers will vary.)

_____

Kinds of Sentences

Place an *S* before each statement, or declarative sentence, a *Q* before each question, or interrogative sentence, and an *E* before each exclamation, or exclamatory sentence.

Examples: _____*S*_____ We saw a very old book in the museum.

_____*E*_____ How brittle its pages were!

_____*Q*_____ Were you allowed to touch it?

The First American Literature

_____*S*_____ 1. At first American colonists were too busy to write books.

_____*S*_____ 2. Some colonists wrote letters to friends in Europe.

_____*E*_____ 3. How different their lives must have seemed to their friends!

_____*Q*_____ 4. Did they keep diaries of everyday events?

_____*Q*_____ 5. What did they write about life in the American colonies?

_____*S*_____ 6. After a while the colonists found time for writing books.

_____*Q*_____ 7. Were most books written by the leaders of the colonies?

_____*S*_____ 8. John Smith wrote about some of the opportunities in America.

_____*Q*_____ 9. Was one of his books a history of Virginia?

_____*S*_____ 10. William Bradford's book told about some of the Pilgrims' adventures.

_____*E*_____ 11. What sad experiences he sometimes wrote about!

_____*S*_____ 12. A history of Pennsylvania was written by William Penn.

_____*S*_____ 13. John Winthrop wrote about the Massachusetts Bay Colony.

_____*Q*_____ 14. Did his book tell about their form of government?

_____*S*_____ 15. The books written by Roger Williams were full of many good ideas.

_____*S*_____ 16. He believed that all people should help govern.

_____*E*_____ 17. How long ago these early colonists wrote!

_____*S*_____ 18. We still learn about life in the first American colonies from their books.

_____*Q*_____ 19. Do some libraries have copies of these books?

Ending Sentences Correctly

🔑 7a, 8a, 9a

Place a period at the end of a statement, a
question mark at the end of a question, and
an exclamation point at the end of an
exclamation.

Examples: People used to get salt from the ocean.

Did they let the water evaporate?

How long that must have taken!

Salt of the Earth

1. Do you sprinkle salt on your food**?**

2. Salt can help make some foods more flavorful**.**

3. What a useful mineral salt is**!**

4. Is it necessary in our diets**?**

5. Body cells cannot work without some salt**.**

6. All animals need salt**.**

7. Many farmers put out salt blocks for their livestock**.**

8. How the cattle gather around the salt block**!**

9. Where does the salt we use come from**?**

10. Some salt is found in oceans and lakes**.**

11. Are there many underground salt deposits**?**

12. How far beneath the earth's surface they lie**!**

13. Miners take this salt out of the earth**.**

14. Does some salt come from wells**?**

15. Is the salt water pumped to the surface**?**

16. Salt comes from many sources**.**

17. There have been many uses for salt throughout history**.**

18. Was salt used to preserve meat and fish**?**

19. In some countries salt was used as a symbol for friendship**.**

20. Weren't Roman soldiers sometimes paid with salt**?**

21. The word *salary* comes from the Roman word for salt**.**

22. American Indians were using salt before European settlers arrived**.**

23. What long distances the Indians traveled to find salt**!**

24. Was salt used for trade with other tribes**?**

25. Oh, how glad they were to trade for it**!**

26. American Indian tribes brought salt to the settlers**.**

Using Capital Letters

➤ 1a, g, h, i, j, 5

The sentences below have been written without capital letters. Study the keys listed above and read the sentences. Underline each word that should begin with a capital letter. (Score: 1 for each word correctly underlined)

Example: on november 19, 1620, a ship named the *mayflower* reached america.

Early Settlements

1.   the oldest town in the united states is st. augustine, florida.
2.   did the spaniards settle in florida?
3.   only a few spanish people settled near the atlantic ocean.
4.   many spanish people settled in mexico and south america.
5.   some groups of french people settled in canada.
6.   many of the settlers along the atlantic ocean came from england.
7.   the settlement of jamestown was named for king james of england.
8.   jamestown was built next to the james river in virginia.
9.   have you ever heard of a man named john smith?
10. john smith was one of the first leaders of jamestown.
11. another group of english people sailed to america on a ship named the *mayflower*.
12. it took many weeks for the *mayflower* to cross the atlantic ocean.
13. on the *mayflower* were about a hundred men, women, and children from england.
14. one reason these people came to america was to practice their faith freely.
15. they built the town of plymouth.
16. the town of plymouth became a part of massachusetts bay colony.
17. the settlers of plymouth chose john carver as their leader.
18. what a cold and lonely winter they had the first year!
19. how they longed to see family and friends they had left in europe!
20. the cold winter months of january and february caused much suffering.
21. in the spring it became warm enough to start planting crops.
22. some american indians living nearby showed the english how to plant corn.
23. the following fall the settlers celebrated their first thanksgiving.
24. they wanted to express thanks for the food they had grown.
25. soon other english colonies were established in connecticut and rhode island.
26. were colonies also established in new hampshire?

Other Things to Do: Using some of the names you underlined above, write two statements, two questions, and two exclamations about early settlers.

Punctuating Sentences

I. The following sentences have been written with some punctuation marks missing. Place periods, question marks, and exclamation points where they are needed. (Score: 33—1 for each punctuation mark correctly used)

Collecting Stamps

1. What a large stamp collection Maria has!
2. Mrs. Tewa has given many stamps to Maria.
3. Maria has bought some stamps from J. R. Rey.
4. What an interesting store Ms. Rey has!
5. Doesn't she sell stamps from all over the world?
6. Did Maria buy those triangular stamps from Dr. Woods?
7. What interesting stamps these are!
8. Did Colonel E. J. Lerman send them to Maria from Germany?
9. Miss Yamato said that many stamps honor famous people.
10. This U.S. stamp has a picture of Amelia Earhart on it.
11. Wasn't Ms. Earhart a well-known airplane pilot in our country?
12. The scientist Albert Einstein is shown on this stamp.
13. Here is a stamp with a picture of Eleanor Roosevelt on it.
14. Mrs. Roosevelt was a great humanitarian.
15. What a beautiful stamp this is!
16. Dr. Martin Luther King, Jr., is honored on this stamp.
17. Wasn't Dr. King a civil rights leader?
18. This stamp from Spain shows a picture of Charles A. Lindbergh.
19. Lindbergh was the first pilot to make a solo flight across the Atlantic Ocean.
20. How interesting a stamp collection can be!

II. Many of the following words can be abbreviated. Write the correct abbreviation on the line following each word. Place an *X* after the words that cannot be abbreviated. (Score: 1 for each abbreviation or *X*)

21.	Monday	**Mon.**	28.	Florida	**Fla., FL**	35.	Judge	**X**
22.	Street	**St.**	29.	October	**Oct.**	36.	Sunday	**Sun.**
23.	January	**Jan.**	30.	East	**E.**	37.	May	**X**
24.	Missouri	**Mo., MO**	31.	Boulevard	**Blvd.**	38.	February	**Feb.**
25.	Avenue	**Ave.**	32.	Thursday	**Thurs.**	39.	Doctor	**Dr.**
26.	Utah	**X, UT**	33.	Pennsylvania	**Pa., PA**	40.	Northwest	**N.W.**
27.	South	**S.**	34.	June	**X**	41.	Saturday	**Sat.**

Recognizing Sentences

7a, 8a, 9a, 41

A *sentence* is a group of words that expresses a complete thought.

Write *Yes* before each group of words below that is a sentence. Place the correct punctuation mark at the end of each sentence. Write *No* in front of each group of words that is not a sentence. (Score: 1 for each *Yes* or *No* and 1 for each punctuation mark)

A Useful Gas

__Yes__   1. Many people have baking soda in their homes.

__No__   2. Also a bottle of a weak acid called vinegar

__No__   3. Can do an experiment with soda and vinegar

__No__   4. A tablespoon of soda in the bottom of a glass

__Yes__   5. Next, pour the vinegar over the soda.

__Yes__   6. What happens to the soda?

__No__   7. Changes to another form

__Yes__   8. The mixture bubbles and looks like it is boiling.

__No__   9. Is making a gas

__Yes__   10. Now hold a burning match over the top of the glass.

__No__   11. Surprising what will happen

__No__   12. Will stop burning

__Yes__   13. Why does the match go out?

__Yes__   14. The gas formed from the soda and vinegar mixture rises to the match.

__No__   15. An odorless, colorless gas called carbon dioxide

__Yes__   16. Carbon dioxide keeps oxygen from the match.

__No__   17. Cannot burn without oxygen

__Yes__   18. How quickly carbon dioxide puts out fires!

__Yes__   19. Some fire extinguishers are filled with this gas in order to put out fires.

Other Things to Do: On a separate sheet of paper make a sentence of each group of words above that is not a sentence.

Recognizing Subjects of Sentences

🔑 14, 41a

Sentences express thoughts about persons, places, or things. A word that tells what a sentence is about is called the *subject* of the sentence.

In each of the following sentences underline the subject of the sentence. (Score: 1 for each word correctly underlined)

Example: Many <u>animals</u> can run fast.

The Amazing Okapi

1. <u>Africa</u> is the home of many interesting animals.
2. The <u>camel</u> is well suited to desert life.
3. The <u>hippopotamus</u> can be found in the swamps and along the rivers.
4. <u>Giraffes</u> are often seen in grassy regions.
5. <u>Zebras</u>, too, are found in areas where grass is plentiful.
6. The <u>okapi</u> is one of the most unusual animals in Africa.
7. This <u>animal</u> stands about 1½ meters (5 feet) high at the shoulders.
8. An <u>okapi</u> has a body similar to a giraffe's body.
9. The <u>okapi's neck</u> is shorter than the giraffe's neck.
10. Its <u>neck</u> looks like the neck of a horse.
11. The <u>okapi</u> lives deep inside the thick African forest.
12. The <u>color</u> of the okapi helps it to hide in the forest.
13. Its <u>body</u> is a dark brown color.
14. The <u>face</u> is brown in the middle and white on the sides.
15. The <u>okapi's legs</u> are white with purplish black stripes.
16. Male <u>okapis</u> have a pair of short horns on their heads.
17. The <u>okapi's eyes</u> can turn in its head.
18. The <u>tongue</u> of this animal is very long and blue.
19. The <u>okapi</u> is very strong and clever.
20. This <u>animal</u> can quickly disappear through a thick forest.
21. <u>People</u> had neither seen nor heard of the okapi until 1900.
22. Some <u>explorers</u> in Africa discovered this rare animal.
23. The <u>picture</u> of the okapi on this page will help you know what the animal looks like.

Other Things to Do: Write ten sentences about an animal you have seen, read, or heard about. Be sure to use correct punctuation marks after the sentences.

Recognizing Nouns

🗝 14

A *noun* is a word that names a person, a place, or a thing.

Underline each noun in the following sentences. (Score: 1 for each word correctly underlined)

Captain John Smith

1. John Smith was an officer in the English army.
2. This man visited many countries with the English army.
3. In 1607 Smith sailed from England to America.
4. John Smith was one of the founders of Jamestown.
5. Jamestown was named after the king of England.
6. Jamestown was the first permanent English settlement in America.
7. Many people settled in Jamestown.
8. Life in Jamestown was very difficult at first.
9. During the long, hard winter many settlers died.
10. The settlers needed homes and food.
11. John Smith became a leader of Jamestown.
12. Smith became president of the colony in 1608.
13. Each person in Jamestown was given a job to do.
14. Trees in the forest were cut down and used to build houses.
15. Forests were cleared and crops were planted.
16. The settlers often traded with nearby tribes for food.
17. Fishing was another source of food.
18. Wasn't tobacco grown in Jamestown and sent to England?
19. After two years, about fifty houses had been built in Jamestown.
20. The settlement was protected by a tall wall that had five sides.
21. Smith traveled a lot and drew a very good map of Virginia.
22. The Powhatan Indian tribe captured John Smith.
23. John Smith's life was saved by a girl named Pocahontas.
24. Pocahontas was the daughter of the Powhatan Indian chief.
25. Smith and Pocahontas became very good friends.
26. After Smith returned to Jamestown, Pocahontas visited him often.
27. Pocahontas brought food and supplies to the settlers.
28. John Rolf and Smith were good friends.
29. Didn't Rolf and Pocahontas marry and go to England?
30. John Smith was hurt in an accident and had to return to England.
31. Many books about America were written by John Smith.

Singular and Plural Nouns   ⚷ 15

I. Fill the blank in each sentence with the plural of the noun in parentheses.

Example: (carrot) Do you like to eat _____*carrots*_____ ?

The Basic Foods

1. (body)   Our _____**bodies**_____ need a variety of foods each day.

2. (egg)   Meat, _____**eggs**_____ , poultry, beans, or fish should be eaten daily.

3. (glass)   Drink several _____**glasses**_____ of milk for vitamins and minerals.

4. (fruit)   Shouldn't we eat some tomatoes or citrus _____**fruits**_____ every day?

5. (orange)   Lemons and _____**oranges**_____ are citrus fruits.

6. (berry)   Other fruits, such as _____**berries**_____ , should be eaten, too.

7. (cereal)   They eat whole-grain breads or _____**cereals**_____ every day.

8. (box)   Many people put raw carrots in their lunch _____**boxes**_____ .

9. (tooth)   They know that raw vegetables are good for their _____**teeth**_____ .

10. (dish)   Many tasty _____**dishes**_____ , such as puddings, are made from milk.

11. (leaf)   Did you know that the _____**leaves**_____ on celery are good to eat?

12. (grocery)   You should plan healthful meals before you buy _____**groceries**_____ .

13. (family)   All _____**families**_____ should eat nutritious foods each day.

14. (shelf)   Keep many nourishing foods on the _____**shelves**_____ .

II. In the blank beside each singular noun write its plural form. In the blank beside each plural noun write its singular form.

15.	knife	**knives**	20. deer	**deer**
16.	ponies	**pony**	21. life	**lives**
17.	peach	**peaches**	22. monkey	**monkeys**
18.	leaf	**leaves**	23. mouse	**mice**
19.	pencils	**pencil**	24. sheep	**sheep**

Possessive Forms of Nouns   🔑 16

To form the possessive of a singular noun or of a plural noun not ending in _s_, add an apostrophe and an _s_ (_'s_). For plural nouns ending in _s_, add an apostrophe only (_'_).

Examples: Beth's camera   a truck's tires   birds' feathers
                     Devon's address   two trucks' tires   mice's tails

I. On the line following each noun write its possessive form.

1. Carlos **Carlos's**   6. dolphins **dolphins'**
2. sheep **sheep's**   7. oxen **oxen's**
3. men **men's**   8. Chris **Chris's**
4. horses **horses'**   9. babies **babies'**
5. cities **cities'**   10. sister **sister's**

II. Fill the blank in each sentence with the possessive of the noun in parentheses.

Traveling Painters

11. (person) A painting of a **person's** face is usually called a "portrait."
12. (America) **America's** early artists often painted portraits.
13. (artist) During the winter the **artist's** time was spent painting pictures.
14. (persons) But **persons'** faces were left out of the pictures.
15. (People) **People's** portraits were finished except for the faces.
16. (painter) By spring the **painter's** homework was done.
17. (artist) The unfinished portraits were put into the **artist's** wagon.
18. (painters) Summer was the **painters'** time to travel.
19. (people) Often the artist stopped at **people's** homes.
20. (wives) Some husbands wanted their **wives'** portraits.
21. (woman) Then the artist painted the **woman's** face on a picture.
22. (child) At times a **child's** face was painted on an unfinished portrait.
23. (wagon) By autumn the **wagon's** stack of paintings had been sold.
24. (winter) Then the **winter's** work of painting began again.

Recognizing Pronouns   🗝 17b

A *pronoun* is a word used in place of a noun.

Examples: *Carla gave the book* to *Miles* and *Tina*. (nouns)
                 She gave *it* to *them*. (personal pronouns)

Underline each personal pronoun in the following sentences. (Score: 1 for each pronoun underlined)

Example: Lois told the children that <u>she</u> would bring <u>her</u> book to <u>their</u> room.

The Covered Bridge

1. Reggie told <u>me</u> that <u>she</u> had read *The Covered Bridge*.
2. "<u>I</u> am sure that <u>you</u> will enjoy the book," Reggie said.
3. <u>It</u> is a story about Connie and <u>her</u> friends.
4. In 1788 <u>they</u> lived alone in a house in Vermont.
5. Ethan Allen was a friend of <u>theirs</u>.
6. Once <u>he</u> came to visit <u>them</u>.
7. <u>You</u> know that <u>he</u> was a soldier in the American Revolution.
8. <u>They</u> heard about <u>his</u> patriotism during the Revolution.
9. Connie had to cross a covered bridge on <u>her</u> way to school.
10. <u>It</u> was a bridge with walls and a roof built over <u>it</u>.
11. "<u>We</u> build bridges to last many years," said a friend of <u>hers</u>.
12. <u>We</u> put roofs over bridges so that <u>they</u> will stay dry.
13. Does the book tell how Peter and <u>his</u> friend saved the bridge?
14. Connie helped <u>him</u> when the river almost swept the bridge away.
15. Sam Breen was a neighbor of <u>theirs</u>.
16. The story tells how <u>they</u> helped <u>him</u> save <u>his</u> sheep from a storm.
17. Connie learned that <u>we</u> always help neighbors when <u>they</u> need <u>us</u>.
18. <u>She</u> and <u>her</u> friends had many good times together.
19. "<u>We</u> have worked hard," Sarah told Connie.
20. Once in the book, Connie and <u>her</u> friends were lost.
21. The night was dark, but <u>they</u> had to go out in the snow.
22. <u>I</u> wonder if Connie was afraid before some animals led <u>them</u> home.
23. <u>I</u> am glad that Reggie told <u>me</u> about this book.
24. <u>You</u> will enjoy reading about Connie and <u>her</u> friends.

Other Things to Do: Circle each noun in the above sentences. Read the sentences above, substituting the correct noun for each pronoun you have underlined.

Using *We* and *Us* in Sentences   ☞ 18a, c

Use the pronoun *we* to tell who did something, or after such words as *it is*, *is it*, or *was it*.

Use the pronoun *us* after such words as *told*, *give*, *heard*, *from*, *to*, *by*, or *with*.

Examples: *We* want to learn more about Lee's hobby.

Lee told *us* about it.

Fill the blank in each sentence with the correct pronoun, *we* or *us*.

Carving Soap

1.   One day ____**we**____ went to Lee's house.

2.   Lee had told ____**us**____ about her hobby.

3.   She showed ____**us**____ some figures she had made.

4.   Lee asked ____**us**____ to guess what the figures were made of.

5.   ____**We**____ could not believe they were carved from a bar of soap.

6.   ____**We**____ decided that we would carve different objects out of soap.

7.   '' ____**We**____ can carve figures of animals,'' said David.

8.   Lee said, '' ____**We**____ can carve many different things out of soap.''

9.   All of ____**us**____ were eager to start carving soap.

10. ____**We**____ each bought a large bar of soap.

11. Our parents let ____**us**____ borrow small knives.

12. The next day Lee showed ____**us**____ how to carve soap.

13. First ____**we**____ drew our design on a piece of paper.

14. Lee showed ____**us**____ how to transfer the design onto the soap.

15. She showed ____**us**____ how to use a stick for drawing the design on the soap.

16. Then ____**we**____ carefully used the knife to cut the soap away from the design.

17. Lee's mother watched ____**us**____ while we used the knives.

18. After that ____**we**____ used our fingers to smooth the rough soap-carving.

Using Pronouns in Pairs   ☞ 18a, b, c

When you tell who does something, use _I_, _he_, _she_, or _they_.

Examples: _He_ and _she_ will give a report to the class.

They and _I_ will tell about our visit.

After such words as _told_, _give_, _heard_, _from_, _to_, _for_, _by_, or _with_, use _her_, _him_, _them_, or _me_.

Examples: Sergio told _her_ and _him_ about his trip.

Gayle gave the pictures to _them_ and _me_.

Underline the pronoun in parentheses that properly completes each sentence below.

Niagara Falls

1. Sergio and Gayle told (him, he) and (she, her) about their trip.
2. (Him, He) and (she, her) went to Niagara Falls last summer.
3. They showed (they, them) and (she, her) some pictures of the falls.
4. The pictures were taken by (him, he) and (she, her).
5. (He, Him) and (they, them) said that the waterfalls are beautiful.
6. (She, Her) and (me, I) asked Sergio how high the waterfalls are.
7. He told (she, her) and (I, me) that they are 53 meters (160 feet) high.
8. (Them, They) and (I, me) were amazed to hear that the falls are that high.
9. (Her, She) and (me, I) asked whether Niagara Falls are the highest falls in the world.
10. Sergio told (him, he) and (me, I) that there are many waterfalls higher than this.
11. Sergio and Gayle told (he, him) and (me, I) why Niagara Falls are important.
12. Sergio explained to (him, he) and (me, I) that the waterfalls generate electricity.
13. He told (them, they) and (I, me) that many factories use the electricity.
14. (Him, He) and (she, her) said that there are many factories near Niagara Falls.
15. Paula asked (him, he) and (I, me) where Niagara Falls are.
16. We showed (she, her) and (they, them) the Niagara River on a map.
17. (He, Him) and (they, them) saw that the falls are between the U.S. and Canada.
18. Gayle asked (them, they) and (I, me) whether the falls ever change size.
19. (Them, They) and (I, me) said that parts of the waterfalls have caved in.
20. (She, Her) and (they, them) said that many people visit Niagara Falls.
21. Gayle said that (she, her) and (they, them) rode in a boat near the falls.
22. We learned many interesting things about Niagara Falls from (he, him) and (her, she).

Other Things to Do: Use the plural forms of the following nouns to write five sentences about traveling: _trip_, _compass_, _leaf_, _country_, and _child_.

Using Pronouns After *Is* and *Was*

🔑 18d

After *it is, it was, is it,* or *was it,* use the pronouns *I, he, she, we,* or *they.*

Underline one of the pronouns in parentheses that properly completes each sentence below.

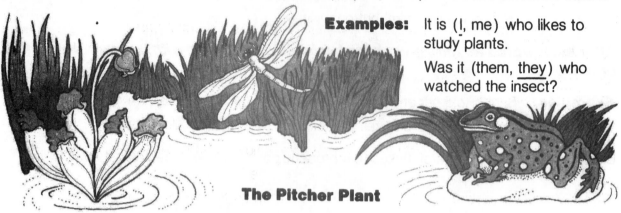

Examples: It is (I, me) who likes to study plants.

Was it (them, they) who watched the insect?

The Pitcher Plant

1. It is (him, he) who told the class about the pitcher plant.
2. But it was (I, me) who learned that there are many kinds of pitcher plants.
3. Was it (them, they) who said that the plant has interesting leaves?
4. It was (I, me) who said some pitcher plants grow in swamps.
5. I think it was (her, she) who said that the leaves are shaped like traps.
6. It was (me, I) who showed how the edges of the leaves fold together.
7. Wasn't it (they, them) who said that the leaves look like pitchers?
8. Then wasn't it (us, we) who explained how the plant traps insects?
9. It is (he, him) who is drawing the picture of the pitcher plant.
10. Was it (them, they) who said that the plant has brightly colored leaves?
11. Yes, but it was (us, we) who said that some pitcher plants have yellow flowers.
12. Wasn't it (her, she) who said that insects are attracted by the plant's sweet smell?
13. Then it was (I, me) who explained that the insects are looking for nectar.
14. Was it (us, we) who told how the insects are trapped inside the leaves?
15. It was (him, he) who said the leaves have tiny hairs growing on them.
16. Then it was (she, her) who said that the hairs hold the insect.
17. It was (me, I) who said all the hairs in the leaves point inward.
18. It was (them, they) who learned that some pitcher plants contain liquid.
19. It was (I, me) who explained that the liquid is rain water.
20. Wasn't it (him, he) who said that the insect falls into this liquid?
21. Then it was (us, we) who guessed that the insect drowns.
22. Was it (they, them) who said that the plant digests the insect?
23. It was (her, she) who told us about the moth who lives in the pitcher plant.
24. Was it (he, him) who told her to read this book about unique plants?
25. Is it (she, her) who will show on the map where these plants grow?

Using Proper Word Forms

In each sentence below underline the proper word form in parentheses.

Blueprints

1. You (can, may) make (an, a) interesting design with blueprint paper.
2. This paper is treated with (a, an) special chemical.
3. (He, Him) and (I, me) knew the chemical makes the paper sensitive to light.
4. Aaron said that he would (teach, learn) (we, us) how to use the paper.
5. I asked (he, him) if architects use blueprint paper to draw building plans.
6. Dana said that it would be fun to (teach, learn) how to make blueprints.
7. Aaron said that (her, she) and (I, me) would need a leaf and some glass.
8. Aaron showed (we, us) how to place the leaf on the top of the paper.
9. Dana asked, ''(May, Can) I lay the piece of glass over the leaf now?''
10. (Us, We) asked why the leaf was put in the bright sunshine.
11. Aaron said that we would (teach, learn) what happens when light shines on the paper.
12. After a minute Aaron told (her, she) and (I, me) to dip the paper in water.
13. ''(Can, May) I hold the paper in the water?'' I asked Aaron.
14. Soon Dana showed the blueprint of (an, a) leaf to (we, us).
15. You (may, can) see that the paper stayed white where the leaf was.
16. It was (me, I) who asked why the rest of the paper was blue.
17. Aaron told (I, me) that light had changed the color of the blueprint paper.
18. ''(May, Can) a light bulb be used instead of sunshine?'' I asked.
19. Dana asked Aaron where she could (learn, teach) more about blueprints.
20. I want to (teach, learn) my friends how to make blueprints.
21. Blueprinting is (an, a) easy hobby that we (can, may) all do.
22. Dana asked, ''(Can, May) I make another print now?''
23. Aaron gave a piece of blueprint paper to (she, her) and (me, I).
24. Then (he, him) and (I, me) cut out a pattern from another piece of paper.
25. Aaron said that (he, him) and (I, me) could make blueprints of these patterns.
26. It was (him, he) who made (a, an) interesting print from the pattern.
27. You (may, can) make (a, an) different design with this pattern.
28. Dana was glad that she had a friend to (learn, teach) her blueprinting.
29. I am glad he could (learn, teach) me how to make blueprints, too.
30. (May, Can) I come again and (learn, teach) more about blueprinting?
31. Dana said (her, she) would make greeting cards with her designs.
32. She asked Aaron and (I, me) what we would do with our designs.
33. Aaron said that (he, him) was going to frame his best design.

Remembering What We Have Learned

1. Write a declarative sentence on the first line below, an interrogative sentence on the second line, and an exclamatory sentence on the third line. 🔑 7a, 8a, 9a, 41b, c, d

   _____(Answers will vary.)_____

   _____(Answers will vary.)_____

   _____(Answers will vary.)_____

2. Write the following sentences correctly. 🔑 1a, b, c, i, 5, 7a, b, c, 8a

   dr a c byrd lives in kentucky ____**Dr. A. C. Byrd lives in Kentucky.**____

   _____

   is buffalo, new york, near lake erie ____**Is Buffalo, New York, near Lake Erie?**____

   _____

3. Write the plural forms of two nouns. 🔑 14, 15

   ____(Answers will vary.)____   ____(Answers will vary.)____

4. Write the possessive forms of a singular noun and of a plural noun. 🔑 14, 16

   ____(Answers will vary.)____   ____(Answers will vary.)____

5. Complete the following sentences by adding a pronoun to each. Use a different pronoun in each sentence. 🔑 17, 18d

   It is ____**I, he, she, we, or they**____.   Was it ____**I, he, she, we, or they**____?

6. On each line below write a sentence, using the words at the left of the line. 🔑 18a, b, c, e, 25, 26

   (her and me) _____(Answers will vary.)_____

   (we) _____

   (us) _____

   (an) _____

   (learn) _____

Writing Sentences

🔑 41

When you write sentences, think of the most effective way to express your thoughts. Decide whether a statement, a question, or an exclamation is needed to express an idea. Write each sentence so that it effectively gives information, asks for information, or expresses feelings.

Read the following examples. Why is the last sentence likely to be the most effective one for getting information?

Examples: How far away is the library?

I want to go to the library.

Do you know where the library is?

What is the address of the library?

1. Imagine that you have just awakened from a frightening dream. Write a sentence that tells how you might feel at that moment. (Score: 5)

(Answers will vary.)

_____

_____

2. A new student meets you at the front door of the school and asks you how to get to the school office. Write a sentence that gives the necessary directions. (Score: 5)

(Answers will vary.)

_____

_____

3. You must write the Mexican Consulate to ask for information about the seaport Veracruz. Write a sentence that asks for the information you need. (Score: 5)

(Answers will vary.)

_____

_____

4. Your best friend has asked you to spend the weekend at a farm, but you are unable to accept the invitation. Write a sentence explaining why you cannot accept. (Score: 5)

(Answers will vary.)

_____

_____

5. Suppose that an inflated balloon pops suddenly near your ear. Write a sentence that expresses your feelings. (Score: 5)

(Answers will vary.)

_____

_____

Recognizing Sentences in Paragraphs   ⚷ 41a, b, c, d

There should be four sentences in each of the paragraphs below. Separate the sentences by putting the correct punctuation mark at the end of each sentence and by underlining the first word of each sentence to show that it should begin with a capital letter. (Score: 1 for each punctuation mark and 1 for each underlined word)

Paul Revere

have you ever heard of Paul Revere? this famous man lived in Boston when England still governed the colonies next to the Atlantic Ocean. Paul Revere's father went to Boston from France. he made his living in America by making many things out of silver.

while working with his father, young Paul Revere became a skilled silversmith. what beautiful silver cups, plates, and jewelry he made. many of Paul Revere's creations can now be seen in museums. this craftsman is also remembered as one of the first people in America to make false teeth.

once England sent some tea to Boston. many Americans did not want this tea to be taken off the ships. they would have to pay taxes to England for the tea. several people, including Paul Revere, threw the tea from the ships into the water.

during the Revolutionary War, Paul Revere was a soldier. he was with the army in Massachusetts, Rhode Island, and Maine. he warned Americans that English soldiers were coming. the poem ''Paul Revere's Ride'' was written about this event.

Other Things to Do: Make a list of the personal pronouns used in the paragraphs above. Next to each pronoun write the noun that it stands for.

Recognizing Parts of Sentences

🔑 14, 17, 18, 19

You have learned that one part of every sentence is the *complete subject*, which tells who or what the sentence is about. The rest of a sentence is the *complete predicate*, which gives information about the subject. The sentences in the examples below have one line under the complete subject of the sentence, and two lines under the complete predicate of the sentence.

Examples: He went to the aquarium.

Many kinds of animals live in the sea.

In each of the following sentences draw one line under the complete subject of the sentence and draw two lines under the complete predicate of the sentence. (Score: 2 for each sentence)

The Interesting Squid

1. The squid lives in the ocean.
2. Some squids are only 1.5 centimeters (¾ inch) long.
3. But other squids may be 13 meters (40 feet) long.
4. These animals have unique bodies.
5. The squid's body is soft and boneless.
6. Ten arms grow out of its body.
7. Two of the arms are longer than the others.
8. These sea animals can swim very rapidly.
9. A squid uses its arms to catch food.
10. Squids usually eat fish.
11. Each arm is covered with rows of small suction cups.
12. The squid's arms are very strong.
13. They can squeeze very tightly.
14. A squid sometimes needs to hide from its enemies.
15. Its body has a small "ink sac."
16. The squid can send out a dark, inky liquid from this sac.
17. This liquid turns the water dark.
18. The squid hides in the dark water.
19. The squid can also change colors.
20. The squid may be lying on the sand.
21. Its color changes to the color of the sand.
22. The squid moves to a rock.
23. Its skin then changes color to look more like the rock.
24. The octopus is related to the squid.
25. But the body of the octopus is shaped differently than the squid's body.

Recognizing Verbs

🔑 19

A *verb* is a word that shows action, being, or state of being.

Examples: Syd *sang* a song for us.   Kelley *was* at school.

The dog *ran* up the street.   I *am* in this room.

Liz *likes* math.   We *were* at home.

They *have* the books.   Sean *is* with his grandmother.

Underline each verb in the sentences below.

Music in America

1. Many people like to sing and dance to music.
2. Music has been written and performed for hundreds of years.
3. Children often sing songs when they play games.
4. Early Americans enjoyed many different kinds of music.
5. Some early settlers brought harpsichords with them from Europe.
6. The harpsichord is an instrument very much like the piano.
7. Seth saw a picture of a harpsichord in a book.
8. People played the harpsichord and sang songs.
9. Some songs passed from one person to another down through the years.
10. These folk songs told stories about people and events.
11. Folk songs were popular in Europe many years ago.
12. Some people from Europe moved to America.
13. They taught folk songs to their children.
14. Some folk songs are hundreds of years old.
15. Songs were written that told about the American Revolution.
16. "Yankee Doodle" is a song about the Revolution.
17. As pioneers moved west, they sang many songs.
18. Many people liked the song "Oh! Susannah."
19. The pioneers danced to such songs as "Turkey in the Straw."
20. Hearing songs like this gave them pleasure.
21. People sang songs as they worked.
22. People who came from different countries brought their music to America.
23. There are many kinds of music in America today.
24. Some people enjoy concert music.
25. Do you listen to music on the radio?
26. Most people are glad that we have many kinds of music.

Principal Parts of Verbs

Verbs have three principal parts. When the third principal part is used, a helping word, such as *has, have, was,* or *had,* must also be used.

I. Write the missing principal parts of the following verbs. (Score: 14)

Example:

do	*did*	*done*
1. eat	**ate**	**eaten**
2. go	**went**	**gone**
3. see	**saw**	**seen**
4. write	**wrote**	**written**
5. give	**gave**	**given**
6. come	**came**	**come**
7. run	**ran**	**run**

II. In each sentence below underline the proper verb form in parentheses.

Valley Forge

8. Last summer Annie (went, gone) on a trip to Valley Forge, Pennsylvania.

9. Perhaps you have (saw, seen) paintings of this famous place.

10. This is where George Washington and the Continental army (came, come) in 1777.

11. They had (did, done) much walking before arriving at Valley Forge.

12. When winter had (came, come), the soldiers were very cold.

13. Washington (gave, given) his army all the food that he had.

14. The soldiers had (ate, eaten) whatever food they could find.

15. Some of them ate berries they (saw, seen) on bushes.

16. But many of them had (went, gone) without food for many days.

17. A few of the soldiers had (ran, run) away from the army.

18. But most of them stayed with Washington and (ate, eaten) little food.

19. The army (did, done) no fighting during the long, cold winter.

20. Some of the soldiers (wrote, written) letters to their families.

21. Washington (saw, seen) that the soldiers were cold and hungry.

22. But Washington never (gave, give) up hope.

23. A Prussian general (came, come) to help Washington train the soldiers.

Using Proper Verb Forms   ⚷ 21

Each sentence below contains two principal parts of the verbs *drink* or *write*. Underline the verb form in parentheses that completes each sentence. (Score: 1 for each word correctly underlined)

Water and Germs

1. Many early Americans (<u>wrote</u>, written) in diaries.
2. They (<u>wrote</u>, written) about events that were joyful and sad.
3. We know about their lives from what they have (wrote, <u>written</u>).
4. These people (<u>drank</u>, drunk) water that they got from wells.
5. Some people (<u>wrote</u>, written) about how they dug their wells.
6. These people did not know whether the water they (<u>drank</u>, drunk) was safe.
7. Sometimes there were germs in the water they had (drank, <u>drunk</u>).
8. Authors (<u>wrote</u>, written) that many people died of fevers.
9. Were these fevers caused by the water the people (<u>drank</u>, drunk)?
10. The people did not know there were germs in the water they (<u>drank</u>, drunk).
11. Early Americans also had (wrote, <u>written</u>) that they used water from rivers.
12. When they had (drank, <u>drunk</u>) this water, many people became ill.
13. They had (drank, <u>drunk</u>) water that had germs in it.
14. When people learned about germs, they (<u>wrote</u>, written) about them.
15. They knew that people who (<u>drank</u>, drunk) water from certain places became ill.
16. Then they found germs in some of the water that people had (drank, <u>drunk</u>).
17. For many years people had (wrote, <u>written</u>) what they knew about germs.
18. Others began to read what was (wrote, <u>written</u>) about these germs.
19. No one thought the water they (<u>drank</u>, drunk) could make them ill.
20. They thought all the water they had (drank, <u>drunk</u>) was safe.
21. At last people began to be concerned about the water that was (drank, <u>drunk</u>).
22. Laws were (wrote, <u>written</u>) to keep the water clean.
23. No one was allowed to throw trash into water that was (drank, <u>drunk</u>).
24. People (<u>wrote</u>, written) about ways to kill the harmful germs in water.
25. Chemicals designed to kill germs were added to water before people (<u>drank</u>, drunk) it.
26. The germs were eliminated before people had (drank, <u>drunk</u>) the water.
27. Authors (<u>wrote</u>, written) less often about people dying of fevers.
28. When they (<u>drank</u>, drunk) pure water, fewer people got sick.
29. Water that is (drank, <u>drunk</u>) in modern times is still purified.
30. Articles are still being (wrote, <u>written</u>) about ways to keep water clean.

Using *Is*, *Are*, *Was*, and *Were*

🔑 20a, b

Use *is* or *was* to tell about one person or thing. Use *are* or *were* to tell about more than one person or thing. Always use *are* or *were* with *you*.

Draw a line under the proper word form in parentheses.

An Experiment With Air

1. Pat and Jeannie (is, <u>are</u>) curious about what air can do.

2. There (<u>is</u>, are) an experiment that shows something that air can do.

3. Jeannie said, "Several things (is, <u>are</u>) needed for this experiment."

4. A large can with a lid (<u>is</u>, are) needed.

5. Pat said that a stove and some water (was, <u>were</u>) also needed.

6. The can that Pat had (<u>was</u>, were) a large metal can.

7. Jeannie said, "That (<u>is</u>, are) a good can to use."

8. A few spoonfuls of water (was, <u>were</u>) in the can.

9. Mrs. Larsen watched while the experiment (<u>was</u>, were) being done.

10. (Is, <u>Are</u>) you ready to set the can on the stove to heat?

11. The sound of water boiling in the can (<u>was</u>, were) heard.

12. Then a cloud of steam (<u>was</u>, were) coming out of the can.

13. "You saw that water (<u>was</u>, were) in the can," said Jeannie.

14. But now the water (<u>is</u>, are) boiling and changing into steam.

15. Very little air (<u>is</u>, are) left inside the can.

16. Jeannie said that the can (<u>was</u>, were) filled with steam.

17. The can (<u>was</u>, were) very hot from the stove.

18. She and Pat (was, <u>were</u>) very careful when they put the top on the can.

19. Pat made sure that the top (<u>was</u>, were) put on tightly.

20. They (was, <u>were</u>) eager to see what would happen.

21. "We (is, <u>are</u>) ready to cool the can now," said Jeannie.

22. They set the can on a shelf that (<u>was</u>, were) outside the room.

23. The air outside the room (<u>is</u>, are) cool.

24. Pat said, "The cool air (<u>is</u>, are) changing the steam back into water."

25. She said that little air pressure (<u>was</u>, were) in the can.

26. But great air pressure (<u>is</u>, are) against the outside of the can.

27. In a short time, the can (<u>was</u>, were) crushed by this air pressure.

Using Proper Verb Forms

📛 20a, b, 30

Use *doesn't, has,* and *hasn't* to tell about one person or thing. Use *don't, have,* and *haven't* to tell about more than one person. Always use *don't, have,* and *haven't* with the words *you* and *I.*

In each sentence below underline the proper word form in parentheses.

Benjamin Franklin

1. Many people (doesn't, don't) know very much about Benjamin Franklin.
2. (Hasn't, Haven't) our country honored Franklin as one of its greatest citizens?
3. (Have, Has) you read any books about Benjamin Franklin?
4. The library (has, have) a copy of his autobiography.
5. (Doesn't, Don't) you remember that Franklin worked for his brother in Boston?
6. They (has, have) forgotten that Franklin moved to Philadelphia.
7. She (doesn't, don't) know that Franklin had a printing shop there.
8. (Haven't, Hasn't) you read *Poor Richard's Almanac*?
9. It (has, have) proverbs in it that Franklin wrote.
10. (Don't, Doesn't) you remember some of Franklin's inventions?
11. They (have, has) read about the stove he invented.
12. But they (haven't, hasn't) read about his invention of the lightning rod.
13. (Don't, Doesn't) some buildings still have lightning rods on their roofs?
14. She (hasn't, haven't) known about the library Franklin started.
15. (Hasn't, Haven't) you read that it was the first library in America?
16. (Doesn't, Don't) he know that Franklin visited England many times?
17. He (has, have) read that Franklin wanted England to repeal the tax on tea.
18. She (haven't, hasn't) read that Franklin was America's first Postmaster General.
19. (Doesn't, Don't) you know that Franklin helped write the Declaration of Independence?
20. They (has, have) seen paintings of him signing the Declaration of Independence.
21. (Don't, Doesn't) the museum have one of those paintings?
22. She (have, has) learned that Franklin was sent to France in 1776.
23. He (hasn't, haven't) read that Franklin asked France to help America in the Revolutionary War.
24. (Don't, Doesn't) you think Franklin had an interesting life?
25. Perhaps you (has, have) read the book *Ben and Me* written by Robert Lawson.
26. (Doesn't, Don't) this book tell a story about a mouse and Benjamin Franklin?
27. Amos, the mouse, (has, have) many interesting adventures with Franklin.
28. If you (hasn't, haven't) read this book, you would enjoy reading it.
29. I think the library (have, has) a copy of this book.

Expressions to Be Avoided   ⚷ 33

In each sentence below underline the proper word form in parentheses.

Early Settlers in Kentucky

1. Have you ever (heard, heered) of Daniel Boone?
2. This pioneer was always (drawed, drawn) to unsettled country.
3. (Ain't, Isn't) he the man who lived by himself in Kentucky?
4. Boone told other people how well crops (growed, grew) in this land.
5. He said that there (isn't, ain't) any land as good as that in Kentucky.
6. Boone felt that everyone should (have, of) moved to this land.
7. Many people who (heered, heard) about this land moved west.
8. Kentucky (drew, drawed) many settlers.
9. (Those, Them) lands were not owned by anyone.
10. Any settler could (of, have) had free land in this country.
11. But some people thought that they (hadn't ought, ought not) to move west.
12. These people (knew, knowed) that life would be difficult in Kentucky.
13. Trees were cut down and (drug, dragged) off fields.
14. But when crops were planted, they usually (grew, growed) well.
15. Wells were dug so that water could be (drawn, drawed) for drinking.
16. People washed clothes in large kettles they (dragged, drug) outside.
17. The children (knowed, knew) that they had to work hard, too.
18. Sometimes the people (heard, heered) stories about animals living in the woods.
19. Everyone (knew, knowed) that bears lived nearby.
20. At any time the settlers might (of, have) decided to leave Kentucky.
21. Some people wished they could (of, have) returned to their old homes.
22. For many months they (heered, heard) no news from their friends and families.
23. They thought that they (ought not, hadn't ought) to have moved.
24. Many of (them, those) people lived far from neighbors.
25. But more and more people were (drawn, drawed) to Kentucky.
26. Soon small towns had (grown, growed) up.
27. Kentucky might never (have, of) been settled.
28. The people could (of, have) stayed in their old homes.
29. But (them, those) early settlers were brave to stay in the unfamiliar land.

Other Things to Do: Write the principal parts of *eat, come, see,* and *do.* Using the second or third principal parts of these verbs, write four sentences about pioneer life.

Writing Quotations

🔑 6, 7h, 8b, 9b, 10f, 42

**Place quotation marks around the
exact words of the speaker.**

In the sentences below place commas,
question marks, exclamation points, and
quotation marks where they are needed.
Underline each word that should begin with
a capital letter.

Example: Tony asked, "isn't deep snow just right for skiing?"

Skiing

1. "I went skiing in Vermont last winter," Tony said.
2. She exclaimed, "what fun I had!"
3. Lee asked, "Is skiing as easy as it looks?" ✗
4. "Falling down when skiing is easy," Tony laughingly replied.
5. "but standing up and moving is not simple," she added.
6. "Some people have hurt themselves while skiing," Louisa said.
7. Lee inquired, "how can you be hurt by falling in snow?"
8. "some skiers go as fast as eighty miles an hour," Tony said.
9. She added," skiers moving that fast could be hurt."
10. Lee asked," Have you ever watched skiers take jumps?"
11. "what fun that must be!" exclaimed Louisa.
12. "jumping while on skis takes many hours of practice," said Tony.
13. Lee inquired, "what are your skis made of, Tony?"
14. Tony answered, "they are made of fiberglass."
15. "A special wax is on the bottom of my skis," she said.
16. Tony explained, "it helps the skis move easily over the snow."
17. Louisa asked, "what are the sticks called that skiers hold?"
18. "they are called ski poles," Tony answered.
19. She explained, "These poles help skiers to make turns."
20. "what sharp turns some people can make on skis!" she exclaimed.
21. "skiers use the poles to push down on the snow," she added.
22. "Does this help people to jump on skis?"asked Louisa.
23. "yes, skiers can push themselves up with the poles," Tony said.
24. "how far can a person jump on skis?"Lee wanted to know.
25. "Some people have jumped over three hundred feet," Louisa said.
26. Lee said, "I would like to go skiing someday."
27. "you would enjoy it," said Tony.

Using Punctuation Marks

When a date is written in a sentence, place a comma between the day of the month and the year, and a comma between the year and the rest of the sentence.

Use a comma to separate the names of a city and a state when they are written in a sentence. Place a comma between the name of the state and the rest of the sentence.

Examples: On December 14, 1983, Julie went to Pendleton, Oregon.

Concord, Massachusetts, was the home of many famous Americans.

Place punctuation marks where they are needed in the sentences below. (Score: 1 for each punctuation mark correctly used)

American Flags

1. "Did you see any pictures of early American flags?" asked Carol.
2. "Yes, I saw several pictures of flags in a book," Ira replied.
3. "Boston, New York, and Charleston used different flags," Ira added.
4. "Bunker Hill, Massachusetts, had an interesting flag," Carol said.
5. "Carol, was this a red flag with a pine tree on it?" asked Ira.
6. "Were red, white, and blue always the colors of the flag?" Ira asked.
7. "No, Ira, many flags had other colors," Carol answered.
8. "Have you heard the story about Betsy Ross?" asked Ira.
9. "Didn't Mrs. Ross live in Philadelphia, Pennsylvania?" asked Carol.
10. "She made a flag decorated with stars and stripes," said Carol.
11. "That may not be a true story, Carol," replied Ira.
12. "Mr. Franklin, Mr. Harrison, and Mr. Lynch designed a flag," Ira said.
13. "On January 2, 1776, George Washington flew this flag," Ira added.
14. Carol explained, "Their flag had stripes and crosses on it."
15. "On June 14, 1777, a new flag was ordered," Carol said.
16. "Red stripes, white stripes, and white stars were on it," she added.
17. "Were stars and stripes added for each new state?" asked Ira.
18. "Yes, after May 1, 1795, the flag had fifteen stripes," replied Carol.
19. "Later the flag had stripes only for the original colonies," Ira said.
20. "From July 4, 1818, there were only thirteen stripes," Ira added.
21. "Was a star added to the flag for each new state?" asked Ira.
22. "Yes, Arizona's star was added in July, 1912, Ira," said Carol.
23. "Stars were later added for Alaska and Hawaii," Ira said.

Other Things to Do: Write the principal parts of *do* and *fly*. Use these six words in sentences about flags.

Using Capital Letters

🔑 1, 2, 5

Use capital letters to make sentences easy to read and understand.

In the sentences below draw a line under each word and abbreviation that should be capitalized. (Score: 1 for each correct underline)

Example: <u>may</u> <u>i</u> go with you, <u>jack</u>?

From Spinning Wheels to Factories

1. <u>maggie</u> and <u>i</u> went to <u>slater museum</u> last <u>saturday</u>.
2. <u>we</u> saw a spinning wheel that was brought to <u>america</u> from <u>england</u>.
3. <u>many</u> people in <u>connecticut</u>, <u>new hampshire</u>, and <u>vermont</u> wove cloth.
4. <u>ms. slater</u> said that the cloth was woven on a loom.
5. <u>many</u> of <u>america</u>'s early settlers had spinning wheels.
6. <u>the</u> pioneers worked very hard every day.
7. <u>during</u> <u>april</u> and <u>may</u>, wool was shorn from the sheep.
8. <u>maggie</u> and <u>i</u> learned how the wool was made into cloth by the people.
9. <u>there</u> were many rivers, such as the <u>connecticut river</u>, in <u>new england</u>.
10. <u>didn't</u> <u>mr. f. c. lowell</u> build a loom that was run by water power?
11. <u>today</u> <u>lowell</u>, <u>massachusetts</u>, is famous for the cloth that is made there.
12. <u>i</u> learned that many factories were built along the rivers.
13. <u>didn't</u> <u>ms. slater</u> say that cloth was made in some of these factories?
14. <u>during</u> <u>july</u> and <u>august</u> the factories were very hot.
15. <u>but</u> in <u>december</u> and <u>january</u> they were often cold.
16. <u>many</u> people came to <u>america</u> from <u>italy</u> and <u>ireland</u>.
17. <u>often</u> these <u>europeans</u> found jobs in the factories.
18. <u>did</u> the people have to work on the <u>fourth</u> of <u>july</u> and <u>new year's day</u>?
19. <u>last</u> <u>june</u> <u>i</u> visited <u>connecticut</u> and <u>massachusetts</u>.
20. <u>on</u> <u>monday</u> <u>dad</u> and <u>i</u> saw many factories in these states.
21. <u>mr. j. f. boat</u> took us into one of the factories.
22. <u>dad</u> asked <u>mr. boat</u> what kind of cloth was made in this factory.
23. <u>he</u> said that cotton was brought from <u>south carolina</u> and <u>alabama</u>.
24. <u>cotton</u> cloth was made in the factory and sent to <u>new york city</u>.

Other Things to Do: Select five verbs that are used above, and write an original sentence with each.

Using Contractions

Place an apostrophe in a contraction to show where letters have been left out.

I. Write the contractions of the following words.

1.	would not	**wouldn't**	6.	he will	**he'll**
2.	we have	**we've**	7.	has not	**hasn't**
3.	you are	**you're**	8.	we are	**we're**
4.	they have	**they've**	9.	she is	**she's**
5.	should not	**shouldn't**	10.	we shall	**we'll**

II. Fill the blank in each sentence with the contraction of the words in parentheses.

11. (Have not) _____ **Haven't** _____ you seen the giant sequoia trees?

12. (is not) This kind of tree _____ **isn't** _____ the size of most trees.

13. (were not) They _____ **weren't** _____ called giant sequoias without reason.

14. (It is) _____ **It's** _____ true that many trees are 30 meters (100 feet) tall.

15. (are not) But _____ **aren't** _____ sequoia trees over 90 meters (300 feet) tall?

16. (that is) Surely _____ **that's** _____ the tallest tree in the world!

17. (will not) Trees _____ **won't** _____ grow that tall in just a few years.

18. (they are) _____ **They're** _____ among the oldest living things in the world.

19. (I have) _____ **I've** _____ heard sequoia trees are hundreds of years old.

20. (Do not) _____ **Don't** _____ these trees grow in parts of California?

21. (you have) Perhaps _____ **you've** _____ seen these trees in Sequoia National Park.

22. (Has not) _____ **Hasn't** _____ a road been made through the trunk of one tree?

23. (you will) I know that _____ **you'll** _____ enjoy reading *Giant Tree.*

24. (Did not) _____ **Didn't** _____ this book tell the story of a giant sequoia?

25. (I shall) Perhaps someday _____ **I'll** _____ see some sequoia trees.

Other Things to Do: Write five of the above sentences as direct quotations.

Using *Sit* and *Set*, *Lie* and *Lay*
🔑 21, 28, 29

To *sit* means to be seated. To *set* means to place or put something.

To *lie* means to rest or recline. To *lay* means to place or put something.

Examples: Chang likes to *sit* there.   *Set* the books on the table.

                 He likes to *lie* on the floor.   Please *lay* the books by me.

Underline the proper verb form in parentheses in each of the following sentences.

1. Most people today (sit, set) in chairs that were bought at a store.
2. We (lie, lay) in beds that were made in a factory.
3. Some pioneer children (sat, set) on chairs that were homemade.
4. Have you ever (sat, set) on a homemade chair?
5. At night they (lay, laid) in homemade beds.
6. Some children (sat, set) on stools when they were in school.
7. They had to (sit, set) very quietly and work hard.
8. The children (lay, laid) their books on their desks.
9. Sometimes they (sit, set) their books on shelves.
10. Many pioneers (lay, laid) on beds that were filled with cornhusks.
11. Have you ever (lain, laid) on a cornhusk bed?
12. Sometimes a feather quilt was (lain, laid) over the bed.
13. People could (lie, lay) under the feather quilt to keep warm.
14. Children often helped (sat, set) the table for meals.
15. Usually no tablecloth was (lain, laid) on the table.
16. The family (sat, set) on stools or chairs around the table.
17. Often the children had to (sit, set) at the table without talking.
18. At night young children sometimes (lay, laid) on a trundle bed.
19. During the day this bed was (sat, set) underneath a large bed.
20. The trundle bed was pulled out when someone was ready to (lie, lay) on it.
21. Very young babies were (lain, laid) in a cradle.
22. Perhaps the cradle was (sat, set) near the spinning wheel.
23. When someone (sat, set) at the spinning wheel, the cradle could also be rocked.
24. At quilting bees the pioneers (sat, set) around a large quilting frame.
25. Later the colorful quilts were (lain, laid) on the beds.
26. How cozy it was to (lie, lay) under a warm quilt on a cold night!
27. People still make quilts which they (lie, lay) on their beds.
28. Do you (lie, lay) your clothes on a shelf or in drawers?
29. Pioneer children were told to (lie, lay) their clothes in a big chest.

Using Proper Verb Forms

⟐ 20, 21, 28, 29, 30

In each sentence below underline the proper verb form in parentheses.

Molly Pitcher

1. Molly Pitcher (was, were) a hero of the American Revolution.
2. Many people have (wrote, written) stories about her.
3. Her real name (wasn't, weren't) Molly Pitcher.
4. (Wasn't, Weren't) her real name Mary Ludwig?
5. Molly and her husband (was, were) from Carlisle, Pennsylvania.
6. (Don't, Doesn't) you know why she was (gave, given) the name Molly Pitcher?
7. Molly had (went, gone) with her husband to the Battle of Monmouth.
8. Often wives (was, were) allowed to stay with their husbands on the battlefield.
9. (Isn't, Aren't) she the woman who brought water to the soldiers?
10. Yes, she (went, gone) to a nearby spring for water.
11. The soldiers (drank, drunk) the water while they fought the battle.
12. (Wasn't, Weren't) Molly afraid of being hurt?
13. All day she never (sat, set) down to rest.
14. She carried pitchers of water and (sit, set) them by the soldiers.
15. The soldiers who had (drank, drunk) the water called her "Molly Pitcher."
16. Suddenly Molly saw her husband (lying, laying) on the ground.
17. She (saw, seen) that he had been hurt.
18. First Molly helped him to (lie, lay) comfortably.
19. Did she (lie, lay) a blanket over him?
20. There (wasn't, weren't) another soldier to take his place at the cannon.
21. (Isn't, Aren't) several people needed to shoot a cannon?
22. Quickly Molly (ran, run) to help.
23. (Wasn't, Weren't) they glad to have her help?
24. She (did, done) the work her husband had done.
25. There (isn't, aren't) many people who would have been as brave.
26. For a long time Molly could not (sit, set) down to rest.
27. At last the soldiers (was, were) successful in the battle.
28. Molly (went, gone) to take care of her husband.
29. She (gave, given) him some water to drink.
30. Soon they had (went, gone) back to their home.
31. Authors (wrote, written) about the brave thing Molly had (did, done).
32. Some money was (gave, given) to her after the Revolution.

Remembering What We Have Learned

1. On the lines below choose three verbs and write their principal parts. 🔑 21

    _____   **(Answers will vary.)**   _____

    _____   _____   _____

    _____   _____   _____

2. On the following lines write three direct quotations. 🔑 6, 7h, 8b, 9b, 10f, 42

    (Answers will vary.)

    _____

    _____

    _____

3. Rewrite the following sentence correctly. 🔑 1, 2, 5, 7, 10

    on july 7 2006 mr kyle and i went to avon connecticut ___**On July 7, 2006,**___

    ___**Mr. Kyle and I went to Avon, Connecticut.**___

4. On the first line write a sentence using the contraction of *have not*. On the second line write a sentence using the contraction of *we will*. 🔑 22

    ___**haven't (Answers will vary.)**___

    ___**we'll (Answers will vary.)**___

5. Write six sentences, using one of the following words in each: *see, run, was, don't, lay,* and *set*. 🔑 20, 21, 28, 29, 30

    (Answers will vary.)

    _____

    _____

    _____

    _____

    _____

    _____

Writing Titles

3, 12a

Use capital letters to begin the first word and each important word in a title.
Underline the titles of books, magazines, movies, plays, and other long works.
Put quotation marks around the titles of songs, poems, short stories, chapters, and other short works.

An unimportant word does not begin with a capital letter unless it is the first word of the title. Such words as *a, the, in, of, by, for, to, from,* and *with* usually are not important words in titles.

Examples:　Have you read Ben and Me?　　　　''A Song of Greatness''
　　　　　　　I saw the movie The Black Stallion.　''The Night of the Leonids''

I.　Write the following titles as they should be written (Score: 31)

1.　james and the giant peach (book) ____ **James and the Giant Peach**

2.　winter morning (poem) ____ **''Winter Morning''**

3.　national geographic (magazine) ____ **National Geographic**

4.　my fair lady (play) ____ **My Fair Lady**

5.　amelia earhart's last flight (song) ____ **''Amelia Earhart's Last Flight''**

6.　what's up, mr. borge? (story) ____ **''What's Up, Mr. Borge?''**

7.　arrow to the sun (book) ____ **Arrow to the Sun**

8.　the crocodile's toothache (poem) ____ **''The Crocodile's Toothache''**

II.　Rewrite each sentence below. Underline or put quotation marks around each title. Capitalize each important word in a title. (Score: 19)

9.　home on the range is a song the chorus sang.

　　''Home on the Range'' is a song the chorus sang.

10.　Did you read the book island of the blue dolphins?

　　Did you read the book Island of the Blue Dolphins?

11.　Gayla and I saw the movie the wizard of oz last week.

　　Gayla and I saw the movie The Wizard of Oz last week.

12.　I read the story joni becomes an artist in our reading book.

　　I read the story ''Joni Becomes an Artist'' in our reading book.

13.　Mr. Napoli read the poem paul revere's ride to the class.

　　Mr. Napoli read the poem ''Paul Revere's Ride'' to the class.

Outlining

🔑 43

An outline is a plan for a report or a story. Complete sentences are not used in an outline; each line begins with a capital letter, but a punctuation mark is not used at the end of the line. Note the following outline and the two paragraphs written from the outline in the example below.

Example:

Town Criers

I. Why their duties were important
  A. Were the only source of news for many people
  B. Told of recent events
  C. Announced meetings
II. How they delivered news
  A. Rang a bell and called out
  B. Attracted a crowd to hear the news

Because there were few newspapers in the American colonies, town criers had an important job. They were the only source of news that most colonists had. They told about recent events and let the people know when town meetings were to be held.

The town criers announced the news from street corners. They rang bells and cried, "Hear ye! Hear ye!" The sound brought people from all around to hear the news.

Listed below are some facts about an animal called the sloth. Use these facts to make an outline for two paragraphs. (Score: 20)

Has tiny ears and a short nose   Moves very slowly

Has coarse grayish hair   Has an interesting walk

Is protected by its color   Can sleep hanging upside down

(Answers will vary.)   **The Sloth**

I. **Its appearance**

  A. **Has tiny ears and a short nose**

  B. **Has coarse grayish hair**

  C. **Is protected by its color**

II. **Its habits**

  A. **Moves very slowly**

  B. **Has an interesting walk**

  C. **Can sleep hanging upside down**

Topic Sentences

🔑 44

A *topic sentence* introduces the subject, or topic, of a paragraph. It begins the paragraph and gives an idea of what the rest of the paragraph is about. All other sentences in the paragraph give more information about the subject.

I. Read the following paragraphs and underline the topic sentences. Answer the questions following the paragraphs. (Score: 5 for each correct answer)

The road runner is a large bird often seen on country roads in the southwestern part of the United States. It gets its name from its habit of running ahead of anyone it meets on the road. It runs in awkward, stiff-legged steps, but it runs swiftly. When it sits upright, its bristly topknot gives it a startled look. Its long, curved beak is a help in hunting food. The road runner is fearless in attacking snakes, lizards, and mice.

Have you ever used a road map? Our country is lined with paved highways, and most drivers depend on such maps. Long ago there were few roads; wagons and carriages had to travel on paths and ruts. People along the way gave directions to travelers. As means of transportation multiplied, the need for better traveling directions grew. Road maps first were printed and sold around 1900. Nowadays many kinds of maps are available to travelers.

1. What is the subject of the first paragraph? ___**The road runner**_____

2. What is the subject of the second paragraph? ___**Road maps**_____

II. Write an interesting topic sentence to introduce the subject of the following paragraph. (Score: 5)

(Answers will vary.)

_____

_____

It lives in the streams of Australia. The platypus has thick, dark brown fur. This unusual-looking animal has a flat tail that resembles a beaver's, and its muzzle looks like a duck's bill. Its short, strong legs and webbed feet are useful in burrowing the hole that serves as its home.

Other Things to Do: Write a title for each of the three paragraphs above.

Make an outline for two paragraphs about your favorite sport. Then write the paragraphs, using an interesting topic sentence to begin each one.

Writing Topic Sentences

☞ 44

After choosing a subject for a paragraph, you must think of how you will introduce that subject. Remember that a topic sentence tells what the paragraph is about. It should introduce your subject in such an interesting manner that it makes a reader want to finish reading the paragraph. Read the examples below and decide whether or not you would want to read paragraphs that began with these topic sentences.

Examples: My first camping trip was a terrible failure.

You should have seen Jim's face when he spied the hornets!

We saw our sand castle disappear under the cool green water.

Have you heard of the wonderful hippogriff?

I know nothing about training a dog.

I.   Write an effective topic sentence for each of the following subjects. (Score: 5 for each sentence)

1.   (A sport I like to play) _____**(Answers will vary.)**_____

_____

2.   (My last vacation) _____**(Answers will vary.)**_____

_____

3.   (Life in the 21st century) _____**(Answers will vary.)**_____

_____

4.   (A frightening dream) _____**(Answers will vary.)**_____

_____

5.   (A favorite TV show) _____**(Answers will vary.)**_____

_____

II.   The topic sentence in the paragraph below is misplaced. Decide which sentence is the best introduction to the paragraph. Write it on the lines below. (Score: 5)

Duane and Mari had asked me to ride to City Park, but they couldn't wait for me to patch that tire. Afterward they told me that they had watched workers stocking City Park Lake with fish. My bicycle had a flat tire at the worst possible time! The workers told them about raising fish. Duane and Mari have been invited to tour the fish hatchery next Saturday.

6.   _____**My bicycle had a flat tire at the worst possible time!**_____

_____

Writing Paragraphs   43, 44

Look at the picture below and think of a subject that the picture suggests. On another sheet
of paper make an outline for two paragraphs about that subject. Then write the paragraphs
on the lines below. (Score: 10 for each paragraph)

(Answers will vary.)

_____

_____

_____

_____

_____

_____

_____

_____

_____

_____

_____

_____

_____

_____

_____

_____

_____

Writing Quotations

🔑 6, 7h, 8b, 9b, 10f, 42

Begin the first word of a direct quotation with a capital letter.

In the sentences below underline each word that should begin with a capital letter. Place periods, question marks, exclamation points, quotation marks, and commas where they are needed.

Example: Jane asked, "what is that?"

Lewis and Clark, Explorers

1. Yoko asked, "who are Meriwether Lewis and William Clark?"
2. "they were famous explorers, I believe," answered Ava.
3. She asked, "didn't they explore part of the United States?"
4. Yoko replied, "yes, they left St. Louis, Missouri, in May, 1804."
5. "There were thirty people in the expedition," she said.
6. Yoko added, "They traveled north to the Mandan Indian villages."
7. "These villages were in North Dakota," she said.
8. "There they met a Frenchman named Charbonneau," Yoko said.
9. She added, "His wife was Sacajawea, a Shoshone Indian."
10. Ava asked, "didn't Sacajawea go with Lewis and Clark?"
11. "Yes, and it was a good thing that she did go," Yoko replied.
12. "They traveled west toward the Pacific Ocean," she said.
13. Yoko explained, "often there was little food to eat."
14. "But Sacajawea showed the explorers how to find food," she said.
15. Ava said, "she knew which nuts and berries were safe to eat."
16. "wasn't she also an interpreter?" Yoko asked.
17. "Sacajawea showed them the best routes to travel," she added.
18. Ava said, "Sacajawea was an important member of the expedition."
19. Yoko said, "horses and food were bought from some Indian tribes."
20. Ava said, "at last the explorers reached the Pacific Ocean."
21. "Then did they return to St. Louis?" Ava wanted to know.
22. "The trip had taken almost two and a half years," replied Yoko.
23. "Sacajawea stayed in the Mandan Indian village," she said.
24. "Lewis and Clark wrote books about their long trip," she added.
25. Ava said, "they also wrote about Sacajawea's great help."

Alphabetizing Words   ⊙— 38a

I. Write the following words in alphabetical order on the lines below.

dart	bear	eagle	lane	oar	map	navy	pearl
hero	ice	arch	flag	quiz	star	urn	ruby
knife	jungle	giant	torch	zero	wharf	verse	yeast

1. **arch**		13. **navy**	
2. **bear**		14. **oar**	
3. **dart**		15. **pearl**	
4. **eagle**		16. **quiz**	
5. **flag**		17. **ruby**	
6. **giant**		18. **star**	
7. **hero**		19. **torch**	
8. **ice**		20. **urn**	
9. **jungle**		21. **verse**	
10. **knife**		22. **wharf**	
11. **lane**		23. **yeast**	
12. **map**		24. **zero**	

II. Arrange the words below in alphabetical order to the second letter.

25. blanket	**because**	28. come	**cannon**
26. buffalo	**blanket**	29. cent	**cent**
27. because	**buffalo**	30. cannon	**come**

III. Arrange these words in alphabetical order to the third letter.

31. absent	**able**	35. differ	**dial**
32. about	**about**	36. ditch	**differ**
33. able	**abroad**	37. dinner	**dinner**
34. abroad	**absent**	38. dial	**ditch**

Using the Dictionary

●━ 37, 38

Words in a dictionary are arranged in alphabetical order so that a word can be found easily and quickly. Guide words at the top of each page of a dictionary show what words are listed on that page.

I. Below are some guide words and the page numbers of a dictionary where these guide words are found. Underneath is a list of words. Write the number of the page on which each word could be found in the dictionary.

Page 5 abet—animal		Page 6 ankle—back		Page 25 nag—noise		Page 26 noisy—nut	
1. nice	**25**	7. able	**5**	13. admit	**5**
2. act	**5**	8. nap	**25**	14. not	**26**
3. number	**26**	9. nose	**26**	15. new	**25**
4. age	**5**	10. answer	**6**	16. ant	**6**
5. name	**25**	11. another	**6**	17. none	**26**
6. ape	**6**	12. angry	**5**	18. add	**5**

II. In Column A below is a list of words. In Column B are the *definitions,* or meanings, of these words. Before each word in Column A, write the number of the definition that fits that word.

Example: _2_ red

1. a tree
2. a color

A		**B**
21	beach	19. a hardwood tree
19	beech	20. an odor
20	scent	21. land next to a body of water
24	cent	22. a swift, long-eared animal
25	bare	23. a large, shaggy animal
23	bear	24. a hundredth part of a dollar
22	hare	25. without covering
26	hair	26. the slender outgrowth from skins

Dividing Words into Syllables   🔑 39

When a word is to be divided at the end of a line, it must be divided only between syllables. Never divide a word of only one syllable.

Use a dictionary to help you divide the following words into syllables. Put an *X* beside any one-syllable word.

Examples:

	baby	*ba-by*		camel	*cam-el*
1.	paper	**pa-per**	21.	cattle	**cat-tle**
2.	baking	**bak-ing**	22.	cabbage	**cab-bage**
3.	cage	**X**	23.	madam	**mad-am**
4.	able	**a-ble**	24.	rabbit	**rab-bit**
5.	zebra	**ze-bra**	25.	better	**bet-ter**
6.	belong	**be-long**	26.	berry	**ber-ry**
7.	hero	**he-ro**	27.	kettle	**ket-tle**
8.	pilot	**pi-lot**	28.	whisper	**whis-per**
9.	pirate	**pi-rate**	29.	ill	**X**
10.	lion	**li-on**	30.	picnic	**pic-nic**
11.	pony	**po-ny**	31.	window	**win-dow**
12.	crow	**X**	32.	pocket	**poc-ket**
13.	polar	**po-lar**	33.	body	**bod-y**
14.	frozen	**fro-zen**	34.	robin	**rob-in**
15.	story	**sto-ry**	35.	doctor	**doc-tor**
16.	over	**o-ver**	36.	solid	**sol-id**
17.	local	**lo-cal**	37.	until	**un-til**
18.	duty	**du-ty**	38.	sunken	**sunk-en**
19.	human	**hu-man**	39.	bump	**X**
20.	music	**mu-sic**	40.	jumbo	**jum-bo**

Choosing Homophones   37

In each sentence below underline the correct homophone in parentheses.

Wolf Boy's Adventure

1. (Their, There) once lived a Kiowa Indian named Wolf Boy.

2. Wolf Boy had (no, know) knife to wear on his belt.

3. His big brother Young Soldier had (one, won) made out of smooth black stone.

4. (Their, There) grandfather had found the knife by the Big River.

5. Wolf Boy wanted very much to own a black stone knife, (to, too).

6. All summer Wolf Boy took the tribe's (herd, heard) of horses to pasture.

7. Now the cool wind (blue, blew), and summer would soon (be, bee) gone.

8. In winter Young Soldier took the horses (to, too) pasture.

9. Young Soldier had (herd, heard) of a place where it was always summer.

10. As he (ate, eight) his stew, Wolf Boy listened to the older boys talk.

11. They told about the land where it was warm the (hole, whole) year.

12. If they went (their, there), they would not have winter chores.

13. Besides, they (new, knew) that Kiowas had never been there.

14. If they found the place, their tribe would think them (great, grate) men.

15. Young Soldier, Cougar, and (too, two) others set out to find this land.

16. They did not (no, know) that Wolf Boy followed them.

17. They did not (here, hear) him or (see, sea) him all the first day.

18. That is how Wolf Boy proved that he should not be (sent, cent) back.

19. In less than a (weak, week) they had traveled into unfamiliar country.

20. They visited (some, sum) members of the Wichita Indian tribe.

21. (Here, Hear) the Indians built their fires in a (hole, whole) in the ground.

22. Wichitas did (not, knot) make houses of buffalo hides as Kiowas did.

23. The boys met many Indian tribes (who's, whose) customs were different from theirs.

24. Young Soldier tied a (not, knot) in a string every day.

25. The string told by (its, it's) knots how many days they had been gone.

26. Did Wolf Boy find a (new, knew) black stone knife for himself?

27. (Your, You're) sure to find out if you read this true story.

28. *The Black Stone Knife* was written (by, buy) Alice Marriott.

29. (Its, It's) full of exciting adventures.

30. Perhaps the school will (by, buy) the book for your library.

Other Things to Do: Write three sentences with *to, too,* and *two.*

Using Proper Verb Forms

21

In each sentence below underline the proper verb form in parentheses.

A Legendary Hero of the West

1. A well-known story tells how Pecos Bill (<u>grew</u>, grown) up.

2. He had (grew, <u>grown</u>) up with wild coyotes in Texas.

3. One day the wind (<u>blew</u>, blown) stronger and stronger.

4. A powerful cyclone (<u>flew</u>, flown) through the air.

5. Cyclones have (blew, <u>blown</u>) away buildings and trees.

6. But Bill (<u>threw</u>, thrown) himself at the cyclone.

7. He had (knew, <u>known</u>) just how to ride on the cyclone's back.

8. Bill and the cyclone had (flew, <u>flown</u>) through the air.

9. Soon the cyclone had (blew, <u>blown</u>) apart into smaller cyclones.

10. Bill had (knew, <u>known</u>) about a wonderful wild horse.

11. Was Bill (threw, <u>thrown</u>) off the horse when he jumped on its back?

12. The horse had (blew, <u>blown</u>) out its breath and had begun to buck.

13. It (<u>flew</u>, flown) across the ground trying to get rid of Bill.

14. One story says that after a week the horse (<u>grew</u>, grown) tired.

15. Before long the horse had (grew, <u>grown</u>) to love Bill.

16. People have (knew, <u>known</u>) other stories about Bill and the horse.

17. Some stories tell about an old man who Bill (<u>knew</u>, known).

18. The story tells how the man was (threw, <u>thrown</u>) from Bill's horse.

19. The horse (<u>knew</u>, known) just how to buck off a rider.

20. Before he knew it, the old man had (flew, <u>flown</u>) through the air.

21. He (<u>flew</u> flown) all the way from Texas to Colorado.

22. But Bill got a rope and (<u>threw</u>. thrown) it to him.

23. The old man (<u>knew</u>, known) never to ride the horse again.

24. After he (<u>threw</u>, thrown) off this man, the horse was named Widow-Maker.

25. These stories say that even the fish (<u>grew</u>, grown) extra large in Texas.

26. One day Sue had (threw, <u>thrown</u>) a rope around a fish.

27. She had (knew, <u>known</u>) how to ride on the back of the fish.

28. Pecos Bill had (grew, <u>grown</u>) to love Sue.

29. She had (knew, <u>known</u>) that only Bill rode Widow-Maker.

30. The horse (<u>blew</u>, blown) out his breath when Sue got on him.

31. Sue was (threw, <u>thrown</u>) into the air, and she (<u>flew</u>, flown) around for a week.

32. Finally Bill (<u>threw</u>, thrown) a rope to her to pull her down.

Reviewing Sentences

I. Place the correct punctuation mark at the end of each sentence. (Score: 8)

The Story of "The Star-Spangled Banner"

1. Do you know all the verses of "The Star-Spangled Banner" **?**
2. Oh, that song is America's national anthem **!**
3. What an interesting history the song has **!**
4. It was written by a man named Francis Scott Key **.**
5. Wasn't it written during the War of 1812 **?**
6. This war was fought with England **.**
7. Key was in Baltimore when he wrote the song **.**
8. How did he happen to write it **?**

II. Write *Yes* before the groups of words that are sentences. Write *No* before the groups of words that are not sentences. (Score: 10)

No _____ 9. English ships in Baltimore harbor

Yes _____ 10. These ships carried large cannons

No _____ 11. Shot the cannons at Fort McHenry

Yes _____ 12. Fort McHenry is near Baltimore

Yes _____ 13. Francis Scott Key went to one of the ships

No _____ 14. Went to help a friend

Yes _____ 15. The British would not let him leave the ship

No _____ 16. Watched Fort McHenry from the British ship

Yes _____ 17. Now and then Key could see the American flag at Fort McHenry

No _____ 18. But sometimes too dark to see the flag

III. Draw one line under the noun that the sentence is about. Draw two lines under the verb in each sentence. (Score: 2 for each sentence)

19. The cannons lighted the dark sky for a moment.
20. The flag still flew from Fort McHenry.
21. Key wrote a poem on a piece of paper.
22. The poem told about his thoughts on that night.
23. The author called the poem "The Star-Spangled Banner."

Reviewing Capitalization and Punctuation ⟜ 1, 2, 5, 6, 7, 8, 9, 10, 12

Underline each word that should begin with a capital letter and place punctuation marks where they are needed. (Score: 1 for each correct underline and 1 for each correct punctuation mark)

Ice Skating

1. Last december fran, ellie, and i learned to ice-skate.
2. The ice on lake haver was 5 centimeters (2 inches) thick.
3. Miss j. r. Jerue said that the ice should be thicker.
4. On wednesday, december 29, Miss Jerue cut a hole in the ice.
5. She said, "the ice is 15 centimeters (6 inches) thick now."
6. Fran, Ellie, and I ran home for our ice skates.
7. Jed and his dogs, skip and rick, went back to the lake with us.
8. "Why do we lace our skates so tightly?" asked Ellie.
9. Jed answered, "tight skates support your ankles."
10. He said that fran and ellie could stand up easier in tight skates.
11. "when did you learn to skate, Miss Jerue?" asked Ellie.
12. On January 10, 1935, I skated at Hyde Park, New York.
13. "I have skated every winter since then," said miss jerue.
14. Jed exclaimed, "what a long time you have been skating!"
15. By March, 1939, I had won a skating contest in Saginaw, Michigan.
16. "Was it a skating race?" asked Jed.
17. "No, but races are popular in the united states," miss jerue said.
18. Races are sometimes held in idaho, colorado, and illinois.
19. "Don't racing skates have long blades?" asked Ellie.
20. "the pointed blade is dug into the ice for a fast start," Jed said.
21. "Hockey skates are good for quick turns, Jed," i said.
22. "yes, and they don't have long blades," he replied.
23. "Figure skates have a rough tip on the blade," said Ellie.
24. "the rough tip helps the skater to do tricks, Ellie," said Jed.
25. Fran exclaimed, "skating is such fun!"
26. I wish that I lived in norway, sweden, or denmark.
27. She explained, "people in those countries have long winters."
28. "I skate outside only in december, january, or february," she said.

Reviewing Proper Word Forms   18, 20, 21, 25, 26, 27, 28, 29, 30

In each sentence below underline the proper word form in parentheses.

A Chemical Experiment

1. When Ian (came, come) to school, he had (a, an) experiment to show us.
2. He wanted to (learn, teach) us something about heat.
3. (We, Us) (saw, seen) that Ian had a magnet.
4. Jan (wrote, written) down the procedures that Ian had (went, gone) through.
5. Ian (lay, laid) a box filled with tiny pieces of iron on (a, an) table.
6. We had (knew, known) that a magnet (may, can) pick up iron.
7. In another box Ian (has, have) some powdered sulphur.
8. His grandfather had (gave, given) the sulphur to (he, him) and (I, me).
9. (She, Her) and (I, me) watched to see what Ian (did, done) next.
10. The iron and the sulphur (was, were) put into a jar.
11. Then Ian told (she, her) and (I, me) to shake the jar.
12. When we had (did, done) this, we (gave, given) the jar to Ian.
13. We had (saw, seen) the iron and the sulphur mix together.
14. Ian (went, gone) to a table and (sat, set) down.
15. He told (we, us) that there (was, were) a magnet on his desk.
16. Ian (threw, thrown) the iron and sulphur mixture on a piece of paper.
17. We saw that the iron had (came, come) to the magnet he held.
18. But the sulphur still (lay, laid) on the paper.
19. The iron and the sulphur (wasn't, weren't) changed by mixing them together.
20. The iron and the sulphur were (threw, thrown) back into the jar.
21. "(May, Can) I (sit, set) there and watch you heat them?" asked Jan.
22. The teacher (sat, set) the jar down carefully on the burner so that the flame was not (blew, blown) out.
23. Now we will (learn, teach) from Ian what happens when the mixture is heated.
24. A magnet (doesn't, don't) pick up the iron any longer.
25. We (knew, known) that the iron in the mixture (wasn't, weren't) just iron anymore.
26. The iron and the sulphur (isn't, aren't) the same as they were before they were heated.
27. The iron and the sulphur (has, have) changed.
28. A new substance (is, are) in the jar now.
29. The iron and the sulphur (doesn't, don't) change when they are simply mixed.
30. We discovered that they change when they (is, are) mixed and heated.
31. (Is, Are) this the report that you (was, were) writing about the experiment?

Reviewing Study of Words   ⊶ 14, 15, 16, 17, 19, 22, 37

I.   Write the plural forms of the nouns in parentheses. (Score: 5)

1.   (army)   The British _____**armies**_____ marched into Washington, D.C.

2.   (person)   _____**People**_____ rushed to their homes.

3.   (family)   They told their _____**families**_____ to hurry out of town.

4.   (box)   The people quickly took _____**boxes**_____ of clothes and ran.

5.   (life)   They were afraid of losing their _____**lives**_____ .

II.   Write the possessive forms of the nouns in parentheses. (Score: 5)

6.   (families)   The streets were full of _____**families'**_____ wagons.

7.   (people)   There were sounds of _____**people's**_____ shouts everywhere.

8.   (Children)   _____**Children's**_____ cries could be heard.

9.   (enemy)   The _____**enemy's**_____ troops were coming closer to the city.

10.   (Madison)   President _____**Madison's**_____ family quickly left town.

III.   Underline the correct homophone in parentheses. (Score: 7)

11.   Do you (<u>know</u>, no) the story about President Madison's wife?

12.   The (hole, <u>whole</u>) family was hurrying from town.

13.   They did (<u>not</u>, knot) take time to pack (there, <u>their</u>) clothes.

14.   They (new, <u>knew</u>) that the British would be in town soon.

15.   There was (<u>one</u>, won) thing that Dolley Madison wanted to save.

16.   She ran back (too, <u>to</u>) the White House to get it.

IV.   Draw one line under each noun below. Draw two lines under each pronoun. Circle each verb. (Score: 19)

17.   <u>Dolley Madison</u> (ran) to a famous <u>picture</u>.

18.   <u><u>She</u></u> (took) <u><u>it</u></u> with <u><u>her</u></u>.

19.   Soon the British <u>troops</u> (marched) into <u>town</u>.

20.   The <u>soldiers</u> (burned) the <u>White House</u>.

21.   But the <u>portrait</u> of <u>George Washington</u> (was saved).

V.   Write the contractions of the following words. (Score: 2)

22.   will not   _____**won't**_____   23.   he will   _____**he'll**_____

49

Reviewing the Paragraph

I.   Some facts about the trap-door spider are listed below. Use these facts to make an outline for a two-paragraph report. (Score: 10)

Found in warm regions   Is large, hairy tarantula

Makes trap door of mud and silk   Uses trap door to catch insects

Digs tunnel for home   Seen usually at night

_____(**Answers will vary.**)_____**The Trap-Door Spider**_____

_____**I. Its description**_____

_____**A. Is large, hairy tarantula**_____

_____**B. Found in warm regions**_____

_____**C. Seen usually at night**_____

_____**II. Its unusual home**_____

_____**A. Digs tunnel for home**_____

_____**B. Makes trap door of mud and silk**_____

_____**C. Uses trap door to catch insects**_____

II.   On the lines below write the two paragraphs you have outlined. Write an interesting title and topic sentence. (Score: 10)

(**Answers will vary.**)   **The Trap-Door Spider**

_____**The trap-door spider is a large, hairy tarantula that lives in warm**

regions. It can usually be seen at night._____

_____**This spider digs a tunnel for its home. It makes a trap door of mud and**

silk. The spider uses the trap door to catch insects._____

_____

_____

_____

_____

_____

Remembering What We Have Learned

1. On the lines below write an outline for a paragraph about a hobby. 🔑 43

   (Answers will vary.)

2. Write the paragraph you outlined above. If you need to divide words at ends of lines, divide them between syllables. Write a title for your paragraph. 🔑 3, 39, 44

   (Answers will vary.)

3. Write the names of six of your friends in alphabetical order. 🔑 38

   (Answers will vary.)

4. Write two sentences, using the homophones *whose* and *who's*. 🔑 37

   (Answers will vary.)

5. Write four sentences, using one of the following words in each: *grown, knew, they're,* and *there*. 🔑 21, 37

   (Answers will vary.)

The key numbers listed at the beginning of each lesson refer to the text material found on the following pages. There are fifty-four keys, many of which are divided into sections. The rules, explanations, and examples given in the keys, together with the explanations on the lesson pages, make it possible to work the exercises with little help from the teacher.

In addition to its purpose as a text for this book, the key section can be used as a guide to review language rules or to get help on special language problems.

Capitalization

1 Writing Names

a. Begin the names of persons with capital letters. Also use capital letters to begin words that are used as names, such as *Mother*.
Examples:
1. **M**ary **A**nn **K**ing 2. **G**randfather 3. **A**unt **L**ouisa

b. Write initials of names with capital letters.
Examples:
1. **J**. **A**. Chan 2. James **A**. Chan 3. **J**. Allen Chan

c. Begin titles of courtesy or their abbreviations with capital letters.
1. **Mr.** is the abbreviation for **Mister**.
2. **Mrs.** (pronounced "Missis") is the abbreviation for **Mistress**.
3. **Dr.** is the abbreviation for **Doctor**.
4. **Miss** and **Ms.** are not abbreviations.
5. Other titles of courtesy may be used for persons holding official positions: **President, Honorable, Governor, Judge, Reverend, Rabbi, Superintendent, Professor, Colonel, General.** These generally are not abbreviated in letters. The title **Judge** is never abbreviated.

d. Begin the names of pets with capital letters.
Examples:
1. **T**abby 2. **P**eppy 3. **R**uff

e. Begin sacred names with capital letters.
Examples:
1. **G**od 2. **J**esus 3. **A**llah

f. Begin the names of the days of the week or their abbreviations with capital letters.
Examples:
1. **S**unday 2. **T**uesday 3. **T**hurs.

g. Begin the names of the months of the year or their abbreviations with capital letters.
Examples:
1. **J**anuary 2. **M**ay 3. **S**ept.

h. Capitalize the first and every important word in the names of holidays and special days.
Examples:
1. **C**hristmas 2. **F**ourth of **J**uly 3. **Y**om **K**ippur
Names of the seasons of the year should *not* be capitalized.
Examples:
1. **s**pring 2. **a**utumn 3. **w**inter

i. Capitalize the first word and every important word in the names of particular places and things.
Examples:
1. **E**urope
2. **C**anada
3. **C**alifornia
4. **C**leveland **C**ounty
5. **S**t. **L**ouis
6. **O**ak **A**venue
7. **W**ilson **S**chool
8. **R**ocky **M**ountains
9. **O**hio **R**iver
10. **L**incoln **P**ark
11. **C**arnegie **L**ibrary
12. **C**ivil **W**ar
13. **H**ill **S**eed **S**tore

j. Capitalize words formed from place names.
Examples:
1. **M**exican 2. **F**rench 3. **A**merican

2   Using the Word I

The word I is always written as a capital letter.

Example:
The pencil I am using does not belong to me.

3   Writing Titles

a. Begin the first word and every important word in a title with a capital letter.

Examples:
1. The Light of Day
2. "A Trip in a Dune Buggy"
3. "Finlandia"

b. Titles of books, plays, magazines, movies, and other long works are underlined.

Examples:
1. Charlotte's Web
2. The Incredible Journey

c. Titles of reports, songs, short stories, poems, and other short works are written with quotation marks.

Examples:
1. "Windy Nights"
2. "Home on the Range"

Note: When a title appears in a sentence or list, quotation marks or underlining is used. Quotation marks or underlining is not used when the title is written above a report, story, or other composition.

4   Writing Lines of Poetry

The first word in each line of a poem or a rhyme usually begins with a capital letter.

Example:
The winter's dress is dark and gray,
   And bare of trim on head or toes.
I like the lack of fuss and frills
   On Nature's drab cold-weather clothes.

5   Beginning Sentences

Begin the first word in every sentence with a capital letter.

Examples:
1. Does Linda like to swim?
2. Yes, and she likes to dive, too.

6   Beginning Quotations

a. Capitalize the first word of a direct quotation.

Examples:
1. Peter said, "My new sweater is very warm."
2. "My new sweater is very warm," said Peter.
3. "My new sweater," Peter said, "is very warm."

b. Do not capitalize the first word of an indirect quotation.

Example:
Dana said that she saw the game on television.

Note: For capitalization in letter writing, see Keys 50 and 51.

Punctuation

7   Using the Period

a. Use a period at the end of a statement, or declarative sentence.

Example:
The falling snow was wet and cold.

b. Use periods after initials of names.

Examples:
1. J. B. Johnson   2. J. B. J.
              3. J. Bryant Johnson

c. Use periods after abbreviated titles of courtesy.

Examples:
1. Mr. Benvenuto   2. Mrs. Land
              3. Dr. Morse

Do not use periods after titles of courtesy that are not abbreviations.

Examples:
1. Miss Williams   2. Judge Montez

d. Use periods after abbreviations of days and months.

Days	
Sunday—Sun.	Thursday—Thurs.
Monday—Mon.	Friday—Fri.
Tuesday—Tues.	Saturday—Sat.
Wednesday—Wed.	

Months	
January—Jan.	July—(none)
February—Feb.	August—Aug.
March—Mar.	September—Sept.
April—Apr.	October—Oct.
May—(none)	November—Nov.
June—(none)	December—Dec.

e. Use periods after abbreviations of directions.

Examples:

1. North—N.
2. South—S.
3. East—E.
4. West—W.
5. Northeast—N.E.
6. Northwest—N.W.
7. Southeast—S.E.
8. Southwest—S.W.

f. Use periods after abbreviations of states.

Note: The names of states should be spelled out when they stand alone or follow a city. The first abbreviation that is listed for states is used most often in lists, maps, footnotes, and bibliographies. The second abbreviation listed is the postal form that is used with ZIP codes and has no period following it.

Examples:

1. Alabama—Ala.—AL
2. Alaska—(none)—AK
3. Arizona—Ariz.—AZ
4. Arkansas—Ark.—AR
5. California—Calif.—CA
6. Colorado—Colo.—CO
7. Connecticut—Conn.—CT
8. Delaware—Del.—DE
9. Florida—Fla.—FL
10. Georgia—Ga.—GA
11. Hawaii—(none)—HI
12. Idaho—(none)—ID
13. Illinois—Ill.—IL
14. Indiana—Ind.—IN
15. Iowa—(none)—IA
16. Kansas—Kans.—KS
17. Kentucky—Ky.—KY
18. Louisiana—La.—LA
19. Maine—(none)—ME
20. Maryland—Md.—MD
21. Massachusetts—Mass.—MA
22. Michigan—Mich.—MI
23. Minnesota—Minn.—MN
24. Mississippi—Miss.—MS
25. Missouri—Mo.—MO
26. Montana—Mont.—MT
27. Nebraska—Nebr.—NB
28. Nevada—Nev.—NV
29. New Hampshire—N.H.—NH
30. New Jersey—N.J.—NJ
31. New Mexico—N.Mex.—NM
32. New York—N.Y.—NY
33. North Carolina—N.C.—NC
34. North Dakota—N.Dak.—ND
35. Ohio—(none)—OH
36. Oklahoma—Okla.—OK
37. Oregon—Oreg.—OR
38. Pennsylvania—Pa.—PA
39. Rhode Island—R.I.—RI
40. South Carolina—S.C.—SC
41. South Dakota—S.Dak.—SD
42. Tennessee—Tenn.—TN
43. Texas—Tex.—TX
44. Utah—(none)—UT
45. Vermont—Vt.—VT
46. Virginia—Va.—VA
47. Washington—Wash.—WA
48. West Virginia—W.Va.—WV
49. Wisconsin—Wis.—WI
50. Wyoming—Wyo.—WY

g. Use periods after other abbreviations.

Examples:

1. Avenue—Ave.
2. Street—St.
3. Boulevard—Blvd.
4. Rural Route—R.R.

h. If a period comes at the end of a direct quotation, place the period inside the end quotation mark.

Example:

Jason said, "Let me show you my chemistry set."

8 Using the Question Mark

a. Use a question mark at the end of a question, or interrogative sentence.

Example:

Have you ever seen a koala?

b. If a question mark comes at the end of a direct quotation, place the question mark inside the end quotation marks.

Examples:

1. Julie asked, "Have you ever seen a koala?"
2. "Have you ever seen a koala?" asked Julie.

9 Using the Exclamation Point

a. Use an exclamation point at the end of an exclamation, or exclamatory sentence.

Example:

Oh, what a beautiful day!

b. If an exclamation point comes at the end of a direct quotation, place the exclamation point inside the end quotation mark.

Examples:

1. "The game is over!" yelled Su-Ling.
2. Drew cried, "What a game!"

10 Using the Comma

a. Use a comma to separate the name of the month from the year.

Examples:

1. October, 1999   2. January, 2003

b. Use a comma to separate the day of the month from the year.

Examples:

1. November 4, 1999   2. July 4, 1776

c. Use a comma to separate the day of the week from the month.

Example:

Monday, November 16

d. When a date is given in a sentence, place a comma after the year, unless the date comes at the end of the sentence.

Examples:

1. On October 12, 1492, Columbus landed in America.
2. Columbus landed in America on October 12, 1492.

e. Use a comma to separate the name of a town or city from the name of a state.

Examples:

1. Topeka, Kansas
2. Leah lives in Topeka, Kansas.

f. Use a comma to separate a direct quotation from the words that tell who said it, unless the quotation is a question or an exclamation that comes before the words that tell who said it.

Examples:

1. Jeff said, "Let's give a mime show."
2. "I'll build a stage," said Rosa, "if you'll make costumes."

g. When you speak to a person in a sentence and call him or her by name, separate the name from the rest of the sentence by one or two commas.

Examples:

1. "Chuck, will you erase the board, please?"
2. "I'll be glad to, Rachel, as soon as I find an eraser."

h. When *yes* or *no* is used at the beginning of a sentence that answers a question, place a comma after the *yes* or *no*.

Examples:

1. Yes, I saw a shark in the aquarium.
2. No, I didn't see a squid.

i. Use a comma to separate words or groups of words in a series.

A *series* is a list of three or more words or groups of words naming persons, things, or actions. A series may also be a list of two or more words or groups of words describing something.

Examples:

1. Kelly, Sandy, Chris, and I went to the park.
2. We swam, ran, and played ball.
3. It was a warm, sunny day.
4. We saw an oak tree, an elm tree, and a pine tree.

j. Use a comma after the greeting of a friendly letter.

Examples:

1. Dear Tina,   2. Dear Uncle Miles,

k. Use a comma after the complimentary close of a letter.

Examples:

1. Your friend,   2. Very truly yours,
3. Sincerely,

11 Using the Apostrophe

a. When you combine two words to form a contraction, use an apostrophe (') to show where letters have been left out.

Examples:

1. we shall—we'll   2. has not—hasn't
See also Key 22.

b. When you form the possessive of a singular word, add an apostrophe and an *s* (*'s*).

Examples:

1. the book's cover   2. Liang's coat

c. When you form the possessive of a plural word that ends in *s*, add an apostrophe only. If the plural does not end in *s*, add an apostrophe and an *s*.

Examples:

1. cars' tires   2. children's stories
See also Key 16.

12 Using Quotation Marks

a. Place quotation marks around titles of stories, poems, songs, and short works that appear in a sentence or a list.

Quotation marks are not placed around the title that is written above a paragraph or a story.

Examples:
1. I think "Paul Revere's Ride" is my favorite poem.
2. Have you finished reading the story "Pecos Bill"?

b. **Book titles are underlined instead of being placed inside quotation marks.**

Example:
1. The Willow Whistle is a book about pioneer life.

c. **Place quotation marks around direct quotations.**

Quotation marks are put outside the comma, period, or other punctuation at the end of a direct quotation.

Examples:
1. Carlos said, "The silver bicycle is mine."
2. "The silver bicycle is mine," said Carlos.

🔑 13 Using the Colon

Use a colon after the greeting in a business letter.

Examples:
1. Dear Sir or Madam:
2. Dear Mr. Bruce:

Parts of Speech

🔑 14 Learning About Nouns

A *noun* is a word that names a person, a place, or a thing. It can act or be acted upon.

Common nouns are general names.

Examples:
1. boy 2. city 3. boat

Proper nouns name particular persons, places, or things.

Examples:
1. Bryan 2. Chicago 3. the *Queen Mary*

🔑 15 Forming Plurals of Singular Nouns

A **singular noun** names one person, place, or thing. A **plural noun** names more than one. There are several ways to form plurals of singular nouns.

a. **The plurals of most words are formed by adding s to the end of the singular word.**

Examples:
1. girl—girl**s**   2. car—car**s**
3. boat—boat**s**

b. **To form the plural of a word ending in ch, sh, s, x, or z add es to the singular word.**

Examples:
1. inch—inch**es**   2. bush—bush**es**
3. box—box**es**

c. **For some words ending in f or fe the plurals are formed by replacing the f or fe with ves.**

Examples:
1. shelf—shel**ves**   2. li**fe**—liv**es**
3. knife—kni**ves**

d. **To form the plural of a word ending in y with a consonant before it, replace the y with i and add es. To form the plural of a word ending in y with a vowel before it, add s.**

Examples:
1. lily—lil**ies**   2. baby—bab**ies**
3. monkey—monkey**s**

e. **To form the plurals of some words, change the spelling of the singular forms.**

Examples:
1. man—**men**   2. mouse—**mice**
3. goose—**geese**

f. **The spelling of some words is the same for both the singular and the plural forms.**

Examples:
1. deer—**deer**   2. sheep—**sheep**

🔑 16 Forming Possessives of Nouns

A **possessive word** is one that shows ownership, possession, or another close relationship.

a. **To form the possessive of a singular word or name, add an apostrophe and an s ('s) to the singular form.**

Examples:
1. the child**'s** book 2. the cat**'s** tail
3. Ross**'s** ball

b. **To form the possessive of a plural noun ending in s, add only an apostrophe. If the plural form does not end in s, add an apostrophe and an s.**

Examples:
1. the cups**'** saucers
2. the cats**'** tails
3. the men**'s** pencils

17 Learning About Pronouns

a. A *pronoun* is a word used in the place of a noun.

b. A *personal pronoun* takes the place of a definite person or thing.

I, me, my, mine, we, us, our, ours, you, your, yours, he, him, his, she, her, hers, it, its, they, them, their, and *theirs* are personal pronouns.

Examples:
Sentences without pronouns:
Randy took Randy's cat to Leah's house. While Randy was there, Randy coaxed Randy's cat to do a trick. The cat walked on the cat's hind feet while Randy dangled a piece of yarn from Randy's fingers. Leah laughed and clapped Leah's hands when Leah saw the trick.

Sentences with pronouns:
Randy took *her* cat to Leah's house. While *she* was there, Randy coaxed *her* cat to do a trick. The cat walked on *its* hind feet while Randy dangled a piece of yarn from *her* fingers. Leah laughed and clapped *her* hands when *she* saw the trick.

18 Using Personal Pronouns

a. To tell who did something, use the pronoun *I, he, she, we,* or *they* (not *me, him, her, us,* or *them*).

Examples:
1. *He* and *I* helped build a hut.
2. Ellie and *she* made some windows.
3. *We* have a clubhouse.
4. Maria and *they* ate lunch in the clubhouse.

b. When you tell about others and yourself in the same sentence, place the nouns and pronouns that name others before the pronoun *I* or *me*.

Examples:
1. Jim and *I* went fishing.
2. Mary, Jason, and *I* were singing.
3. That puppet belongs to Joe and *me*.
4. Dad gave Mia, Bill and *me* a dollar.

c. After such words as *told, give, heard, from, to, for, by,* or *with,* use the pronoun *me, him, her, us,* or *them* (do not use *I, he, she, we,* or *they*).

Examples:
1. Joe gave the kite to Bill and *me*.

2. The art was done by *her* and *me*.
3. The bakery gave cookies to *us*.
4. Bob went with Jack and *them*.

d. After *it is, it was, is it,* or *was it,* use *I, he, she, we,* or *they.*

Examples:
1. It is *I* who wanted that book.
2. It was *he* at the door.
3. Was it *we* who won the game?
4. Is it *they* who are too noisy?

e. The word *self* is combined with personal pronouns to form *myself, yourself, himself, herself, itself, ourselves, yourselves,* and *themselves.*

Examples:
1. Ira went to the woods by *himself.*
2. They drew funny pictures of *themselves.*

19 Learning About Verbs

Words that show action, being, or state of being are *verbs.*

Examples:
Verbs that show action:
1. The angry dog *barked.*
2. Allen *jumped* over the fence.

Verbs that show being or state of being:
3. Tony *was* in the yard.
4. I *am* ten years old.
5. Carla *seems* ready for the test.

20 Using Singular and Plural Verbs

a. Use a *singular verb* to tell about one person or thing. Use a *plural verb* to tell about more than one person or thing.

Is, was, and *has* are singular verbs; *are, were,* and *have* are plural verbs.

Examples:
1. Toby *is* a good swimmer.
2. She *was* the first one in the pool.
3. The water *was* not cold.
4. One of the swimmers *is* Tad.
5. *Are* the diving boards good?
6. We *were* on the edge of the pool.
7. Our pools *have* lifeguards.
8. *Have* they left the pool?

b. Use a plural verb with the pronoun *you* or *I.*

Examples:
1. *Were you* at the party?
2. *You are* a very fast runner.

3. *You have* a first-aid kit.
4. *I have* an interesting book.
Note: Two exceptions to this rule are *I am* and *I was.*
Examples:
1. *I am* happy.
2. *I was* at the library today.

29. set	set	set
30. sing	sang or sung	sung
31. sit	sat	sat
32. take	took	taken
33. teach	taught	taught
34. throw	threw	thrown
35. write	wrote	written

🔑 21 Using Principal Parts of Verbs

a. **Verbs have three principal parts. The third principal part always needs a helping word.**

b. **Helping words are also verbs. Verbs that may be used as helping words are *is, are, was, were, has, have,* and *had.***

One or more words may separate a helping word from the word it helps.

Examples:
1. I *went* to the museum yesterday.
2. I *have gone* by myself many times.
3. *Have* you ever *gone* to the museum?
4. Mia *had* never before *seen* the exhibits.

Note the principal parts of the following verbs:

1. become	became	become
2. begin	began	begun
3. blow	blew	blown
4. break	broke	broken
5. bring	brought	brought
6. come	came	come
7. do	did	done
8. draw	drew	drawn
9. drink	drank	drunk
10. drive	drove	driven
11. eat	ate	eaten
12. fall	fell	fallen
13. fly	flew	flown
14. freeze	froze	frozen
15. give	gave	given
16. go	went	gone
17. grow	grew	grown
18. hear	heard	heard
19. know	knew	known
20. lay	laid	laid
21. learn	learned	learned
22. lie	lay	lain
23. raise	raised	raised
24. ride	rode	ridden
25. ring	rang or rung	rung
26. rise	rose	risen
27. run	ran	run
28. see	saw	seen

🔑 22 Writing Contractions

Contractions are shortened word forms made by leaving out one or more letters. A contraction is a single word formed by combining a verb with a pronoun or a verb with the word *not.*

Use an apostrophe to show where letters have been left out of a contraction.

Examples:
1. are not—aren't
2. cannot—can't
3. could not—couldn't
4. did not—didn't
5. do not—don't
6. does not—doesn't
7. had not—hadn't
8. has not—hasn't
9. have not—haven't
10. he is—he's
11. he will—he'll
12. I am—I'm
13. I have—I've
14. I will—I'll
15. is not—isn't
16. it is—it's
17. she is—she's
18. she will—she'll
19. should not—shouldn't
20. that is—that's
21. they are—they're
22. they have—they've
23. they will—they'll
24. was not—wasn't
25. we are—we're
26. we have—we've
27. we will—we'll
28. were not—weren't
29. who is—who's
30. will not—won't
31. would not—wouldn't
32. you are—you're
33. you have—you've
34. you will—you'll

23 Using Adjectives and Adverbs

a. Words that *describe* nouns or pronouns tell *what kind, how many,* or *which one.* Such describing words are called *adjectives.*

Examples:
1. I read an *exciting* story.
2. *That* girl has mowed *two* lawns.
3. He is too *hot* and *tired* to go to the store.

b. Some describing words tell something about a verb. They often tell *how, when,* or *where.* Such describing words are called *adverbs.*

Examples:
1. She writes *well.*   2. Kuo left *early.*
       3. Jaime lives *here.*

24 Using Conjunctions

a. Conjunctions are words used to connect two other words or groups of words.

And, but, or, if, when, after, because, and *while* are words often used as conjunctions. A conjunction is sometimes used at the beginning of a sentence.

Examples:
1. Robert *or* Alice will make the bench.
2. They will sand *and* paint the bench *after* it is made.
3. Robin will bring the bench to school *and* put pots of flowers on it.
4. *If* the plants are watered, they will grow.
5. Our room is pretty now, *but* it will be prettier *when* the flowers bloom.
6. *While* the plants are growing, everyone will be interested in watching them.

b. Use conjunctions to combine short sentences into longer, more interesting ones.

Examples:
1. *Too many short sentences:* Robert will make a bench. Alice will make the bench, too. They will sand the bench. They will paint the bench.

   Two better sentences: Robert and Alice will make a bench. They will sand and paint the bench.

2. *Too many short sentences:* Robin will bring some pots of flowers. She will put the flowers on the bench. Our room is pretty now. It will be prettier when we have flowers.

   Two better sentences: When Robin brings some pots of flowers, she will put them on the bench. Our room is pretty now, but it will be prettier when we have flowers.

c. Avoid using too many *and*s.

A long sentence using too many *and*s is usually boring and hard to read. Use shorter sentences and a variety of conjunctions to make writing interesting and easy to read.

Examples:
Too many ands: Susan and Marie made a patio and Susan mixed the cement and Marie laid the bricks.

Two better sentences: Susan and Marie made a patio. While Susan mixed the cement, Marie laid the bricks.

Using Words Correctly

25 Using *A* and *An*

a. The word *an* is usually used before a word that begins with a vowel sound. The letters of the alphabet that are vowels are *a, e, i, o,* and *u. An* is not used before words beginning with the sound of long *u.*

Examples:
1. *an* apple   4. *an* ocean
2. *an* egg   5. *an* uncle
3. *an* idea   6. *an* hour

b. The word *a* is usually used before a word that does not begin with a vowel sound. The word *a* is also used before words beginning with the sound of long *u.*

Examples:
1. *a* bicycle   2. *a* horse   3. *a* uniform

26 Using *Teach* and *Learn*

a. To *teach* means to help someone learn.

b. To *learn* means to find out about something or to find out how to do something.

Examples:
1. I want to *learn* to ski.
2. Dad will *teach* me to ski.

27 Using *May* and *Can*

a. Use *may* to ask or give permission.

b. Use *can* to show that someone is able to do something.

Examples:
1. **May** I go to Charley's house?
2. Yes, you **may** go now.
3. I **can** juggle three balls.
4. A seal **can** swim fast.

⚷ 28   Using *Sit* and *Set*

a. To *sit* means to rest or take a seat. The principal parts of this verb are *sit, sat,* and *sat.*

Examples:
1. Please **sit** here.
2. Mary **sat** here yesterday.
3. I have **sat** in this chair for an hour.

b. To *set* means to put or place something. The principal parts of this verb are *set, set,* and *set.*

Examples:
1. **Set** the box here.
2. Yesterday I **set** the box there.
3. I have **set** it there each day.

⚷ 29   Using *Lie* and *Lay*

a. To *lie* means to rest or recline. The principal parts of this verb are *lie, lay,* and *lain.*

Examples:
1. I told the dog to **lie** down.
2. Then he **lay** down before the fire.
3. Ruff has **lain** there all evening.

b. To *lay* means to place or put something. The principal parts of this verb are *lay, laid,* and *laid.*

Examples:
1. Please **lay** the books on the table.
2. Hwang **laid** the books on the table.
3. Hwang has **laid** the books on the table.

⚷ 30   Using *Doesn't* and *Don't*

Use *doesn't* to tell about one person or thing. Use *don't* to tell about more than one person or thing. Use *don't* with the word *you* and the word *I.*

Examples:
1. Jason **doesn't** like to fish.
2. **Don't** the other children bait his hook?
3. **Don't** you like to eat fish?
4. I **don't** like to scale them.

⚷ 31   Using *In* and *Into*

Use *into* to tell about movement from the outside to the inside of something. Use *in* to tell about the inside.

Examples:
1. Gary went **into** the shed to get a tool.
2. He was **in** the shed when she called.

⚷ 32   Unnecessary Words

Leave out any word that is not necessary to the meaning of a sentence.

Use:	Barbara has a new bike.
Instead of:	Barbara she has a new bike.
Use:	The chorus sang a song.
Instead of:	The chorus they sang a song.
Use:	I have a book.
Instead of:	I have got a book.
Use:	He told me.
Instead of:	He went and told me.
Use:	Bring the box here.
Instead of:	Go bring the box here.
Use:	This baseball is mine.
Instead of:	This here baseball is mine.
Use:	He took the dish off the table.
Instead of:	He took the dish off of the table.

⚷ 33   Expressions to Be Avoided

Certain expressions should be avoided in speaking and in writing.

Use:	these rocks, those rocks*
Instead of:	them rocks
Use:	is not, am not, are not
Instead of:	ain't
Use:	ate, eaten
Instead of:	et, eaded
Use:	bought
Instead of:	buyed
Use:	heard
Instead of:	heered
Use:	dragged
Instead of:	drug
Use:	drew, drawn
Instead of:	drawed
Use:	grew, grown
Instead of:	growed

*Use **these** to tell of things near you. Use **those** to tell of things away from you.

Use:	knew, known
Instead of:	knowed
Use:	might have
Instead of:	might of
Use:	should have
Instead of:	should of
Use:	couldn't have
Instead of:	couldn't of

34 Double Negatives

Words such as **no, not, none, nothing, never, hardly,** and **scarcely** and contractions made from **not** are negative words.

Use only one negative word to tell about one thing.

Use:	Jill **doesn't have any** chalk.
	Jill **has no** chalk.
Instead of:	Jill **doesn't have no** chalk.
Use:	I **haven't** bought **anything.**
	I **have** bought **nothing.**
Instead of:	I **haven't** bought **nothing.**
Use:	**None** of them **were** here.
	No one was here.
Instead of:	**None** of them **weren't** here.
	Not no one was here.
Use:	Ann **has never** seen ducks.
	Ann **hasn't ever** seen ducks.
Instead of:	Ann **has never** seen **no** ducks.
	Ann **hasn't never** seen ducks.
Use:	He **can hardly** walk.
Instead of:	He **can't hardly** walk.

35 Using Synonyms

Synonyms are words that mean the same or nearly the same thing.

Examples:

1. afraid—frightened
2. aid—help
3. amusing—funny
4. awkward—clumsy
5. begin—start
6. below—beneath or under
7. big—large
8. bold—brave
9. bottle—jar
10. brief—short
11. bright—sunny or shiny
12. certain—sure
13. close—shut or near
14. cry—weep
15. cut—slash
16. difficult—hard
17. enjoy—like
18. enormous—huge
19. flabby—soft
20. fly—soar
21. fret—worry
22. genuine—real
23. grasp—seize
24. hunt—search
25. ill—sick
26. impolite—rude
27. look—see or watch
28. neat—orderly
28. odd—strange
30. part—piece
31. ran—raced
32. remain—stay
33. rich—wealthy
34. say—speak
35. small—tiny
36. speak—talk or say
37. stroll—walk
38. throw—toss or pitch

36 Using Antonyms

Antonyms are words that have opposite meanings.

Examples:

1. add—subtract
2. after—before
3. ancient—new or modern
4. appear—disappear
5. artificial—real
6. ashamed—proud
7. awkward—graceful
8. behind—before
9. bought—sold
10. buy—sell
11. careful—careless or **reckless**
12. cloudy—sunny
13. clumsy—graceful
14. correct—incorrect or **wrong**
15. day—night
16. dull—glossy or bright
17. ending—beginning or **starting**
18. enemy—friend
19. expensive—cheap or **inexpensive**
20. fresh—stale

21. give—get, receive, or take
22. glad—sad
23. hard—soft
24. heavy—light
25. huge—tiny
26. imaginary—real
27. large—small
28. last—first
29. long—short
30. loose—tight
31. lose—win or find
32. loud—quiet or soft
33. often—seldom
34. old—young or new
35. polite—rude
36. poor—rich
37. pretty—ugly
38. thick—thin
39. safe—unsafe or dangerous
40. strong—weak
41. well—sick

🔑 37 Using Homophones

a. *Homophones* **are words that sound alike or almost alike but have different spellings and different meanings.**

b. **When you use a homophone, be sure to spell the word that gives the meaning you intend.**

   Examples:
   1. ate—eight
      Bruce *ate* carrots for lunch.
      There were *eight* people here for the meeting.
   2. bare—bear
      The table was *bare.*
      Mr. Thompson saw a *bear* at the zoo.
   3. beach—beech
      We played on the *beach* before we went swimming.
      We had our picnic under the *beech* tree.
   4. be—bee
      Can you *be* home by two o'clock?
      The *bee* stung Robert's finger.
   5. blew—blue
      The wind *blew* the door open.
      The color of the sky is *blue.*
   6. buy—by
      Did you *buy* milk at the store?
      We walked slowly *by* the bakery.
   7. cent—sent—scent
      I spent my last *cent* for a new book.

Mom *sent* Jack to the store.
Do you like the *scent* of roses?
   8. dear—deer
      I wrote to one of my *dear* friends.
      A baby *deer* is called a fawn.
   9. fair—fare
      It was a *fair* day when Jim started his trip.
      Jim paid his own *fare* on the bus.
   10. grate—great
       The *grate* in the stove is broken.
       Elsie wanted to be early for the *great* celebration.
   11. hare—hair
       The *hare* hopped into the forest.
       John stood in front of the mirror to comb his *hair.*
   12. hear—here
       Did you *hear* the canary singing?
       Your book is *here* on the table.
   13. heard—herd
       I *heard* the chatter of a squirrel.
       There is a *herd* of buffalo in this park.
   14. hole—whole
       I have a *hole* in my pocket.
       The *whole* family went to the fair.
   15. its—it's
       The snake shed *its* skin.
       It's raining while the sun is shining.
   16. knew—new
       I *knew* how to work the math problem.
       Jane bought a *new* book yesterday.
   17. knot—not
       I tied a *knot* in my rope.
       I'm *not* going to the show today.
   18. know—no
       Does anyone *know* where the pencils are?
       There are *no* pencils in the box.
   19. one—won
       Jason and Alva played *one* game of chess.
       Who *won* the game?
   20. sea—see
       Have you ever been for a sail on the *sea*?
       I can *see* the snow-covered mountain.
   21. some—sum
       There are *some* visitors in our class.
       The *sum* is found by adding numbers.
   22. son—sun
       Mr. Harada bought his *son* a new shirt.
       The *sun* is shining brightly today.
   23. stair—stare
       A board in the *stair* is broken.
       Why did you sit and *stare* into space?
   24. tail—tale

Lou's dog has a short, stubby **tail.**
I read a **tale** about a legendary hero.

25. their—there—they're
Their house is made of lumber.
Our house is **there** on the corner.
They're going to the museum today.

26. threw—through
Alice **threw** the basketball.
Did the ball go **through** the hoop?

27. to—too—two
Joe went **to** the library.
He brought home **too** many books.
Adam went **to** the library, **too.**
Adam brought **two** books home.

28. weak—week
You often feel **weak** after an illness.
Betty has been sick for a **week.**

29. who's—whose
Who's going to the library?
Whose book is this?

30. your—you're
Don't forget **your** book.
You're going to the library, aren't you?

Using the Dictionary

38   Locating Words

a. **Words in a dictionary are arranged so that their first letters are in the order of the alphabet: *a, b, c, d, e, f, g, h, i, j, k, l, m, n, o, p, q, r, s, t, u, v, w, x, y, z.* Words beginning with the same first letter are arranged according to the second and following letters.**

Examples:

1. *an*telope
2. *as*h
3. *b*ell
4. *c*otton
5. *d*ollar
6. *ea*r
7. *ey*e
8. *fa*ther
9. *fe*ather
10. *fi*re
11. *gi*nger
12. *gl*ass
13. *ha*wk
14. *ho*bby
15. *ice*
16. *icy*
17. *j*anitor
18. *k*angaroo
19. *la*wn
20. *le*opard
21. *ma*de
22. *mi*lk
23. *n*est
24. *ok*ra
25. *ow*l
26. *p*arrot
27. *q*uail
28. *r*adio
29. *saili*ng
30. *sailo*r
31. *ti*ger
32. *u*mbrella
33. *v*iolin
34. *wind*
35. *wint*er
36. *x*ylophone
37. *y*ear
38. *z*ebra

b. **There are two *guide words* at the top of each dictionary page. They indicate that those two words and all words that can be arranged alphabetically between them appear on that page.**

39   Dividing Words into Syllables

a. **When it is necessary in writing to divide a word at the end of a line, divide it only at the end of a syllable. Use a dictionary to find where a word is divided into syllables. Never divide a word of one syllable.**

b. **Place a hyphen at the end of a syllable. Then write the rest of the word on the next line.**

Examples:

1. bat (one syllable)
2. broth-er (two syllables)
3. tel-e-phone (three syllables)

c. **To aid in pronunciation, each word in a dictionary is divided into syllables.**

1. The syllable that is most stressed when the word is spoken is shown by an **accent mark (´).**
2. Many of the sounds of the vowels *a, e, i, o,* and *u* are shown by diacritical markings. The sounds of the vowels are often illustrated by key words in the pronunciation guide at the bottom of a dictionary page.

40   Spelling Words

When you are unsure of the spelling of a word, check it in a dictionary. See also Keys 15, 16, 22, and 37.

Writing

41   Using Sentences

When you talk, you usually put your thoughts into sentences. When you write letters, stories, and reports, you use sentences. Properly written sentences help the reader understand what you mean.

a. **A sentence is a group of words that tells something or asks something. It makes sense when you say it, hear it, or read it.**

Examples:
1. Is that an oak tree?
2. No, that is an elm tree.

Below are groups of words that are not sentences. Each group has something missing and does not make sense.

Examples:
1. An angrily buzzing bee
2. Flew here and there

b. **A sentence that tells something is called a** *statement,* **or** *declarative sentence.* **Its end punctuation is a period.**

Example:

The gray squirrel is gathering acorns.

c. **A sentence that asks something is called a** *question,* **or** *interrogative sentence.* **Its end punctuation is a question mark.**

Examples:
1. What kind of animal is that?
2. Did we frighten the gray squirrel?

d. **A sentence that shows surprise, fear, excitement, or other sudden or strong feeling is called an** *exclamation,* **or** *exclamatory sentence.* **Its end punctuation is an exclamation point.**

Examples:
1. What a big squirrel that is!
2. How we frightened it!

e. **Do not use too many short sentences. Often two or more sentences can be put together to make one interesting sentence.**

Examples:
1. *Too many short sentences:* Jill is holding a hammer. It is a heavy hammer.

   One better sentence. Jill is holding a heavy hammer.
2. *Too many short sentences:* Luis has a ball. It is new. He has a bat. It is new. He has a glove. It is old.

   One better sentence: Luis has a new ball, a new bat, and an old glove.

42 Writing Quotations

Direct quotations are the exact words thought, spoken, or written by someone. *Indirect quotations* tell what someone thought, said, or wrote but are not the exact words. When you use direct quotations in your writing, begin a new paragraph each time a different person speaks.

a. **Capitalize the first word of a direct quotation. Place quotation marks at the beginning and end of a direct quotation.**

Examples:
1. "The sun is bright," he said.
2. He said, "The sun is bright."

A direct quotation is sometimes divided by the words that tell who spoke. Capitalize the first word and place quotation marks around the exact words spoken in a divided direct quotation. Use commas to separate the words that tell who spoke from the direct quotation.

Example:

"The sun," Jack remarked, "is bright."

b. **Indirect quotations do not begin with a capital letter. Quotation marks are not used with indirect quotations.**

Example:

He said that the sun was bright.

43 Outlining

An *outline* is a brief plan for a report or story. It lists the topics of paragraphs to be written and shows the order in which they will be explained. Each paragraph topic is numbered with a roman numeral. Statements telling how the topic is to be explained are identified by capital letters.

Make an outline when planning a report or story.

Note the arrangement of the topics and subtopics in the following outline.

Title:

Making and Flying Your Own Kite

Topic of first paragraph:

I. The fun of kites
   A. Flying kites in the spring
   B. Designing, making, and experimenting with kites

Topic of second paragraph:

II. Making a diamond kite
   A. Designing a diamond kite
   B. Gathering materials
   C. Making the kite

Topic of third paragraph:

III. Flying the kite
   A. Finding a good field on a windy day
   B. Staying away from power lines
   C. Trying some tricks with your kite

44 Writing Paragraphs

Most stories, letters, and reports are divided into parts. Each part is called a **paragraph.** A paragraph explains one idea about the subject. A new paragraph is begun each time a new idea is introduced. Sometimes a subject can be explained in one paragraph, but often several paragraphs are needed to explain a broader subject. Each paragraph includes a **topic sentence**, an interesting sentence that tells what the paragraph will be about.

a. A paragraph is made up of one or more sentences that tell about one thing.

Example:

The Wren

The wren is a small gray, brown, and white bird. It is always moving busily about. Its song makes it welcome in our backyard.

b. Follow these rules in writing a paragraph.

1. Write a title that gives an idea of the subject. Begin the first word and each important word in the title with a capital letter.
2. Indent the first line of each paragraph. To **indent** means to begin the first line about 2½ centimeters (1 inch) to the right of the left margin. Begin all other lines in the paragraph at the margin.
3. Leave margins about 2½ centimeters (1 inch) wide at the top, at the bottom, and on each side of the paper. Keep these margins as straight as you can.
4. Begin the paragraph with an interesting sentence.
5. Begin each sentence with a capital letter, and end it with the correct punctuation mark.
6. Be sure that you write complete, correct sentences.
7. Begin a new paragraph each time you introduce a new idea.

45 Making Reports

Making a **report** is writing about something you saw, heard, read, or did. The thing you write about is the **topic** of the report.

a. Choose a topic that is interesting and worthwhile.

1. Will the report help the readers learn something they would like to know?

2. Limit your subject. "Soap" is not a good subject because you cannot tell everything about all kinds of soap. "How Pioneers Made Soap" is a good subject because you can tell all the important facts.

b. Plan your report before you write it.

1. Ask yourself questions about the subject. The questions will help you select interesting and important ideas to write.
2. Find interesting information about your subject in reference books.
3. Write only those ideas and facts that are needed to tell about your subject.

c. Write your report neatly and correctly.

1. Begin the report with an interesting sentence that introduces the subject. Tell more about the subject in each of the other sentences. Write a title that will make people want to read your report.
2. Write neatly, so that your words are easy to read.
3. Proofread the finished report for spelling, capitalization, and punctuation.
4. Read your report to find out whether another person is likely to understand what you want to tell.

46 Writing Notices and Announcements

Sometimes information needs to be given to a large number of people. Then a notice must be written to be read aloud, placed on a bulletin board, or delivered.

In an announcement or notice be sure to include all necessary information.

1. Tell what the event is.
2. Tell when and where the event will be held.
3. Tell who may attend and who is having the event.

Example:

The fifth grade will have a photography exhibit in their room after school on Monday, January 15. Everyone is invited to view the exhibit.

47 Writing Stories

A **story** tells something that happens to a person or a thing. The people or things told about may be real or imaginary. Usually a story tells about a problem and how it is solved. Most stories have more than one paragraph.

a. Plan the story before you write it.
1. Think of a problem and its exciting or interesting solution.
2. Decide what you must tell about your story in order that the reader may understand it. Leave out any idea not needed to tell the story.
3. Arrange the events of the story in the order they happened.

b. Write the story in an interesting and correct way.
1. Write an interesting title in the center of the first line.
2. Write an interesting sentence to begin the story.
3. Tell all the important events in the order in which they happen.
4. When you tell something new, put it in a new paragraph.
5. Try to use words that say exactly what you mean.
6. Be sure that the last sentence ends the story in an interesting and satisfying way.

c. Check your story after it is written.
1. Have you told everything necessary for a reader to understand the story? Have you told anything that you do not need to tell?
2. Look for short, choppy sentences, and combine them.
3. Proofread the spelling, punctuation, and capitalization in your story.
4. Make sure that your writing is neat and easy to read.

🔑 48 Writing Addresses

a. An *address* tells where a person lives or receives mail.
1. A person in a city usually has a street address. The ZIP code follows the name of the state.
2. A person or a business may use a post office box instead of a street address. *P.O. Box* is the abbreviation for *Post Office Box.*
3. A person who lives in the country may have a rural route number instead of a street address. *R.R.* is the abbreviation for *Rural Route.*

Examples:
1. Mr. Roy M. Ross
   38 Brooks Street
   Augusta, Maine 04330
2. Ace Hobby Company
   P.O. Box 2313
   Tiro, Ohio 44807
3. Dr. B. D. Arnt
   R.R. 1
   Crewe, Virginia 23930

b. In an address begin all words, abbreviations, and initials with capital letters.

c. Use a comma to separate the name of a city from the name of a state if they are on the same line in an address. No comma is used before a ZIP code, but the space of two letters should be left between the name of the state and the ZIP code.

Examples:
1. Barre, Vermont 05641
2. Albany, Oregon 97321

d. Two-letter state abbreviations may be used in addresses. Both letters are capitalized, and no period follows.

Note: See Key 7f for a list of the two-letter abbreviations.

🔑 49 Addressing Envelopes

a. Write the address and name of the sender in the upper left corner of the envelope.

b. In the center of the envelope write the title of courtesy, the name, and the address of the person who is to receive the letter. Place a comma between the name of the city and the name of the state only if they are written on the same line. Do not place a comma between the state and the ZIP code.

Example:

```
Cecil Howe
R.R. 3
Lyons, New York  14489



                    Miss Ann Lewis
                    41 Ashley Drive
                    Buhl, Idaho  83316
```

50 Writing Friendly Letters

A *friendly letter* is an informal letter written to a friend or a relative. It may be written to send a personal message, a thank-you for a gift or kindness, or an invitation to a social event.

a. A friendly letter has five parts.
1. The *heading* gives the address of the person writing the letter and the date.
2. The *greeting* tells to whom the letter is written and greets that person.
3. The *body,* or *main part,* gives the writer's message.
4. The *closing,* or *complimentary close,* is a polite or affectionate way to say goodbye.
5. The *signature* is the name of the writer.

b. Follow these rules for capitalization in a friendly letter.
1. In the heading begin all words with capital letters.
2. Begin the first word of the greeting with a capital letter.
3. Begin all names and all sentences with capital letters.
4. Begin the first word of the complimentary close with a capital letter.

c. Follow these rules for punctuation in a friendly letter.
1. In the heading place a comma between the name of the city and the name of the state, and between the day of the month and the year.
2. Place a comma after the greeting.
3. End each sentence with the correct punctuation mark.
4. Place a comma after the complimentary close.

Example:

Heading:	633 Dauphine Street New Orleans, LA 70112 February 3, 2010
Greeting:	Dear Fred,
Body:	Mom and Dad gave me a bike for my birthday. It's really a beauty! I want to try my new bicycle in the open country. Let's ride our bicycles in Audubon Park next Sunday.
Complimentary close:	Your friend,
Signature:	Dawn

51 Writing Business Letters

a. A business letter has six parts.
1. The *heading* tells where and when the letter is written.
2. The *inside address* tells the title of courtesy and the name and address of the person the letter is written to. A company's name may be used instead of a title of courtesy and a person's name.
3. The *greeting* is a polite way to greet the person who is to receive the letter.
4. The *body* gives the writer's message.
5. The *complimentary close* expresses courtesy in ending the letter.
6. The *signature* is either the full name or the initials and last name of the person who writes the letter.

b. Follow these rules for capitalization in a business letter.
1. In the heading begin all words with capital letters.
2. In the address begin all words, abbreviations, and initials with capital letters.
3. Begin the first word of the greeting with a capital letter.
4. Begin the first word of the complimentary close with a capital letter.

c. Follow these rules for punctuating a business letter.
1. Place a colon *(:)* after the greeting.
2. In the inside address place a period after an abbreviated title of courtesy. Place a comma between the name of the city and the state.
3. Follow Key 50 for punctuating the heading, body, and complimentary close of a business letter.

Example:

Heading:	282 Nye Street Rockport, IN 46617 January 24, 2010
Address:	Adams Hobby Company 4486 North Appleton Street Chicago, Illinois 60610
Greeting:	Dear Sir or Madam:
Body:	Please send a copy of your latest catalogue. Enclosed is seventy cents for postage.
Complimentary close:	Very truly yours,
Signature:	Eric Minelli

Speaking And Listening

52 Speaking and Listening to Other People

a. Make a report interesting by following these suggestions.
1. Choose a worthwhile topic.
2. Decide what you will say about your topic.
3. Write an interesting beginning sentence.
4. Be sure that every sentence tells about the topic.
5. Speak clearly and correctly.

b. Tell a story in an entertaining way by following these suggestions.
1. Choose an interesting story. Make up your own, or tell one you have read.
2. Know your story well before you tell it.
3. Tell the title of your story.
4. Make the beginning of your story interesting so that people will listen.
5. Tell all the important events in the order in which they happen.
6. Use words that say exactly what you mean.
7. Choose a good ending sentence.
8. Look at your listeners.
9. Do not use too many **and**s.
10. Speak clearly, correctly, and loudly enough for everyone to hear.

c. Listen carefully to others when they talk, tell stories, or give reports.
1. Look at the speaker to show you are listening.
2. Decide what you should gain from the talk. Are you listening for fun, or are you listening to learn something?
3. Listen to discover the topic of the talk.
4. Listen to decide which of the speaker's ideas are important enough to remember.
5. Think of questions to ask after the talk. But do not interrupt while someone is speaking.
6. Decide which things the speaker did well. Did the speaker express ideas so that they were easily understood? Was the talk interesting?

d. Do your part in the discussion by following a few simple rules.
1. Choose an interesting topic.
2. Learn all you can about this topic before the discussion.
3. Stick to the topic being discussed.
4. Give others an opportunity to talk.
5. Avoid talking too long at a time.
6. Avoid interrupting others.
7. Respect the rights and opinions of others.
8. Try to disagree politely.
9. Ask intelligent questions.

53 Broadcasting

Broadcasting means talking about the pictures you see in this book and the many interesting things you see around you in the world. Before you broadcast, look carefully and think.

Broadcasters on television and radio tell people about some things that are happening all over the world, both near us and far away.

When you broadcast in this book, it means that you ask and try to answer questions about various subjects. Talking about new ideas can be fun and you can learn something, too.

What kinds of questions can you ask about the pictures and the world? Here are some of them.

What do you see?
What is happening?
Who do you see?
What are they doing?
Why are they doing it?
Have you ever done that?
How are they feeling? Why?
How would you feel? Why?
What are they saying?
What do you think will happen next?

What other questions could you ask about each separate picture?

What kinds of questions could you ask about other things?

54 Recognizing Different Ways to Speak

Many different languages are spoken on earth. Each of these languages can be spoken in a variety of ways, called dialects. English, for example, has hundreds of dialects. In the United States, different dialects are often spoken by people from different parts of the country. Even within a single neighborhood, there may be several ways of speaking.

Some people at your school may speak a dialect different from yours. All the dialects that you hear are part of our language, and one dialect is not better than another. In school, however, we learn a common way of speaking. It is important that we master this common, shared dialect so that we may be easily understood by anyone who speaks our language.

Writing Quotations

● 42

   Direct and indirect quotations are useful in writing about what someone thought, said, or wrote. Stories are usually more effective when you use both direct and indirect quotations. Remember that quotation marks are not used to punctuate indirect quotations.

Examples: Chet cried, ''I'm scared!''   Chet said that he was scared.
             ''Are you scared?'' asked Chet.   Chet asked whether I was scared.
             ''Why am I scared?'' Chet wondered.   Chet wondered why he was scared.

I.   Rewrite the following sentences as direct quotations. (Score: 25)

1.   Renaldo said that he saw petrified trees in Arizona.   **(Answers will vary.)**

      Renaldo said, ''I saw petrified trees in Arizona.''

2.   Bette wanted to know what causes trees to petrify.

      ''What causes trees to petrify?'' asked Bette.

3.   Alex's reply was that these trees were once driftwood.

      Alex replied, ''These trees were once driftwood.''

4.   Renaldo explained that this wood gradually was covered with mud.

      Renaldo explained, ''This wood gradually was covered with mud.''

5.   He added that minerals in the mud replaced the trees' cells.

      ''Minerals in the mud replaced the trees' cells,'' he added.

II.   Rewrite the following sentences as indirect quotations. (Score: 20)

6.   ''Why does petrified wood feel like rock?'' Bette asked.   **(Answers will vary.)**

      Bette asked why petrified wood feels like rock.

7.   ''It is rock,'' Alex explained, ''that still looks like wood.''

      Alex explained that it is rock that still looks like wood.

8.   Renaldo exclaimed, ''What pretty streaks of color it has!''

      Renaldo exclaimed that it has pretty streaks of color.

9.   ''The colors come from the minerals,'' said Alex.

      Alex said that the colors come from the minerals.

III.   Write a direct quotation about how things change in nature. (Score: 5)

10.   **(Answers will vary.)**

Using Periods in Writing Abbreviations

⚬━ 1c, f, g, 7c, d, e, f, g

Use a period after abbreviations.

Write the abbreviation of each of the following words.

Examples:

Tuesday _____ *Tues.* _____   Missouri _____ *Mo.* _____

1. Sunday	**Sun.**	20. Mister	**Mr.**
2. Monday	**Mon.**	21. Mistress	**Mrs.**
3. Wednesday	**Wed.**	22. Doctor	**Dr.**
4. Thursday	**Thurs.**	23. General	**Gen.**
5. Friday	**Fri.**	24. President	**Pres.**
6. Saturday	**Sat.**	25. Avenue	**Ave.**
7. January	**Jan.**	26. Street	**St.**
8. February	**Feb.**	27. Boulevard	**Blvd.**
9. March	**Mar.**	28. Alabama	**Ala.**
10. April	**Apr.**	29. Arkansas	**Ark.**
11. August	**Aug.**	30. Vermont	**Vt.**
12. September	**Sept.**	31. Illinois	**Ill.**
13. October	**Oct.**	32. Indiana	**Ind.**
14. November	**Nov.**	33. Oregon	**Oreg.**
15. December	**Dec.**	34. Louisiana	**La.**
16. West	**W.**	35. Michigan	**Mich.**
17. North	**N.**	36. California	**Calif.**
18. Southeast	**S.E.**	37. Texas	**Tex.**
19. Northwest	**N.W.**	38. Virginia	**Va.**

Other Things to Do: Write the abbreviation of the state that you live in and the abbreviations of all the states that border yours.

Writing Titles of Courtesy
1b, c, 7c

I. Rewrite the following names, using the proper title of courtesy before each. Abbreviate the titles that can be abbreviated.

Example: J. Leroy Bryan (a lawyer)   _Mr. J. Leroy Bryan_

1. Diane Chow (a woman) — **(Ms.), (Miss), or (Mrs.) Diane Chow**

2. P. B. Jimenez (a physician) — **Dr. P. B. Jimenez**

3. Marcia Dean (a judge) — **Judge Marcia Dean**

4. Roger Simon (a rabbi) — **Rabbi Roger Simon**

5. Raphael T. Sanchez (a senator) — **Sen. Raphael T. Sanchez**

6. M. C. Jackson (a farmer) — **Mr. M. C. Jackson**

7. W. L. Cohen (a professor) — **Prof. W. L. Cohen**

8. Phyllis Acers (an actress) — **(Ms.), (Miss), or (Mrs.) Phyllis Acers**

9. D. E. Munari (a general) — **Gen. D. E. Munari**

10. F. H. Hwang (a minister) — **Rev. F. H. Hwang**

II. Write the titles of courtesy and the names of the following persons. Abbreviate titles of courtesy whenever possible.

11. Your father — **(Answers will vary.)**

12. Your mother

13. Your teacher

14. A woman friend

15. Your family doctor or dentist

16. The principal of your school

17. The governor of your state

18. The President of the United States

Other Things to Do: Use your dictionary to check the spelling or abbreviation of each title of respect you are not sure of.

Parts of a Friendly Letter   🔑 50a

I. Complete the following sentences by writing the names of the five parts of a friendly letter and an explanation of the use of each part. (Score: 10) **(Answers will vary.)**

1. The **first part is the heading** , which tells **the address of** **the person writing the letter and the date the letter is written.**

2. The **second part is the greeting** , which tells **to whom the** **letter is written and which greets that person.**

3. The **main part is the body** , which tells **the writer's** **message.**

4. The **fourth part is the closing** , which tells **good-bye in** **a polite or affectionate way.**

5. The **last part is the signature** , which tells **the name of** **the writer.**

II. On the lines below write the names of the parts of the following letter. (Score: 10)

6. **Heading** _____
   [415 Fosdyke Street
     Providence, RI 02914
     January 16, 2019

7. **Greeting** _____
   [Dear Chang,

8. **Body (or main part)** _____
   [I saw an interesting television program yesterday. It was about Robinson Crusoe, who was marooned on an island for four years. The ways he found food and built a shelter were exciting to learn about.
     I plan to read the book *Robinson Crusoe* by Daniel Defoe. If you read it too, perhaps we can talk about it when I visit you next month.

9. **Closing** _____
   [Your friend,

10. **Signature** _____
    [Harris

Other Things to Do: Write a letter to a friend or relative who lives in another town.

Writing a Friendly Letter

🔑 48, 50b, c

I. Place commas where they are needed in the following letter. Underline each word that should begin with a capital letter. (Score: 13)

<u>rural</u> <u>route</u> 3

<u>montgomery</u>, <u>alabama</u>   36110

<u>june</u> 6, 2003

<u>dear</u> Cynthia,

<u>thank</u> you for inviting me to visit you. I'll bring my tennis racket, as you suggested. Dad will bring me, and we should arrive at about six o'clock next Friday evening.

<u>your</u> <u>friend</u>,

<u>sharon</u>

II. On the lines below write a letter to one of your friends telling about a movie, an art exhibit, or an exciting sports event that you have seen. Use your own address and today's date in the heading. (Score: 15)

_____

_____

_____

_____

(Answers will vary.)

_____

_____

_____

_____

_____

_____

_____

Other Things to Do: Pretend that your class is going to have a program. Write an invitation to one of your neighbors to attend the program.

Parts of a Business Letter   48, 51

Rewrite the following business letter, writing the six parts in their proper places. Use capital letters and punctuation marks where they are needed. (Score: 1 for each capital letter, 1 for each punctuation mark, and 3 for each part of the letter correctly placed)

56 strongs drive roswell new mexico 88201 march 9 1985 davis seed company 604 west fifth street amarillo texas 79106 dear sir or madam please send me your new seed catalogue i am interested in flowers that grow well in dry, sunny places i would appreciate your suggestions about kinds of flowers that grow well in such places i would also like to have your free booklet on preparing soil for planting flowers very truly yours amy bryce

56 Strongs Drive

Roswell, New Mexico 88201

March 9, 2007

Davis Seed Company

604 West Fifth Street

Amarillo, Texas 79106

Dear Sir or Madam:

Please send me your new seed catalogue.

I am interested in flowers that grow well in dry,

sunny places. I would appreciate your

suggestions about kinds of flowers that

grow well in such places. I would also

like to have your free booklet on preparing

soil for planting flowers.

Very truly yours,

Amy Bryce

Writing a Business Letter

○━ 48, 51

On the lines below write a letter to answer one of the following advertisements. Use your address and today's date in the heading.

For a free booklet on starting a hobby, write to Baker Hobby Shop, 440 High Street, Wichita, Kansas 67214. A catalogue of hobby ideas and supplies will be sent on request.

Get your own plastic globe of the world. Send two dollars and the top from a box of Bran Cereal to Bran Cereal Company, P.O. Box 1624, Minneapolis, Minnesota 55440.   **(Answers will vary.)**

_____   **(Student's address)**

_____   **(Today's date)**

Baker Hobby Shop

440 High Street

Wichita, Kansas   67214

        or

Bran Cereal Company

P.O. Box 1624

Minneapolis, Minnesota   55440

_____

(Greeting): _____

_____

                    (The body of the letter)

_____

_____

_____

                    (Closing),

                    (Student's signature)

_____

_____

Addressing Envelopes   48, 49

In order for a letter to reach the person it is written to, the envelope must be correctly addressed.

I. Address the envelope below to Miss Angela Stevens, 317 Bestor Street, Denton, Texas 77201. The letter is from Robert Ayres, Rural Route 2, Fort Smith, Arkansas 72901. (Score: 10)

Robert Ayres

Rural Route 2

Fort Smith, Arkansas   72901

                          Miss Angela Stevens

                          317 Bestor Street

                          Denton, Texas (TX)   77201

II. Address the envelope below to Mr. Glenn Lopez, 622 Northwest Park Street, East St. Louis, Illinois 62205. Use your own return address. (Score: 10)

(Student's address)

                          Mr. Glenn Lopez

                          622 Northwest Park Street

                          East St. Louis, Illinois (IL)   62205

Capitalization and Punctuation

The sentences below tell about a famous American ship. In each sentence underline every word that should begin with a capital letter. Put punctuation marks where they are needed.

Old Ironsides

1. The *constitution* is one of america's oldest and most famous ships.
2. *old ironsides* is the nickname of the *constitution*.
3. This ship first sailed from boston, massachusetts.
4. Construction on the ship was finished on september 20, 1797.
5. The *constitution* was used against pirates in the atlantic ocean.
6. Then the united states fought against england in the War of 1812.
7. The *constitution* met the *guerrière*, a british ship.
8. captain isaac hull was in command of the american ship.
9. Carmen asked, "was the Constitution in a battle?"
10. Randy replied, "yes, the battle was fought on August 19, 1812."
11. How happy the american people were when the Constitution won!
12. In december, 1812, there was another famous sea battle.
13. The *constitution* fought the british ship *java*.
14. Every american citizen heard news of the battle.
15. Randy exclaimed, "How pleased they must have been!"
16. Carmen said, "i am sure they were thankful for the victory."
17. Why was the ship called *old ironsides*?
18. The british cannon balls bounced off the sides of the *constitution*.
19. "That is why the ship was called *old ironsides*," explained Ali.
20. After many years, the old ship sailed back to boston, massachusetts.
21. Carmen explained, "The old ship was to be torn apart."
22. But on september 14, 1830, a poem was printed in a Boston newspaper.
23. The title of the poem was "old ironsides," by Oliver w. Holmes.
24. mr. Holmes remembered the War of 1812.
25. He reminded the american people how well the ship had fought.
26. people from all over the united states sent pennies, dimes, and dollars.
27. Ali asked, "was the ship saved, Carmen?"
28. "Yes, Ali, *old ironsides* can be seen today in boston," Carmen replied.
29. "Tourists can visit it in boston harbor," she said.

Recognizing and Using Pronouns

I. Underline each personal pronoun in the following sentences. (Score: 21—1 for each pronoun underlined)

Sam Houston

1. Joan gave us her book about Sam Houston.
2. "You will find it an interesting book," she said.
3. She told me about this dynamic man.
4. When he was a teenager, Sam left his home.
5. We heard how he lived with the Cherokee Indian tribe.
6. Joan said that he was adopted by the Cherokee Indian chief.
7. Sam learned their language, skills, and customs.
8. Sam used the name "Black Raven" when he lived with the tribe.
9. He was well known in Tennessee.
10. I have heard that Houston was a congressman for that state.
11. I am sure you know that he was governor of Tennessee.
12. We know he helped shape American history.

II. Underline one of the pronouns in parentheses that properly completes each of the following sentences. (Score: 1 for each word correctly underlined)

13. (We, Us) learned that Sam moved to Texas.
14. It was (he, him) who had a trading post in this country.
15. Joan told (he, him) and (me, I) that Texas was part of Mexico.
16. (Her, She) and (I, me) knew that many Americans settled in Texas at that time.
17. It was (me, I) who knew that they wanted to be independent from Mexico.
18. Joan told (us, we) that Houston organized and led the Texas army.
19. Many Americans sent help to (him, he) and (they, them).
20. (He, Him) and (they, them) defeated the Mexican army.
21. (Us, We) knew that Texas gained its independence from Mexico in 1836.
22. (Her, She) and (I, me) learned that Houston was president of the Republic of Texas.
23. It was (he, him) who wanted Texas to join the United States.
24. Joan told (she, her) and (I, me) that Texas joined the Union in 1845.
25. Wasn't it (he, him) who was one of the first senators of Texas?
26. Joan told (her, she) and (me, I) that Houston worked hard for his state.
27. (He, Him) and (I, me) know that a city in Texas was named in honor of Sam Houston.

Other Things To Do: Make a list of five nouns and five verbs used in the sentences above. Use those nouns and verbs to write five sentences.

Using **I** or **Me** With Other Nouns and Pronouns   ⊙—— 18a, b, c, d

I. In each sentence below underline the proper words in parentheses.

The Jungles of Brazil

1.   (Me and Amy, <u>Amy and I</u>) have been reading about Brazil.

2.   (<u>She and I</u>, Her and I) read that Brazil is in South America.

3.   Our teacher told (<u>her and me</u>, she and I) about the jungles in Brazil.

4.   (I and Amy, <u>Amy and I</u>) knew that it is always hot in the jungle.

5.   (<u>She and I</u>, Her and I) learned that plants grow all year long.

6.   Tad told (<u>her and me</u>, me and her) that there is no cold weather to kill insects.

7.   (<u>Amy and I</u>, I and Amy) knew that hundreds of insects live in the jungle.

8.   Tad had told Amy and (I, <u>me</u>) that some of these insects spread diseases.

9.   (<u>She and I</u>, I and she) saw some pictures of the jungle.

10. (Amy and me, <u>Amy and I</u>) saw how the tall trees grow close together.

11. Tad told (me and Li-Chen, <u>Li-Chen and me</u>) that long vines hang from the trees.

12. (<u>She and I</u>, I and she) saw how the trees keep the sun from shining in the forest.

13. The picture showed (me and her, <u>her and me</u>) how dim the light is.

14. (Li-Chen and me, <u>Li-Chen and I</u>) knew that the forest is quiet during the day.

15. But Tad told (<u>her and me</u>, she and I) that it is noisy at night.

16. (<u>She and I</u>, I and she) knew that birds and animals make the noises.

17. (Her and me, <u>She and I</u>) knew that monkeys chatter in the trees.

18. Tad told (<u>her and me</u>, I and she) that many kinds of monkeys live there.

II. Write **I** or **me** in each blank.

19. It was _____**I**_____ who asked what other animals live in the jungle.

20. Tad told Amy and _____**me**_____ that snakes and bats live there.

21. Amy and _____**I**_____ knew that some varieties of parrots live in the jungle.

22. Tad told _____**me**_____ that the jungle is also the home of some anteaters.

23. It was _____**I**_____ who asked if the Brazil nut grows in the forest.

24. Amy explained to her and _____**me**_____ that the nut comes from an evergreen tree.

25. Tad explained to _____**me**_____ that oil crushed from the nut is used for salads.

26. He told Li-Chen and _____**me**_____ that the Brazil nut is delicious.

27. Amy and _____**I**_____ want to taste the Brazil nut.

Using *Them*, *These*, and *Those*   🔑 33

Them is a pronoun used alone in the
place of two or more nouns. The
words *these* and *those* are used
to point out other words.

Examples: Are *these* books yours?

No, but *those* pictures are mine.

I brought *them* from home.

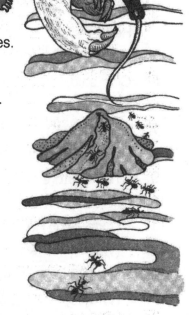

In each sentence below underline the proper word form in parentheses.

The Anteater

1. Perhaps you have seen (them, <u>those</u>) animals called anteaters.

2. Some zoos have several of (<u>them</u>, those).

3. People are fascinated with (them, <u>those</u>) long, thin noses!

4. Do you know where (<u>these</u>, them) animals live?

5. (<u>These</u>, Them) anteaters in our zoo came from Brazil.

6. (Them, <u>These</u>) anteaters usually eat white ants, or termites.

7. Do all of (them, <u>those</u>) have such long tongues?

8. (<u>Those</u>, Them) long tongues are very sticky.

9. The sticky tongue helps the animal pick up (<u>those</u>, them) ants.

10. Did you know that (them, <u>those</u>) anteaters have no teeth?

11. (Them, <u>Those</u>) insects build large mud nests on the ground or in trees.

12. Look at the long claws on (<u>these</u>, them) anteaters!

13. The long claws help (these, <u>them</u>) tear open the ants' nests.

14. (<u>These</u>, Them) anteaters in the zoo are about .6 meters (2 feet) long.

15. Usually you will find (<u>them</u>, those) living in trees.

16. They use (them, <u>those</u>) hind feet to hang from a limb of the tree.

17. (<u>These</u>, Them) anteaters have long tails.

18. The tails also help (those, <u>them</u>) hang from trees.

19. (<u>These</u>, Them) anteaters are smaller than other species of anteaters.

20. Have you seen (them, <u>those</u>) anteaters that are 2.1 meters (7 feet) long?

21. Most of (<u>them</u>, those) live on the ground, don't they?

22. (<u>Those</u>, Them) long claws make it hard for the animals to walk.

23. Aren't (<u>these</u>, them) animals also called ant bears?

24. Ant bears are (<u>those</u>, them) anteaters that live in South America.

25. (<u>These</u>, Them) ant bears are very large animals.

26. Don't (<u>those</u>, them) animals have black, shaggy fur?

27. Each of (<u>them</u>, these) has a white stripe on its shoulder.

Troublesome Words   ⚬➔ 20a, 27, 30, 37

In each sentence below underline the proper word form in parentheses. (Score: 1 for each correct word underlined)

Annie Sullivan

1. ''I read a book about Annie Sullivan (your, <u>you're</u>) sure to enjoy,'' said Clay.

2. ''(<u>It's</u>, Its) about a teacher of blind and deaf people,'' he said.

3. Steve asked, ''Isn't Annie Sullivan the person who went (<u>to</u>, too) Alabama to teach Helen Keller?''

4. ''(<u>Don't</u>, Doesn't) you remember that Helen Keller was blind and deaf?'' asked Lynn.

5. Clay said, ''(<u>You're</u>, Your) right, and Annie Sullivan taught Helen to read and speak.''

6. ''Wasn't it Annie (<u>whose</u>, who's) eyesight was also poor as a child?'' Steve asked.

7. Clay said, ''Yes, she was about (to, <u>two</u>) years old when she got very sick.''

8. He added, ''She couldn't see very well with her (<u>blue</u>, blew) eyes after her illness.''

9. ''The doctors didn't think (there, <u>their</u>) operations could help Annie's eyes,'' said Lynn.

10. She said, ''There were many people (<u>whose</u>, who's) help was important to Annie.''

11. ''(<u>One</u>, Won) doctor in Boston operated on Annie's eyes,'' said Clay.

12. ''(Who's, <u>Whose</u>) house did Annie stay in after her operation?'' asked Steve.

13. Clay said, ''She went (<u>to</u>, too) Mrs. Hopkin's house.''

14. ''(Whose, <u>Who's</u>) Mrs. Hopkins?'' asked Lynn.

15. ''A teacher (<u>whose</u>, who's) home was on Cape Cod,'' said Clay.

16. Steve asked, ''(May, <u>Can</u>) you tell us what school Annie went to?''

17. ''(<u>It's</u>, Its) a school that is still in Boston,'' Lynn answered.

18. Clay asked, ''(<u>Have</u>, Has) you ever heard of the Perkins School for the blind?''

19. ''This school (have, <u>has</u>) helped many blind people,'' he said.

20. ''Is it famous for (<u>its</u>, it's) way of teaching blind people to read?'' asked Steve.

21. Lynn said, ''(<u>It's</u>, Its) a school that was founded by Dr. Howe in 1832.''

22. ''Annie went (<u>to</u>, too) Perkins when she was fourteen years old,'' said Clay.

23. He said, ''Annie learned (too, <u>to</u>) read braille at Perkins.''

24. ''Blind people read braille with (<u>their</u>, there) fingers,'' Clay added.

25. ''(<u>It's</u>, Its) interesting to read about Annie's work with Helen Keller,'' he said.

26. ''Have you read the book, (to, <u>too</u>)?'' asked Lynn.

27. Steve asked, ''(<u>Who's</u>, Whose) the author of the book you read?''

28. ''The book's title is *Annie Sullivan, a Portrait* and (<u>its</u>, it's) author is Terry Dunahoo,'' said Clay.

29. Lynn asked, ''Would you (by, <u>buy</u>) a copy of this book?''

30. ''I think (<u>it's</u>, its) in the library,'' said Clay.

31. ''Have you read any other books written (<u>by</u>, buy) that author?'' asked Lynn.

Uses of the Dictionary   ⚷ 38

I. Arrange the following words in alphabetical order.

act	acid	rat	lily	inlet	mail	race	lamb
dark	nod	cage	jam	gulf	leaf	end	meal
exit	hole	cake	net	sand	sash	home	pit

1. **acid**
2. **act**
3. **cage**
4. **cake**
5. **dark**
6. **end**
7. **exit**
8. **gulf**
9. **hole**
10. **home**
11. **inlet**
12. **jam**
13. **lamb**
14. **leaf**
15. **lily**
16. **mail**
17. **meal**
18. **net**
19. **nod**
20. **pit**
21. **race**
22. **rat**
23. **sand**
24. **sash**

II. The guide words from four pages of a dictionary are listed below. On each line write the number of the page where the word listed could be found.

Page 1 a—act	Page 2 action—bat	Page 3 batch—bead	Page 4 beak—can
25. bag **2**	29. began **4**	33. bath **3**	
26. bay **3**	30. bear **4**	34. bean **4**	
27. absent **1**	31. actor **2**	35. also **2**	
28. about **1**	32. battle **3**	36. calf **4**	

III. Write the number of the definition in Column B in front of the word in Column A that matches the definition. Use a dictionary to find any definition you do not know.

A		B
39 run	37.	seven consecutive days
38 grave	38.	serious or important
40 weak	39.	to move quickly
37 week	40.	not strong

Dividing Words into Syllables

38a, 39

An accent mark shows which syllable of the word is given the most force when the word is spoken.

Examples: fa ′ ther   yes ′ ter-day   bas ′ ket

Below is a list of words. In the first column arrange the words in alphabetical order. In the second column rewrite the words, dividing them into syllables. Place an accent mark after the accented syllable. Refer to your dictionary if you need help.

1.	airplane	airplane	air ′ plane
2.	doctor	baggage	bag ′ gage
3.	baggage	cement	ce-ment ′
4.	funny	doctor	doc ′ tor
5.	cement	express	ex-press ′
6.	helper	funny	fun ′ ny
7.	express	helper	help ′ er
8.	keeper	idle	i ′ dle
9.	idle	Japan	Ja-pan ′
10.	liberty	keeper	keep ′ er
11.	Japan	liberty	lib ′ er-ty
12.	multiply	multiply	mul ′ ti-ply
13.	question	painter	paint ′ er
14.	sister	question	ques ′ tion
15.	painter	receive	re-ceive ′
16.	select	select	se-lect ′
17.	receive	sister	sis ′ ter
18.	turtle	turtle	tur ′ tle

Other Things to Do: Use your dictionary to find five words that you do not know. Arrange the words in alphabetical order. Find their meanings and pronunciations and write five sentences using one of the words in each sentence.

Choosing Proper Word Forms

In each sentence below underline the proper word form in parentheses.

American Astronaut

1. A page in our country's history was (wrote, <u>written</u>) on February 20, 1962.
2. On that day the first American (<u>flew</u>, flown) into orbit around the earth.
3. Early that morning an astronaut (<u>took</u>, taken) his place inside a space capsule.
4. The astronaut, (who's, <u>whose</u>) name was John Glenn, was calm.
5. But (<u>who's</u>, whose) able to think of such a flight without some excitement?
6. Everyone knew what great courage it (<u>took</u>, taken).
7. Glenn had (flew, <u>flown</u>) jet planes.
8. He had (rode, <u>ridden</u>) in many modern aircraft.
9. He had (broke, <u>broken</u>) a speed record flying coast to coast.
10. Glenn had (took, <u>taken</u>) three years to train as an astronaut.
11. He (<u>knew</u>, known) what tremendous dangers he faced.
12. The space capsule Glenn (<u>rode</u>, ridden) in was named *Friendship 7*.
13. Every precaution was (took, <u>taken</u>) in planning his flight.
14. The rocket stood ready, (<u>its</u>, it's) nose high in the air.
15. At last the rocket (<u>broke</u>, broken) away from the ground in a perfect liftoff.
16. The morning stillness was (broke, <u>broken</u>) by the roar of the engines.
17. Lumps of ice that had (froze, <u>frozen</u>) to the rocket tumbled to the ground.
18. The astronaut (<u>rode</u>, ridden) higher and higher away from our planet.
19. Never before had an American (rode, <u>ridden</u>) as fast or as high.
20. Glenn was puzzled by icy crystals that (<u>froze</u>, frozen) on his spacecraft.
21. The particles that had (froze, <u>frozen</u>) glowed like tiny lights.
22. Glenn (<u>took</u>, taken) many pictures of his flight through space.
23. He sent back reports as he (<u>rode</u>, ridden) in orbit.
24. His observations were (wrote, <u>written</u>) down.
25. Many of the things he (<u>wrote</u>, written) helped later astronauts.
26. Three times he (<u>rode</u>, ridden) around the earth before landing safely in the ocean.
27. After landing, Glenn was (flew, <u>flown</u>) back to the U.S.
28. When Glenn had (rode, <u>ridden</u>) back to the earth he was famous.
29. Enthusiastic cheering (<u>broke</u>, broken) out wherever he appeared.
30. Authors (<u>wrote</u>, written) articles in praise of him.
31. John Glenn had (took, <u>taken</u>) a ride that made history.

Other Things to Do: Pretend you are an astronaut who has taken a flight in space. Using five of the word forms underlined above, write five sentences about your imaginary space flight.

Remembering What We Have Learned

1. On the lines below write a business letter to an imaginary company. Ask for information about their product or service. 🔑 48, 51

   (Answers will vary.)

   _____

   _____

   _____

   _____

   _____

   _____

   _____

   _____

   _____

   _____

   _____

2. Write the names of four fruits in alphabetical order, divide the words into syllables, and place an accent mark after each accented syllable. 🔑 38, 39

   (Answers will vary.)

   _____   _____

   _____   _____

3. Write the abbreviations for a day of the week and a month of the year. 🔑 7d

   (Answers will vary.)

   _____

4. On each line below write a sentence, using one of the words at the left of the line. 🔑 18, 21, 33, 37

   (them, those) _____ **(Answers will vary.)** _____

   (to, too, two) _____

   (wrote, written) _____

   (I, me) _____

Adjectives

Adjectives are words that are used to describe nouns or pronouns. Adjectives tell how something looks, feels, smells, tastes, or sounds. Using adjectives can help what you say and what you write be more interesting.

I. Underline the adjectives in each of the following sentences. (Score: 24)

1. Rubia has an <u>interesting</u> collection of <u>unusual</u> shells.
2. Many of the shells are <u>large</u> and <u>lustrous.</u>
3. These shells are a <u>soft</u>, <u>shiny</u>, <u>cream</u> color.
4. The <u>big</u> shell of the abalone is a <u>sparkling</u> <u>blue</u> color.
5. How <u>smooth</u> and <u>cool</u> it feels!
6. The shell of the conch has a <u>unique</u>, <u>spiral</u> shape.
7. Hold this <u>large</u>, <u>round</u> shell near your ear.
8. It sounds like the <u>loud</u>, <u>roaring</u> ocean.
9. This shell came from a <u>warm</u>, <u>sunny</u> beach in Florida.
10. It is a <u>long</u>, <u>slender</u> shell.
11. Have you seen the <u>dark</u>, <u>rough</u> shell of the oyster?

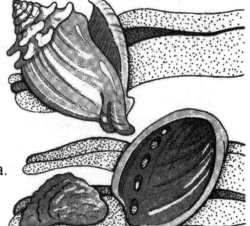

II. After each noun in Column A write two adjectives from Column B that describe the noun. Some of the words in Column B will be used more than once. (Score: 24)

A	(Answers will vary)	B
12. train	**noisy, shrill, huge, loud, rugged**	warm
13. leopard	**clever, fierce, huge, roaring, noisy**	juicy
14. rock	**warm, bright, huge, smooth, hard**	clever
15. mountain	**huge, rugged, bright, smooth**	fierce
16. light bulb	**warm, bright, smooth, glowing**	shrill
17. whistle	**shrill, loud, noisy**	bright
18. glass	**smooth, hard, glowing**	huge
19. orange	**juicy, delicious, sweet**	smooth
20. summer day	**warm, bright, noisy, glowing**	sweet
21. apple	**juicy, smooth, delicious, sweet**	delicious
22. siren	**shrill, roaring, loud, noisy**	roaring
23. fire	**warm, fierce, bright, glowing**	loud
		noisy
		glowing
		hard
		rugged

Using Conjunctions

⊶ 24

A conjunction is often used to combine two short, choppy sentences into one more effective sentence. Notice where the conjunctions are placed in the examples below.

Examples: I hit the ball. Loren ran to catch it.

I hit the ball, *and* Loren ran to catch it.

When I hit the ball, Loren ran to catch it.

Use one of the conjunctions below to combine the short sentences that follow. Try to use a different conjunction in each sentence. (Score: 3 for each sentence) **(Answers will vary.)**

| and | if | while | although | for | where |
| but | as | when | because | after | that |

1. I was in Florida. I learned about saw grass. __**While I was in Florida,**__
   __**I learned about saw grass.**__

2. It is difficult to walk through saw grass. It has sharp edges. __**It is**__
   __**difficult to walk through saw grass because it has sharp edges.**__

3. One edge of the grass is smooth. The other edge is sharp. __**One edge of**__
   __**the grass is smooth, but the other edge is sharp.**__

4. Alligators can live in this grass. They have tough skins. __**Alligators can**__
   __**live in this grass, for they have tough skins.**__

5. People walk through the grass. They may be cut by it. __**If people walk**__
   __**through the grass, they may be cut by it.**__

6. Pools of water are in the saw grass. Alligators live in them. __**Pools of water are**__
   __**in the saw grass, and alligators live in them.**__

7. Underwater plants are in the pools. The alligators eat them. __**The alligators eat**__
   __**the underwater plants that are in the pools.**__

8. People go to this country. They observe the alligators. __**People observe the**__
   __**alligators when they go to this country.**__

9. The grass is tall. Special cars are used to drive through it. __**Because the**__
   __**grass is tall, special cars are used to drive through it.**__

Combining Sentences

⟜ 24

Use one of the following conjunctions to combine the short sentences below. Try to use each word only two times. Conjunctions are not always placed between the sentences. You may need to leave out some words in order to form more effective sentences. (Score: 3 for each sentence) **(Answers will vary.)**

| but | until | that | after | as |
| when | where | which | because | and |

Robert E. Lee

1. Robert E. Lee was born in Virginia. Virginia is a beautiful state. **Robert E. Lee was born in Virginia which is a beautiful state.**

2. He went to school at West Point. He fought in the Mexican War. **After he went to school at West Point, he fought in the Mexican War.**

3. Lee was sent to Texas. He was a young soldier. **Lee was sent to Texas when he was a young soldier.**

4. He let his slaves go free. He did not believe in slavery. **He let his slaves go free because he did not believe in slavery.**

5. Lee loved Virginia. His home was there. **Lee loved Virginia because his home was there.**

6. The War Between the States began. Lee joined the Union army. **When the War Between the States began, Lee joined the Union army.**

7. He left the Union army. He could not fight Virginia. **He left the Union army because he could not fight Virginia.**

8. Lee always rode a gray horse. It was named Traveller. **Lee always rode a gray horse, which was named Traveller.**

9. He led the Confederate army. The war ended. **He led the Confederate army until the war ended.**

10. He returned home. He urged the South to be friendly with the North. **After he returned home, he urged the South to be friendly with the North.**

Separating Sentences

5, 7a, 24c

Rewrite the two paragraphs below, separating the sentences with punctuation marks. Use capital letters where they are needed. (Score: 2 for each sentence)

Whales

A whale may grow to be more than 30 meters (100 feet) long it is the largest animal in the world although the whale lives in the ocean, it breathes air. Sometimes a whale can be located by the tall spout of cloudy vapor that it shoots into the air this spout is the air that the whale is blowing out of its lungs.

A whale may grow to be more than 30 meters (100 feet) long. It is the

largest animal in the world. Although the whale lives in the ocean, it

breathes air. Sometimes a whale can be located by the tall spout of cloudy

vapor that it shoots into the air. This spout is the air that the whale is

blowing out of its lungs.

Whaling

In the 19th century many ships sailed from New England seaports to hunt whales the ships were often away from home for several years. When a whale was spotted, a small boat was lowered into the water the sailors rowed close to the whale they threw a harpoon, or spear, at it the wounded whale dived back under the water and swam rapidly away the boat was pulled along behind the whale until the whale stopped swimming whaling is no longer permitted by most countries.

In the 19th century many ships sailed from New England seaports to hunt

whales. The ships were often away from home for several years. When a

whale was spotted, a small boat was lowered into the water. The sailors

rowed close to the whale. They threw a harpoon, or spear, at it. The

wounded whale dived back under the water and swam rapidly away. The

boat was pulled along behind the whale until the whale stopped swimming.

Whaling is no longer permitted by most countries.

Avoiding Too Many *Ands*   24a, c

The sentences in the paragraphs below contain too many *and*s. Rewrite the paragraphs, using shorter, clearer sentences. (Score: 2 for each correct sentence)

The Banyan Tree

There is an unusual tree that grows in Asia and it is called the banyan tree. This tree grows to be about 30 meters (100 feet) tall and long branches grow down from the tree toward the ground. These branches reach the ground and roots begin to grow from the branches into the ground. The branches form new trunks for the tree and sometimes one tree may have as many as one hundred trunks.

There is an unusual tree that grows in Asia. It is called the banyan tree. This tree grows to be about 30 meters (100 feet) tall. Long branches grow down from the tree toward the ground. These branches reach the ground. Roots begin to grow from the branches into the ground. The branches form new trunks for the tree. Sometimes one tree may have as many as one hundred trunks.

The Crab

The crab lives in many different parts of the ocean and this animal is covered with a shell and as the crab grows larger, its shell becomes too tight. Then the animal sheds its shell and forms a new, soft shell and sometimes you can find an old crab shell lying on the beach and a crab that has a new shell is called a soft-shelled crab and a crab that is in an old shell is called a hard-shelled crab.

The crab lives in many different parts of the ocean. This animal is covered with a shell. As the crab grows larger, its shell becomes too tight. Then the animal sheds its shell and forms a new, soft shell. Sometimes you can find an old crab shell lying on the beach. A crab that has a new shell is called a soft-shelled crab. A crab that is in an old shell is called a hard-shelled crab.

Capitalization and Punctuation

○━ 1–3, 5–7c, 8–12

In the sentences below circle each word that should begin with a capital letter. Underline and place punctuation marks where they are needed.

1. *Five Bushel Farm* is a book by (elizabeth) (coatsworth).
2. The story is about Andrew, Sally, and their friends.
3. Andrew's father was (captain) Patterson.
4. Captain Patterson sailed on a ship named the (fair) (american).
5. Once he sailed to the (caribbean) (sea).
6. Andrew stayed in (philadelphia), (pennsylvania).
7. Didn't he stay with Mr. and Mrs. (b). Titcomb?
8. Mr. and Mrs. Titcomb took Andrew to (maine).
9. They thought that (captain) (patterson) was lost at sea.
10. Andrew said, "(i) know that my father will come back."
11. "How will he know where (i) have gone?" asked Andrew.
12. Was Andrew very sad when he went to (maine)?
13. You'll enjoy reading about his trip in a covered wagon.
14. Soon he became the friend of a man from (germany) named Franz
15. Andrew made a model of his father's ship.
16. Yes, and what a beautiful model it was!
17. Didn't he go to live with (sally), (deborah), and (nannie)?
18. They had a young bear cub named (hannibal).
19. In (may), 1790, Sally's Aunt Esther was married.
20. Sally and Andrew gathered wild strawberries in (june).
21. "Sally, be careful when you play with (hannibal)," said Aunt Nannie.
22. Sally and Andrew met some (american) (indians).
23. Yes, she and Andrew had many good times that summer.
24. Did Andrew's father ever return?
25. How grateful Captain Patterson was!
26. (he) told Andrew about his long trip to (cuba).
27. Sally said, "(let) Andrew stay here awhile, Captain Patterson."
28. Part of (five) (bushel) (farm) tells about a house-raising.
29. Neighbors came to build a house for Sally, Nannie, and Eben.
30. Has (elizabeth) (coatsworth) written any other books?
31. Yes, she wrote (away) (goes) (sally).
32. Can we find these books in the library?

Other Things to Do: Write three direct quotations. Make one quotation a statement, one a question, and one an exclamation.

Writing Descriptions   ☞ 23

Skillful descriptions help to express thoughts clearly and interestingly. Choose adjectives carefully as you write descriptions; be sure they add necessary information. Decide which sentence in the examples is the most effective description.

Examples: Things were on the table.

The old table was painted blue and was piled with some pans.

The wobbly table sagged under a pile of battered pans.

I.   Write a descriptive sentence about each subject listed below. (Score: 25)

1. (A bicycle) _____ **(Answers will vary.)** _____

_____

2. (A rainy day) _____

_____

3. (A lemon) _____

_____

4. (A hot sidewalk) _____

_____

5. (Yourself) _____

_____

II.   Write a paragraph describing what you see, hear, and smell when you enter a supermarket. (Score: 25)

(Answers will vary.)

_____

_____

_____

_____

_____

_____

_____

_____

Using Antonyms

I. Write an antonym for each word listed below. **(Answers will vary.)**

Example: always _____*never*_____

1.	before	**after**	13.	seldom	**often**
2.	bought	**sold**	14.	prompt	**tardy**
3.	clumsy	**graceful**	15.	huge	**tiny**
4.	disappear	**appear**	16.	rude	**polite**
5.	large	**small**	17.	soft	**hard**
6.	pretty	**ugly**	18.	win	**lose**
7.	happy	**sad**	19.	glossy	**dull**
8.	thin	**fat**	20.	long	**short**
9.	sick	**well**	21.	loose	**tight**
10.	first	**last**	22.	sunny	**cloudy**
11.	strong	**weak**	23.	heavy	**light**
12.	reckless	**careful**	24.	ancient	**new**

II. Fill in the blank with an antonym of the word in parentheses. **(Answers will vary.)**

25. (man)   There is a poem about a _____**woman**_____ named Barbara Frietchie.

26. (glad)   She was _____**sad**_____ when the War Between the States began.

27. (night)   One _____**day**_____ the Confederate army came into her town.

28. (behind)   They saw a United States flag _____**before**_____ Barbara's house.

29. (safe)   It might be _____**dangerous**_____ to show this flag.

30. (ashamed)   But Barbara was _____**proud**_____ of her country's flag.

31. (give)   She would not let the soldiers _____**take**_____ it away.

32. (cowardly)   The soldiers admired this _____**brave**_____ woman.

33. (friend)   She was their _____**enemy**_____ , but she was brave.

34. (entered)   The soldiers soon _____**left**_____ the town.

Using Synonyms

I. Write a synonym for each of the words below. **(Answers will vary.)**

Example: ancient ___*old*___

1.	say	speak	14.	impolite	rude
2.	glad	happy	15.	part	piece
3.	aid	help	16.	damp	wet
4.	begin	start	17.	afraid	frightened
5.	big	large	18.	talk	speak
6.	sick	ill	19.	sure	certain
7.	shut	close	20.	remained	stayed
8.	walk	stroll	21.	bold	brave
9.	cry	weep	22.	funny	amusing
10.	huge	enormous	23.	look	see
11.	clumsy	awkward	24.	fly	soar
12.	throw	toss	25.	genuine	real
13.	search	hunt	26.	difficult	hard

II. Write a synonym for the word in parentheses in each blank. **(Answers will vary.)**

27. Cacao trees grow in (bright) ___sunny___ South America.

28. These trees are planted in (orderly) ___neat___ rows.

29. They grow (below) ___under___ taller trees that give them shade.

30. (Odd) ___Different___ looking pods grow from the tree trunk and stems.

31. Workers (seize) ___grasp___ the pod and cut it from the tree.

32. Sharp knives are used to (cut) ___slash___ open the pod.

33. Inside the pod there are many (small) ___little___ seeds.

34. Many people (like) ___enjoy___ cocoa, which is made from the seeds.

Other Things to Do: Write an antonym for ten of the words in the list above.

Plurals, Possessives, and Contractions
🔑 15, 16, 22

I. Write the plural forms of the following nouns.

1.	wolf	**wolves**	8.	penny	**pennies**
2.	farm	**farms**	9.	half	**halves**
3.	wish	**wishes**	10.	inch	**inches**
4.	life	**lives**	11.	deer	**deer**
5.	city	**cities**	12.	boat	**boats**
6.	foot	**feet**	13.	woman	**women**
7.	donkey	**donkeys**	14.	pencil	**pencils**

II. Write the possessive forms of the nouns below.

15.	Charles	**Charles's**	21.	Sheri	**Sheri's**
16.	Canadian	**Canadian's**	22.	boy	**boy's**
17.	pilots	**pilots'**	23.	baby	**baby's**
18.	pioneers	**pioneers'**	24.	officer	**officer's**
19.	sheep	**sheep's**	25.	monkeys	**monkeys'**
20.	children	**children's**	26.	airplanes	**airplanes'**

III. Write the contractions of the words listed below.

27.	had not	**hadn't**	34.	they will	**they'll**
28.	could not	**couldn't**	35.	were not	**weren't**
29.	he is	**he's**	36.	do not	**don't**
30.	did not	**didn't**	37.	she is	**she's**
31.	you are	**you're**	38.	you are	**you're**
32.	does not	**doesn't**	39.	it is	**it's**
33.	she will	**she'll**	40.	you have	**you've**

Choosing Homophones

When two words sound alike but have different spellings and meanings, be sure to use the one that fits the meaning of the sentence. In each of the following sentences underline the correct homophones in parentheses.

Traveling Through Space

1. Do you (no, <u>know</u>) what happens when a candle burns in a sealed jar?
2. Soon (<u>there</u>, their, they're) is no oxygen left in the jar.
3. The flame goes out when (<u>there</u>, their) is (<u>no</u>, know) oxygen.
4. Oxygen is (won, <u>one</u>) element that fuel needs in order to burn.
5. People (new, <u>knew</u>) long ago that there is no oxygen outside the earth's atmosphere.
6. Perhaps some of (<u>your</u>, you're) books tell about spacecraft.
7. These spacecraft carry (there, <u>their</u>, they're) own oxygen.
8. The spacecraft carries the oxygen in (it's, <u>its</u>) (<u>tail</u>, tale).
9. The oxygen is cooled until (<u>it's</u>, its) a pale (blew, <u>blue</u>) liquid.
10. This liquid oxygen does (knot, <u>not</u>) take up much space in the rocket.
11. It is (<u>sent</u>, cent) through the spacecraft and mixed with fuel.
12. The mixture makes a (grate, <u>great</u>) hot flame that moves the spacecraft.
13. A trip to another planet would take much longer than a (<u>week</u>, weak).
14. You can (sea, <u>see</u>) that a great deal of fuel would be needed.
15. Many fuels would take up (<u>too</u>, to) much space in a rocket.
16. A spacecraft cannot carry enough gasoline (<u>to</u>, too) fly to another planet.
17. What fuel could carry people (<u>through</u>, threw) space?
18. There are some people (who's, <u>whose</u>) lives are spent working on spacecraft.
19. Perhaps (<u>they're</u>, their) trying to find (sum, <u>some</u>) new kind of fuel.
20. Would you like to (<u>meet</u>, meat) a person (<u>who's</u>, whose) a scientist?
21. Some of (<u>your</u>, you're) stories are about other planets.
22. There are many (tails, <u>tales</u>) about other planets.
23. We know that (their, <u>they're</u>) not like the planet Earth where we live.
24. If (<u>you're</u>, your) ever on another planet, you'll see interesting things.
25. The (<u>sun</u>, son) does not make some of the planets very warm.
26. There would be no (<u>seas</u>, sees) and only (<u>bare</u>, bear) land on others.
27. Do you know anyone (whose, <u>who's</u>) planning to be a scientist?

Unnecessary Words

⚓ 32

Draw a line through all unnecessary words in the following sentences.

Paul Bunyan

1. Do you know where Paul Bunyan lived ~~at~~?
2. This ~~here~~ imaginary man was a giant who lived in the northern woods.
3. Paul ~~he~~ was a great lumberjack.
4. America has ~~got~~ many legends about this giant.
5. The legends ~~they~~ tell about his amazing deeds.
6. Once Paul ~~went and~~ got a small pine tree.
7. Didn't he use that ~~there~~ tree to comb his beard?
8. Do you know where the Mississippi River is ~~at~~?
9. Once the Mississippi ~~it~~ was six rivers instead of one.
10. Paul wanted to ~~go~~ take some logs to the Mississippi.
11. Where were the logs going ~~to~~?
12. Paul ~~he~~ wanted to float them down the river to New Orleans.
13. But the logs ~~they~~ got on the wrong Mississippi.
14. Where do you suppose the logs floated ~~to~~?
15. That ~~there~~ river took the logs to New Mexico.
16. "I have ~~got~~ an idea," said Paul Bunyan.
17. He ~~went and~~ dug a new Mississippi River.
18. Once a mosquito took Paul's cow off ~~of~~ the ground.
19. Then the mosquito ~~it~~ flew away with the cow.
20. These ~~here~~ mosquitoes were very large insects.
21. Paul ~~he~~ had an ox named Babe.
22. This ~~here~~ ox was dark blue and very large.
23. Babe could ~~go and~~ haul a whole forest of logs.
24. Babe was thirsty, so Paul ~~went and~~ dug the Great Lakes.
25. Once the ox lost a shoe off ~~of~~ its foot.
26. A blacksmith had to ~~go~~ bring a new shoe for the ox.
27. The shoe ~~it~~ was a very heavy thing to carry.
28. That ~~there~~ man sank into solid rock up to his knees.
29. Paul had ~~got~~ a huge frying pan on which pancakes were cooked.
30. "~~Go~~ bring some slabs of bacon," Paul told some workers.
31. These ~~here~~ slabs of bacon were tied to the workers' feet.
32. Then the workers ~~went and~~ skated all over the pan.
33. The workers ~~they~~ did this to grease the pan for pancakes.

Double Negatives

Words such as *no, not, nothing, none, never, hardly,* and *scarcely* are called *negative words.* Only one negative word should be used to tell about one thing.

In each sentence below underline the proper word form in parentheses.

An Animal in Armor

1. There isn't (no, any) animal much stranger looking than the armadillo.
2. These animals aren't (ever, never) found in cold climates.
3. They don't live (nowhere, anywhere) except in warm parts of the world.
4. Don't (none, any) of them live in South America?
5. In the U.S. armadillos are hardly (ever, never) seen north of Texas.
6. Haven't you (ever, never) heard they live underground?
7. They hardly (ever, never) come out during the day.
8. They (can't, can) hardly see at all.
9. But it (is, isn't) no helpless animal.
10. Don't (none, any) of them roll up into small balls?
11. They don't leave (nothing, anything) showing but a hard shell.
12. Haven't you (ever, never) seen the shell of an armadillo?
13. A needle wouldn't (ever, never) go through its shell.
14. Other animals (can, can't) scarcely do anything to harm it.
15. You (can't, can) hardly see any skin on its back or sides.
16. There is not (nothing, anything) much sharper than its claws.
17. There isn't (nothing, anything) that helps an armadillo more than its claws.
18. You (wouldn't, would) hardly believe how fast it can dig a hole.
19. It (could, couldn't) scarcely find a better hiding place.
20. The armadillo's legs aren't (any, no) more than a few inches long.
21. You would think it couldn't (never, ever) run fast.
22. But you haven't (ever, never) seen an animal run much faster.
23. Aren't (any, none) of them good swimmers?
24. The armadillo (is, isn't) no brave animal.
25. It isn't eager to meet (any, no) strangers.
26. Armadillos hardly (ever, never) grow more than one meter (3 feet) long.
27. One kind of armadillo (is, isn't) no more than 15 centimeters (6 inches) long.

Using *Himself, Themselves, Their,* and *There*   ⚷ 18e, 37

Underline the proper word form in parentheses to complete each of the following sentences.

Raising Cattle in the Early Days

1.   (There, Their) were few people living in Texas before the Civil War.
2.   People often built (there, their) homes far from each other.
3.   Some people, like Joe Downs, lived by (theirselves, themselves) on ranches.
4.   The people usually had many head of cattle on (there, their) ranches.
5.   Joe often worked on the ranch all day by (himself, hisself).
6.   Usually (their, there) were no fences surrounding a ranch.
7.   The cattle could find food and water by (theirselves, themselves).
8.   During the Civil War many people left (their, there) ranches to join the army.
9.   They found (theirselves, themselves) far from home.
10. The cattle took care of (themselves, theirselves) in Texas.
11. (Their, There) was plenty of grass for them to eat.
12. After the war, ranchers found thousands of cattle on (their, there) land.
13. (There, Their) ranches weren't large enough for so many cattle.
14. But (their, there) was no place nearby to sell the cattle.
15. They knew that (there, their) was a need for cattle in the North.
16. Some of the ranchers decided to take (there, their) cattle to Kansas.
17. Joe could not move a thousand cattle by (hisself, himself).
18. (There, Their) were people who could be hired to help with the work.
19. Some ranchers took (their, there) cattle on the Chisholm Trail to Kansas.
20. They found (theirselves, themselves) working hard on the trip.
21. The ranchers were away from (their, there) homes for many weeks.
22. (There, Their) large herd of cattle walked about 16 kilometers (10 miles) a day.
23. (Their, There) was little time to rest on a cattle drive.
24. If (there, their) was a storm, the cattle might run away.
25. They could swim across a river by (theirselves, themselves).
26. But (their, there) was often trouble at a very deep river.
27. At night Joe Downs would often sing to (hisself, himself).
28. Music helped the workers keep (their, there) cattle quiet.
29. At night they sat around a campfire and ate (their, there) dinner.
30. At last they drove (there, their) cattle into Abilene, Kansas.
31. The cattle were sold, and the workers could finally enjoy (theirselves, themselves).
32. Joe could amuse (himself, hisself) or rest for a few days.
33. Then the ranchers, like Joe Downs, returned to (there, their) homes in Texas.

Choosing Proper Word Forms

○━ 18e, 21, 37

Practice choosing proper word forms, verb forms, and homophones. Underline the proper word form in parentheses in each sentence below. (Score: 1 for each sentence)

An Early American Artist

1. John Audubon was an artist (whose, who's) paintings of birds are well known.

2. He often (drew, drawn) pictures when he was a boy.

3. John was a boy (whose, who's) early years were spent in France.

4. He (became, become) interested in the birds that he saw.

5. When he saw a bird, he would (lay, lie) on the ground near it.

6. He (wood, would) study the bird carefully.

7. Pictures of that bird were (drew, drawn) from memory after he went home.

8. "You should study (your, you're) school lessons," his parents said.

9. His parents thought he spent (to, too, two) much time drawing.

10. They decided to send (there, their) son to America.

11. John went to Pennsylvania by (himself, hisself) in 1803.

12. Soon he had (became, become) known as an artist.

13. John (drew; drawn) pictures of all the birds he saw.

14. Before long he had (fell, fallen) in love and was married.

15. He and his wife went to Kentucky by (themselves, theirselves).

16. Sometimes they had little food in (there, their) home.

17. His wife (became, become) a teacher and earned some money.

18. (There, Their) was an idea forming in John's mind.

19. He (became, become) more and more interested in his drawing.

20. He wanted (to, too, two) draw pictures of every bird in North America.

21. The pictures would be published in a book after they were (drew, drawn).

22. John made many trips through the wilderness by (hisself, himself).

23. One trip was to Louisiana, where he (drew, drawn) pictures of the native birds.

24. Sometimes he (drew, drawn) portraits of people to earn extra money.

25. He often worked late at night until he finally (fell, fallen) asleep.

26. At last his stack of drawings had (became, become) very large.

27. He had (drew, drawn) pictures of hundreds of birds.

28. Didn't he go to England (to, too, two) have his pictures published?

29. Many people bought the books of pictures he had (drew, drawn).

30. Many of the pictures John (drew, drawn) are in museums.

Remembering What We Have Learned

1. Use conjunctions to write three sentences. Use *and* in the first sentence, *but* in the second, and *when* in the third. ⚷ 24

    (Answers will vary.)

    _____

    _____

2. Write four sentences to describe your favorite sport. Use at least two adjectives in each sentence. ⚷ 23

    (Answers will vary.)

    _____

    _____

    _____

    _____

3. On the line below write two words that are synonyms. ⚷ 35

    (Answers will vary.)

    _____

4. On the line below write two words that are antonyms. ⚷ 36

    (Answers will vary.)

    _____

5. On each line write a sentence, using one of the words in parentheses at the left of the line. ⚷ 21, 34, 37

    (their, there) _____ **(Answers will vary.)** _____

    (to, too, two) _____

    (your, you're) _____

    (whose, who's) _____

    (became, become) _____

    (fell, fallen) _____

    (drew, drawn) _____

    (hardly, scarcely) _____

Writing Stories

Plan a story about a funny, frightening, or surprising incident. Limit your story to only one incident. Plan to use at least two direct quotations in your story. Write the title and the story on the lines below. (Score: 50)

(Answers will vary.)

Outlining

Information about the life of Harriet Tubman is given below. Use the information to outline two paragraphs about this brave woman. In the outline for the first paragraph list information about her childhood and escape to freedom. In the outline for the second paragraph include information about her life after she left the South. (Score: 20)

Born a slave in Dorchester County, Maryland
Worked as a maid, woodcutter, and field hand
Escaped to Philadelphia in 1849
Worked for the "Underground Railroad"
Helped more than 300 slaves escape to freedom
Bought a small farm in Auburn, New York
Served as a spy for the Union army
Used her farm as a home for orphans

(Answers will vary.)   **Harriet Tubman**

I. Early life

    A. Born a slave in Dorchester County, Maryland

    B. Worked as a maid, woodcutter, and field hand

    C. Escaped to Philadelphia in 1849

II. Life after leaving the South

    A. Worked for the "Underground Railroad"

    B. Helped more than 300 slaves escape to freedom

    C. Bought a small farm in Auburn, New York

    D. Served as a spy for the Union army

    E. Used her farm as a home for orphans

Other Things to Do: Write the two paragraphs about Harriet Tubman that you outlined above. Write an interesting title for your paragraphs.

Writing Reports

🔑 43, 45

A report tells about something you have seen, done, or read. A report should begin with an interesting topic sentence. Each sentence of the report should give information about the topic. Outlining the report before it is written helps you decide what ideas you will use and the order in which you will write them.

Choose one of the topics listed below. On another sheet of paper make an outline for a report about the topic you chose. Write the report on the lines below. (Score: 50)

Working with clay   An unsuccessful experiment

How to make a skateboard   My favorite sport

My favorite book   Cars of the future

(Answers will vary.)

Other Things to Do: Make an outline for a report that tells about a book you have read. Then ask your teacher to let you give the report orally.

Combining Sentences

🔑 24, 41e

Rewrite each pair of sentences below to make one better sentence. You may wish to use conjunctions such as: *where, because, but, since, and,* and *which*. (Score: 3 for each sentence correctly written)

The Sea Horse

1. Rebecca went to the aquarium. She saw an interesting fish. **(Answers will vary.)**

   Rebecca went to the aquarium, where she saw an interesting fish.

2. ·It is called a sea horse. Its head looks like a horse's head._____

   It is called a sea horse because its head looks like a horse's head.

3. This fish cannot fight. It is fairly safe from its enemies._____

   This fish cannot fight, but it is fairly safe from its enemies.

4. It looks like seaweed. A sea horse is hard to see._____

   Because it looks like seaweed, a sea horse is hard to see.

5. It wraps its tail around a seaweed. It clings to the plant._____

   It wraps its tail around a seaweed and clings to the plant.

6. The sea horse sucks food into its mouth. Its mouth is shaped like a pipe._____

   The sea horse sucks food into its mouth, which is shaped like a pipe.

7. One species of sea horse lives in the Atlantic Ocean. It is only 15 centimeters (6

   inches) long. **One species of sea horse that is only 15 centimeters**

   (6 inches) long lives in the Atlantic Ocean.

Punctuation and Capitalization

🔑 1–3, 5–8, 10–12

Underline each word that should begin with a capital letter in the sentences below. Place punctuation marks where they are needed.

Traffic in the Air

1. Ted R. Fleming works as an aircraft controller in phoenix, arizona.
2. Isn't that a very difficult job?
3. Yes, an aircraft controller has to make important decisions quickly.
4. A controller's instructions help pilots take off and land planes safely.
5. Controllers use radios, computers, and radar to direct aircraft traffic.
6. Ted works at the sky harbor international airport in phoenix.
7. he works with 50 other controllers in a large, dark room.
8. A radarscope sits on the top of each controller's desk.
9. Ted often sees five, ten, or fifteen signals on the radarscope.
10. each signal represents an aircraft in flight.
11. Data tags for each aircraft are shown on a computer terminal.
12. These tags show each plane's flight number and destination.
13. ted talks to the aircraft pilots through a telephone headset.
14. What do Ted and the pilots say to each other?
15. A pilot might say, "this is Flight 256. Am I cleared for landing?"
16. Ted might answer, "yes, Flight 256, on runway 2."
17. Where did Ted learn to be an aircraft controller?
18. He went to the Federal Aviation Academy in oklahoma city.
19. He trained for three more years at the Sky Harbor International Airport.
20. Air traffic control hasn't always been as it is today.
21. years ago people waved flags on runways to show pilots where to land their planes.
22. aircraft traffic was controlled by cities and towns.
23. On july 6, 1936, the federal government took charge of air traffic control.
24. The federal Aviation Administration operates all aircraft control centers.
25. The united states has 22 aircraft control centers.
26. Three are in chicago, washington, D.C., and indianapolis.
27. Are there european control centers for international flights?
28. creighton peet has written an interesting book about aircraft controllers.
29. *eye on the sky* is the title of the book.

Using *In, Into, These, Those,* and *Them*

31, 33

Use *into* to tell about movement from the outside to the inside of something. Use *in* to refer only to the inside of something.

These points out a group of persons or things near the speaker. *Those* points out a group of persons or things not near the speaker. *Them* refers to two or more persons or things and is not used to point out something.

In each sentence below underline the proper word form in parentheses.

1. Kim was (in, into) the house when Lucia called her.
2. Lucia went (in, into) the house to find her.
3. (Those, Them) children outside are going swimming.
4. Get (into, in) the car and come with us.
5. I've been painting (those, them) pictures that are on the table.
6. (These, Those) paintbrushes in my hand will have to be cleaned.
7. Kim went (in, into) the kitchen to clean the brushes.
8. I'll put them (into, in) the box where I keep them.
9. Please tell (those, them) that I'll be out soon.
10. It's so hot it will feel good to be (into, in) the water.
11. Lucia went outside and got (into, in) the car.
12. The swimming pool was (into, in) the park.
13. The swimmers went (into, in) the bathhouse to take a shower.
14. (These, Them) showers help to keep the water in the pool clean.
15. Do I need to wear a bathing cap (into, in) the pool?
16. Will you dive (in, into) the water?
17. How good it feels to be (in, into) the water!
18. Look at (those, these) people diving from the diving board over there.
19. It is not easy to make (those, them) swan dives.
20. (Them, Those) lifeguards sometimes give swimming lessons.
21. Watch (these, those) swimmers here at the side of the pool.
22. They are floating with their faces (in, into) the water.
23. Have you seen anyone swim like (those, these) people over there?
24. They swim (into, in) the water while on their backs.
25. (Them, Those) people are doing the backstroke.
26. (These, Those) girls and boys next to me are splashing each other.
27. (Them, Those) lifeguards are telling them to stop.
28. It's time for us to go (into, in) the locker room to change our clothes.
29. You may put your wet bathing suit (in, into) my plastic bag.

Using Proper Word Forms   ☛ 20, 21, 26, 27, 31, 37

In each sentence below underline the proper word form in parentheses.

The Northern Lights

1. Does (you're, <u>your</u>) book about Alaska describe the northern lights?
2. Many people (<u>haven't</u>, hasn't) seen this interesting sight.
3. (Your, <u>You're</u>) amazed if you ever see these lights.
4. (Their, <u>They're</u>, There) often seen in the sky at night in the far north.
5. The northern lights (is, <u>are</u>) called *aurora borealis.*
6. These lights (<u>are</u>, is) often seen in September and March.
7. (<u>It's</u>, Its) not known for certain what causes them.
8. They have (became, <u>become</u>) famous all over the world.
9. Often a noise is heard before the lights have (<u>begun</u>, began).
10. The sound (are, <u>is</u>) something like the rustling of silk.
11. Then the dark sky is (broke, <u>broken</u>) by the shining lights.
12. It looks as though someone (<u>threw</u>, thrown) Roman candles into the air.
13. (<u>Aren't</u>, Isn't) the lights sometimes like a fan in the sky?
14. The sky may look as though (<u>there</u>, their) are searchlights turned on.
15. Sometimes the lights last for only a minute or (to, <u>two</u>, too).
16. Sometimes they may be seen (<u>in</u>, into) the sky for several hours.
17. (<u>Isn't</u>, Aren't) green the most common color seen in the lights?
18. Many people have (wrote, <u>written</u>) about this beautiful sight.
19. People (<u>became</u>, become) interested in the lights years ago.
20. They wanted to (<u>learn</u>, teach) what caused the lights.
21. Experiments could (learn, <u>teach</u>) them many interesting things.
22. A scientist uses a glass tube that has a stopper in (it's, <u>its</u>) top.
23. Most of the air is (drew, <u>drawn</u>) out of the tube.
24. Soon the tube (haven't, <u>hasn't</u>) much air left in it.
25. Then electricity is passed (threw, <u>through</u>) the tube.
26. Nothing else is put (in, <u>into</u>) the tube.
27. Suddenly there (<u>are</u>, is) lights inside the tube.
28. It looks as though the northern lights have (flew, <u>flown</u>) into the tube.
29. Scientists believe that it takes electricity (<u>to</u>, too) make the northern lights.
30. (Whose, <u>Who's</u>) book tells about this experiment?
31. (Can, <u>May</u>) I borrow it to read about the experiment?
32. (Are, <u>Is</u>) there a copy of the book in the library?

Reviewing Sentences

7a, 8a, 9a, 41a–d

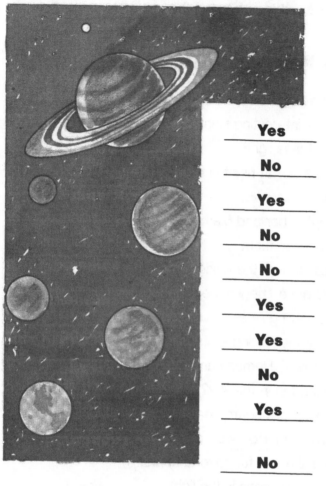

I. Write *Yes* before each group of words that is a sentence. Write *No* before each group of words that is not a sentence. (Score: 10)

Planets That Circle the Sun

Yes	1.	Most people are curious about planets
No	2.	Nine planets circling the sun
Yes	3.	What are the faraway planets like
No	4.	Not very much like Earth
No	5.	The planet Mercury closest to the sun
Yes	6.	People wouldn't want to visit Mercury
Yes	7.	One side of the planet is burning hot
No	8.	The other side freezing cold
Yes	9.	We know very little about the planet Venus
No	10.	Cannot see through its thick clouds.

II. Put the correct punctuation mark at the end of each sentence. (Score: 14)

11. What a beautiful planet Mars is **!**
12. Doesn't it have a reddish color **?**
13. Scientists believe that crude plants could grow on Mars **.**
14. How cold we would be if we visited there **!**
15. Would space suits keep us warm **?**
16. Jupiter is the largest planet that is known **.**
17. Imagine a planet almost 1,400 times larger than Earth **. (or !)**
18. If there is air on Jupiter, it is probably frozen **.**
19. Have you ever looked at Saturn through a large telescope **?**
20. What a beautiful sight it is **!**
21. This planet has beautiful rings around it **.**
22. Do you know the names of some other planets **?**
23. Some other planets are Uranus, Neptune, Pluto, and Earth **.**
24. Scientists think many of these planets except Earth are very cold **.**

Reviewing Paragraphs   ⊶ 24, 41e, 44

I. Rewrite the following "run-on" sentence to make four more effective sentences. Write the sentences in paragraph form. (Score: 20—5 for each sentence)

How amazing a globefish is it can swell its spine-covered body until it is shaped like a large ball and the spines make the fish look like a porcupine and other fish would have a hard time trying to eat this large ball of spines.   **(Answers will vary.)**

How amazing a globefish is! It can swell its spine-covered body until it is

shaped like a large ball. The spines make the fish look like a porcupine.

Other fish would have a hard time trying to eat this large ball of spines.

II. Rewrite the following short, choppy sentences to make five longer, more interesting sentences. Use conjunctions where they are needed. Write a title for the paragraph. (Score: 30—5 for the title and 5 for each sentence)

There are some fish called rays. They are very unusual. Their eyes are on top of their bodies. Their mouths are under the bodies. One kind of ray has a long tail. The tail has spikes on it. The ray uses its tail. It uses the tail to fight its enemies. Skin divers try to avoid the giant ray. It is very dangerous.   **(Answers will vary.)**

Rays

There are some fish called rays that are very unusual. Their eyes are on

top of their bodies. One kind of ray has a long tail that has spikes on it. The

ray uses its tail to fight its enemies. Skin divers try to avoid the giant ray

because it is very dangerous.

Capitalization and Punctuation

🗝 1–3, 5–12

Underline each word that should begin with a capital letter. Place punctuation marks where they are needed. (Score: 1 for each word correctly underlined and 1 for each punctuation mark correctly placed)

A Book About a Horse

1. *justin morgan had a horse* is a very interesting book.
2. Its author is marguerite henry.
3. I read this book on monday, august 19.
4. Justin and Joel walked to springfield, massachusetts.
5. Justin got two horses named ebenezer and little bub.
6. Then he and Joel took the horses to randolph, vermont.
7. Couldn't they travel in Vermont on sunday?
8. No, a law would not allow people to travel on that day.
9. People said, "little bub is too small to be worth much."
10. But how Joel loved the frisky, quick pony!
11. He wanted the horse as a gift for christmas.
12. But Little Bub was Justin's horse.
13. Yes, but one day the horse was sold.
14. "Perhaps i can buy the horse," said Joel to himself.
15. Joel didn't have enough money to buy Justin's horse.
16. Didn't someone take Little Bub from randolph?
17. Weeks, months, and years went by.
18. On june 18, 1812, the united states declared war.
19. this was the War of 1812, which was fought against england.
20. The book tells about Joel's adventures with the american army.
21. Was he at the battle near lake champlain?
22. Yes, he thought that Little Bub might be in the battle.
23. Joel hoped the horse would be safe.
24. In december, 1814, a treaty of peace was signed.
25. "I still believe that i'll find Little Bub," said Joel.
26. one cold, bitter day in winter, he saw the horse.
27. "At last i can buy him," said Joel.
28. mr. chase said, "i'll lend you the money, Joel."
29. didn't president monroe ride the horse one day?
30. today, Morgan horses are famous all over the united states.
31. They're known for their strength and speed.

Word-Study Review   ⚷ 14–17, 19, 22

I. Draw one line under each noun, two lines under each pronoun, and a circle around each verb. (Score: 20)

1. Many interesting animals (live) in Australia.

2. Koalas (swing) in the tall trees there.

3. Ho-san (told) us about these animals.

4. We also (saw) pictures of them.

5. They seldom (walk) in the forest.

6. The animals (sleep) most of the day.

II. Write the plural form of the word in parentheses.

7. (life) Koalas lead very easy _____**lives**_____ .

8. (leaf) They eat _____**leaves**_____ from the trees in which they live.

9. (foot) The koala uses its _____**feet**_____ to hold onto the branches.

10. (lunch) Koalas do not hunt for their _____**lunches**_____ .

11. (enemy) This animal has few _____**enemies**_____ .

III. Write the possessive form of the word in parentheses.

12. (mothers) The young are carried in their _____**mothers'**_____ pouches.

13. (cub) The _____**cub's**_____ mother may later carry it on her back.

14. (people) Are these animals ever _____**people's**_____ pets?

15. (koala) A _____**koala's**_____ height is about 1/2 meter (2 feet).

IV. Write the contraction of the two words in parentheses.

16. (Are not) _____**Aren't**_____ koalas sometimes called teddy bears?

17. (Is not) _____**Isn't**_____ that a strange name for an animal that's not a bear?

18. (It is) _____**It's**_____ related to the opossum instead of the bear.

19. (they will) Is it true that _____**they'll**_____ drink no water?

20. (That is) _____**That's**_____ what I have read.

Word-Study Review   👕 35, 36, 37

I. Underline the correct homophone in parentheses.

1. In 1800 there were (know, <u>no</u>) trains in the United States.
2. Horatio Allen was (<u>sent</u>, scent) to England in 1828.
3. Didn't he (<u>buy</u>, by) a train engine?
4. It made (won, <u>one</u>) trip before it broke.
5. Do you (no, <u>know</u>) how fast this train went?
6. It traveled at the (<u>great</u>, grate) speed of 16 kilometers (10 miles) an hour.
7. But the engine was (<u>too</u>, to) heavy (<u>to</u>, too) run on wooden tracks.
8. (<u>New</u>, Knew) iron tracks were put over the wooden tracks.
9. The train's wheels (through, <u>threw</u>) out sparks as it went (<u>by</u>, buy).

II. Fill the blank with a synonym of the word in parentheses. **(Answers will vary.)**

10. (frightened) Most people were _____**afraid**_____ of a large, loud train.

11. (enjoyed) They _____**liked**_____ traveling in a quiet stagecoach.

12. (bright) One _____**sunny**_____ day there was a race near Baltimore.

13. (awkward) The _____**clumsy**_____ train raced a fast horse.

14. (grasped) The engineer _____**seized**_____ large pieces of wood.

15. (tossed) The wood was _____**thrown**_____ on the blazing fire.

16. (hard) It was _____**difficult**_____ for the train to go faster.

17. (large) But slowly the _____**huge**_____ engine moved ahead of the horse.

18. (piece) Then suddenly a _____**part**_____ of the engine broke.

III. Fill the blank with an antonym of the word in parentheses. **(Answers will vary.)**

19. (soft) With a _____**loud**_____ crash the train stopped running.

20. (slowly) The horse _____**quickly**_____ caught up to the train.

21. (lost) The horse easily _____**won**_____ the race.

22. (often) People had _____**seldom**_____ seen such an exciting race.

23. (before) How they laughed at trains _____**after**_____ this race!

24. (sell) Few people would _____**buy**_____ tickets to ride on one.

Reviewing the Use of Pronouns

In each sentence below underline the proper word forms in parentheses.

Learning About Oxygen

1. (Raul and I, Me and Raul) learned many things about air.
2. Raul had learned several things about air by (hisself, himself).
3. He showed (we, us) a book he had read about air.
4. Lori told (him and me, he and I) that oxygen is found in air.
5. (He, Him) and (me, I) knew that there are many gases in the air.
6. It was (I, me) who asked whether oxygen is a gas.
7. Lori told (us, we) that oxygen is a gas found in the air.
8. She told (they, them) that nitrogen is another gas found in the air.
9. It was (she, her) who said that nothing alive could live without oxygen.
10. Do you see (those, them, these) trees and animals outside?
11. All of (them, those) things need oxygen to live.
12. (We, Us) knew that we breathe the oxygen in the air.
13. Raul asked (she, her) and (me, I) what oxygen is like.
14. (She, Her) and (me, I) knew that oxygen cannot be seen.
15. It was (I, me) who said that oxygen has no color or odor.
16. But Lori told (he, him) and (me, I) that the gas is everywhere.
17. (He, Him) and (them, they) knew that there is oxygen in water and plants.
18. It was (he, him) who said that soil also contains oxygen.
19. Raul asked (her, she) and (I, me) whether oxygen is the only gas in the air.
20. It was (we, us) who said that many other gases mix with oxygen in the air.
21. (We, Us) knew that oxygen can be harmful to certain things.
22. (I and she, She and I) asked Raul whether he knew what causes metal to rust.
23. (Us, We) have all seen rusty nails and other types of metal.
24. It was (he, him) who said that oxygen causes rust on metal.
25. (Her and me, She and I) said that oxygen mixes with the iron in the metal.
26. When (these, them) two things mix, rust is formed.
27. (Raul and I, Me and Raul) knew that steel bridges are always painted.
28. (Us, We) knew that the paint keeps the bridge from rusting.
29. (He, Him) and (me, I) asked how paint can stop rust.
30. "Bridges don't rust by (theirselves, themselves)," said Lori.
31. It was (she, her) who said that paint protects the steel from oxygen.
32. "Keeping oxygen from the steel prevents rust," she told (us, we).
33. It was (us, we) who said that steel in buildings is also painted.

Reviewing Proper Word Forms

In each sentence below underline the proper word form in parentheses.

Death Valley

1. (There, Their) is a desert in California called Death Valley.
2. Death Valley (lies, lays) 85 meters (282 feet) below sea level.
3. The land there is (to, too, two) dry for people to farm.
4. There (is, are) tall mountains surrounding Death Valley.
5. Because of these mountains, clouds (don't, doesn't) go over the valley.
6. Very little rain has (fell, fallen) there.
7. No rivers or lakes (is, are) in Death Valley.
8. Wild burros have (ran, run) in this desert for years.
9. A burro (doesn't, don't) need to drink much water.
10. The land (is, are) too dry for trees to grow.
11. Early settlers going to California (came, come) across this desert.
12. (Them, Those) early pioneers (ridden, rode) in wagons.
13. They (knew, known) how dangerous it was to cross the valley.
14. People had told (them, these) about the terrible desert.
15. The water the people (drank, drunk) had to be carried with them.
16. They (took, taken) barrels filled with water.
17. They (sat, set) the barrels in (their, there) wagons.
18. At last the long trip was (began, begun).
19. Day after day the people (sat, set) in the hot wagons.
20. No animals were (seen, saw) except for lizards and burros.
21. Sometimes all the water was (drank, drunk) before the trip ended.
22. There (was, were) no place (to, too) get more water.
23. This is why the desert was (knew, known) as Death Valley.
24. The settlers knew that rivers (was, were) on the other side of the desert.
25. How happy they were when they had (came, come) out of the valley.
26. The animals (ran, run) to the first river they (saw, seen).
27. The trip across Death Valley had (took, taken) many days.
28. Today people (may, can) quickly drive across the desert in automobiles.
29. There (is, are) a paved highway that crosses the valley.
30. People have (rode, ridden) across the desert in a few hours.
31. But a person (who's, whose) crossing the desert should try to drive at night.
32. It would be very hot if the trip (began, begun) during the day.
33. Summer temperatures of 51.6°C (125°F) (is, are) common.

Reviewing Proper Word Forms   🔑 18e, 20, 21, 28, 29, 31, 33, 37

Underline the proper word or verb form in parentheses to complete each of the following sentences. (Score: 1 for each word correctly underlined)

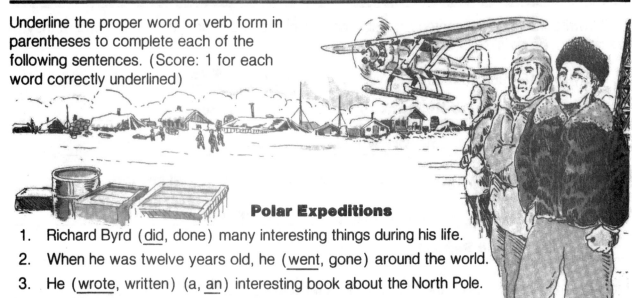

Polar Expeditions

1. Richard Byrd (<u>did</u>, done) many interesting things during his life.

2. When he was twelve years old, he (<u>went</u>, gone) around the world.

3. He (<u>wrote</u>, written) (a, <u>an</u>) interesting book about the North Pole.

4. Admiral Byrd (were, <u>was</u>) the first pilot to fly over the North Pole.

5. He (<u>flew</u>, flown) over this area on May 9, 1926.

6. When Byrd was a child, he had (became, <u>become</u>) interested in the North Pole.

7. He wanted to (teach, <u>learn</u>) more about this part of the world.

8. At last he was (gave, <u>given</u>) a chance to go to the South Pole.

9. (Wasn't, <u>Weren't</u>) several people with him at the South Pole?

10. No food (<u>grew</u>, grown) in this bare, cold land.

11. There (was, <u>were</u>) no cities or stores at the South Pole.

12. Byrd (<u>gave</u>, given) an order to take food for the trip.

13. They (has, <u>have</u>) the wood for building their houses.

14. The workers built the buildings by (theirselves, <u>themselves</u>).

15. But nails were (froze, <u>frozen</u>) in the cold air.

16. When the hammer hit the nails, the nails (<u>broke</u>, broken).

17. The nails were (lay, <u>laid</u>) by a fire to warm.

18. When (<u>they're</u>, there) warm, nails won't break.

19. There was a building where the workers could (<u>sit</u>, set) and relax.

20. The camp also (<u>has</u>, have) a building where the airplanes are kept.

21. The ground (<u>froze</u>, frozen) hard during the winter.

22. The wind had (blew, <u>blown</u>) snow over (them, <u>those</u>) buildings.

23. (<u>Wasn't</u>, Weren't) a tunnel built between the buildings?

24. The workers went (in, <u>into</u>) the tunnel to go from one building to another.

25. What food do you think they (<u>ate</u>, eaten)?

26. Some hunting was (did, <u>done</u>) nearby.

27. Seal and whale meat were (ate, <u>eaten</u>) quite often.

Remembering What We Have Learned

1. Rewrite the following sentences, using capital letters and punctuation marks where they are needed. 🔑 1–3, 5–12

on friday june 15 1985 adele went to visit mr j r drew ___**On Friday,**___

___**June 15, 1985, Adele went to visit Mr. J. R. Drew.**___

mr drews farm is in ohio ___**Mr. Drew's farm is in Ohio.**___

adele worked played and rested ___**Adele worked, played, and rested.**___

what fun she had with the dog named peppy ___**What fun she had with**___

___**the dog named Peppy!**___

mr drew i must go home on the fourth of july said adele ___**"Mr. Drew, I**___

___**must go home on the Fourth of July," said Adele.**___

wasnt adeles vacation one that most people would enjoy ___**Wasn't Adele's**___

___**vacation one that most people would enjoy?**___

2. On the lines below write two sentences. Use at least one noun, one pronoun, and one verb in each sentence. Then, on another piece of paper, combine the sentences into one long sentence by using a conjunction. 🔑 14, 17, 19, 24, 41

(Answers will vary.)

_____

_____

3. On the first row of lines below write the singular and plural forms of two nouns. On the second row of lines write the possessive forms of the four words. 🔑 15, 16

(Answers will vary.)

_____ _____ _____ _____

_____ _____ _____ _____

4. On the first row of lines below write the three principal parts of a verb. On the second row of lines write three contractions. 🔑 21, 22

(Answers will vary.)

_____ _____ _____ _____

_____ _____ _____ _____

5. Write a sentence describing an animal that you have seen. 🔑 23

(Answers will vary.)

_____

_____

6. Write two pairs of synonyms on the first row of lines below, two pairs of antonyms on the second row, and two pairs of homophones on the third row. 🔑 35, 36, 37

_____ _____ **(Answers will vary.)** _____ _____

_____ _____ _____ _____

_____ _____ _____ _____

7. Write the names of four animals in alphabetical order. 🔑 38

_____ _____ **(Answers will vary.)** _____ _____

8. Write three two-syllable words, and put hyphens between the syllables. Place an accent mark after the accented syllable of each word. 🔑 39

_____ **(Answers will vary.)** _____

9. On each line below write a sentence, using one of the words or sets of words in parentheses at the left of each line. 🔑 18, 20, 21, 26, 27, 29, 31, 33, 37

(he and I, him and me) _____ **(Answers will vary.)** _____

(we, us) _____

(himself, themselves) _____

(was, were) _____

(teach, learn) _____

(may, can) _____

(lie, lay) _____

(in, into) _____

(them, those) _____

(began, begun) _____

(threw, thrown) _____

(knew, known) _____

(to, too, two) _____

(its, it's) _____

(their, there) _____

Index of Lessons

NOTE: Numbers following the entries are page numbers. Only pages on which the subject is emphasized are listed.

Index of Informational Topics and Stories in Lessons

NOTE: Numbers following the entries are page numbers.

Index of The Text

NOTE: Numbers following the entries refer to key numbers, not to page numbers.

Keys to Good Language

TEST BOOKLET

Phoenix Learning Resources, LLC.

Pretest 1

I. In the sentences below underline each word, abbreviation, or initial that should begin with a capital letter. Place periods, question marks, and exclamation points where they are needed. (Score: 16—1 for each underlined word and 1 for each punctuation mark)

1. how we enjoyed the fourth of july**!**
2. We visited mrs**.** ellen l**.** harris in philadelphia**.**
3. She told us how the french celebrate their national holiday**.**
4. Did you know that my aunt once lived in paris**?**

II. Write *Yes* before each of the following groups of words that is a sentence. Write *No* before each group that is not a sentence. Then draw a line under each noun, and draw a circle around each pronoun in the groups of words. (Score: 19)

___**Yes**___ 5. Ted said that (his) family had an exciting trip

___**No**___ 6. Taking pictures with (his) camera

___**Yes**___ 7. (Their) car was so heavy that (it) stuck in the mud on a dirt road

___**No**___ 8. A very clear picture of Ted and the car

III. Write the plural form of each word below. (Score: 4)

9. flag ___**flags**___   11. firefly ___**fireflies**___

10. calf ___**calves**___   12. child ___**children**___

IV. Write the possessive form of each word below. (Score: 2)

13. woman ___**woman's**___   14. swimmers ___**swimmers'**___

V. Write the abbreviations for the following words. (Score: 2)

15. Thursday ___**Thurs.**___   16. Avenue ___**Ave.**___

VI. In the sentences below underline the proper word form in parentheses. (Score: 9)

17. Ted's parents said the trip would (teach, learn) Ted about our country's history.
18. Their vacation was educational both for (he, him) and (they, them).
19. Ted thought that it was (he, him) who had learned the most.
20. (We, Us) enjoyed hearing about his experiences.
21. He has one picture of (a, an) old Pennsylvania barn.
22. (May, Can) we see your other pictures, Ted?
23. Ted said that (her, she) and (I, me) might see them.

1

Post Test 1

I. In the sentences below underline each word, abbreviation, or initial that should begin with a capital letter. Place punctuation marks where they are needed. (Score: 18—1 for each underlined word and 1 for each punctuation mark)

1. <u>rhode</u> <u>island</u> is the smallest state in our country.

2. Many <u>canadians</u> went there to live.

3. <u>what</u> beautiful beaches the state has!

4. Did <u>dr</u>.<u>tam</u> <u>y</u>.<u>ling</u> move to <u>newport</u> after <u>new</u> <u>year's</u> <u>day</u>?

II. Write *Yes* before each of the following groups of words that is a sentence. Write *No* before each group that is not a sentence. Then draw a line under each noun, and draw a circle around each pronoun in the groups of words. (Score: 18)

No _____ 5. In (his) book, a <u>navigator</u> named Verrazano

Yes _____ 6. Did (he) give the <u>state</u> a <u>name</u>

No _____ 7. American <u>Indians</u> from several <u>tribes</u> in the <u>region</u>

Yes _____ 8. <u>Fish</u> and <u>grain</u> were (their) <u>principal</u> <u>foods</u>

III. Write the plural of each word below. (Score: 4)

9. city _____ **cities** _____   11. valley _____ **valleys** _____

10. foot _____ **feet** _____   12. loaf _____ **loaves** _____

IV. Write the possessive form of each word below. (Score: 2)

13. donkeys _____ **donkeys'** _____   14. Tess _____ **Tess's** _____

V. Write the abbreviations for the following words. (Score: 2)

15. Southeast _____ **S.E.** _____   16. September _____ **Sept.** _____

VI. In the sentences below underline the proper word form in parentheses. (Score: 8)

17. Angel and (<u>I</u>, me) made a notebook about Roger Williams.

18. (<u>We</u>, Us) learned that he had (a, <u>an</u>) interesting life.

19. It was (<u>he</u>, him) and his followers who founded Providence.

20. Didn't the Narragansett Indians (<u>teach</u>, learn) him their language?

21. He was fair to (they, <u>them</u>), and they always had respect for (he, <u>him</u>).

22. Anyone who is interested (<u>may</u>, can) look at our notebook.

2

Pretest 2

I. Rewrite each of the following sentences, using capital letters, periods, question marks, exclamation points, quotation marks, and commas where they are needed. (Score: 40—1 for each capital letter and 1 for each punctuation mark)

1. fran do you play tennis asked miss b b jones _____**"Fran, do you play tennis?"**

asked Miss B. B. Jones. _____

2. fran replied yes my father sister and i will play on memorial day _____**Fran replied,**

"Yes, my father, sister, and I will play on Memorial Day." _____

3. on may 28 1982 mark saw the french championships in paris france _____**On May**

28, 1982, Mark saw the French championships in Paris, France. ___

4. how exciting it must have been cried fran _____**"How exciting it must have**

been!" cried Fran. _____

II. Underline each verb in the following sentences. (Score: 3)
5. Fred tossed the ball into the air.
6. Then swiftly he swung his racket.
7. The tennis ball sailed over the net.

III. Write the other two principal parts of the following verbs. (Score: 4)

8. do _____**did**_____ _____**done**_____   9. eat _____**ate**_____ _____**eaten**_____

IV. Fill the blank in each sentence below with the contraction of the words in parentheses at the left of the sentence. (Score: 2)

10. (does not) Pamela _____**doesn't**_____ play tennis well.

11. (Cannot) _____**Can't**_____ Sue teach her the game?

V. In the sentences below underline the proper verb form in parentheses. (Score: 6)
12. Pam (came, come) to the tennis court for her lesson.
13. Phil and Sue (was, were) already there.
14. Pam thought they might (of, have) forgotten to come.
15. She (sat, set) down for a while to watch them play.
16. Then Phil (lay, laid) on the grass to watch the tennis lesson.
17. They (drank, drunk) plenty of water when the lesson was over.

Post Test 2

I. Rewrite each of the following sentences, using capital letters and punctuation marks where they are needed. (Score: 39—1 for each capital letter and 1 for each punctuation mark)

1. americans once thought that alaska had only snow ice and polar bears _____

   Americans once thought that Alaska had only snow, ice, and polar bears.

2. mr j d cruz exclaimed yes but what riches were discovered there _____ **Mr. J. D.**

   Cruz exclaimed, "Yes, but what riches were discovered there!"

3. on january 3 1959 alaska became the forty-ninth state i said _____ **"On January 3,**

   1959, Alaska became the forty-ninth state," I said.

4. next independence day we'll visit juneau alaska said jan _____ **"Next**

   Independence Day we'll visit Juneau, Alaska," said Jan.

II. Underline each verb in the following sentences. (Score: 3)

5. Eskimos and Aleut Indians first lived in Alaska.
6. Several Europeans explored this remote territory.
7. Many Russians settled near Kodiak.

III. Write the other principal parts of the following verbs. (Score: 4)

8. give _____ **gave** _____ **given** _____   9. write _____ **wrote** _____ **written** _____

IV. Fill the blank in each sentence below with the contraction of the words in parentheses at the left of the sentence. (Score: 2)

10. (Should not) _____ **Shouldn't** _____ there be more farms in Alaska?

11. (cannot) Farming _____ **can't** _____ be done until the land is cleared.

V. In the following sentences underline the proper verb form in parentheses. (Score: 7)

12. Books and songs have been (wrote, written) about Alaska's gold rush.
13. The valuable ore had (laid, lain) in the earth for millions of years.
14. A few (came, come) to Alaska and (was, were) to make fortunes from this gold.
15. Many others liked to (sit, set) and dream of finding gold.
16. It would (of, have) been an exciting time to be in Alaska.
17. (Doesn't, Don't) you wish you could search for gold?

Pretest 3

I. Write *T* beside the true statements below. Write *F* beside the false statements below. (Score: 6)

T   1.   An outline is a plan for a report or story.

T   2.   The sentences in a paragraph should tell about only one subject or main idea.

F   3.   The second sentence in a paragraph should introduce the subject.

F   4.   The last sentence in a paragraph should introduce a new subject.

T   5.   The topic sentence should be an interesting one to catch the reader's attention.

T   6.   The first sentence of a paragraph should be indented.

II. Place an *X* before each statement below that lists a use of the dictionary. (Score: 6)

X   7.   To find how to spell a word   _____   10.   To find how to write a paragraph

_____   8.   To find how to outline   **X**   11.   To find how to pronounce a word

X   9.   To find how to divide a word   **X**   12.   To find how to define a word

III. In the following sentences draw a circle around each letter that should be capitalized. Underline or punctuate titles when necessary. (Score: 9)

13.   Was the story, "(a) (C)areless (g)iant" written by David Harrison?

14.   The book (i)n (Y)ards and (g)ardens is in our library.

IV. Arrange the following words in alphabetical order: *trim, try, tree, true.* (Score: 4)

15.   _____**tree**_____   17.   _____**true**_____

16.   _____**trim**_____   18.   _____**try**_____

V. Rewrite the words below by placing hyphens between the syllables. (Score: 4)

19.   ladder _____**lad-der**_____   21.   pilot _____**pi-lot**_____

20.   hammer _____**ham-mer**_____   22.   basket _____**bas-ket**_____

VI. In the sentences below underline the proper word form in parentheses. (Score: 8)

23.   The tiny tree in the (<u>red</u>, read) bowl was (flew, <u>flown</u>) from Japan.

24.   For hundreds of years the Japanese have (knew, <u>known</u>) how to grow dwarf plants.

25.   Even miniature fruit trees can (<u>be</u>, bee) raised in flower pots.

26.   Some flower growers (hear, <u>here</u>) have developed dwarf plants, (to, <u>too</u>).

27.   Perhaps you have (grew, <u>grown</u>) dwarf zinnias or marigolds in your garden.

28.   My brother has (threw, <u>thrown</u>) all his energy into growing these plants.

Post Test 3

I. Write *T* beside the true statements below. Write *F* beside the false statements below. (Score: 6)

F 1. Each sentence in a paragraph should tell about a different subject.

T 2. The first sentence in a paragraph should introduce the subject.

T 3. The topic sentence of a paragraph should be an interesting one.

F 4. The last line of a paragraph should be indented.

F 5. A paragraph cannot contain more than one sentence.

T 6. An outline is a written plan for a report or story.

II. Place an *X* before each statement below that lists a use of the dictionary. (Score: 6)

X 7. To find how to define a word   **X** 10. To find how to divide a word

X 8. To find how to spell a word   _____ 11. To find how to write a story

_____ 9. To find how to outline   **X** 12. To find how to pronounce a word

III. In the following sentences draw a circle around each letter that should be capitalized. Underline or punctuate titles when necessary. (Score: 9)

13. The song, "(t)he (S)tar (S)pangled (b)anner" tells about American history.

14. Isn't (W)atchwords of (L)iberty an interesting book?

IV. Arrange the following words in alphabetical order: *love, long, low, lot.* (Score: 4)

15. _____**long**_____   17. _____**love**_____

16. _____**lot**_____   18. _____**low**_____

V. Rewrite the words below by placing hyphens between the syllables. (Score: 4)

19. bubble ___**bub-ble**___   21. motor ___**mo-tor**___

20. winter ___**win-ter**___   22. cradle ___**cra-dle**___

VI. In the sentences below underline the proper word form in parentheses. (Score: 8)

23. Our government is (knew, known) as a democracy.

24. Lawmakers in a democracy are elected (by, buy) the people.

25. We have (grew, grown) accustomed (to, too) our democratic freedom.

26. (Its, It's) easy to forget how people struggled for (their, there) rights.

27. Have you (herd, heard) or read stories of how freedom was gained?

28. The American flag is (flown, flew) on national holidays.

Pretest 4

I. Fill each blank below with a word that will make each sentence give accurate information about writing letters. (Score: 4)

1. A friendly letter has _____**five**_____ parts.

2. A business letter has _____**six**_____ parts.

3. The greeting of a friendly letter is followed by a _____**comma**_____.

4. The greeting of a business letter is followed by a _____**colon**_____.

II. Write the following address as it should be written. (Score: 13)

5. dr k j ingraham   **Dr. K. J. Ingraham**_____

   821 east park street   **821 East Park Street**_____

   cincinnati ohio 45242   **Cincinnati, Ohio 45242**_____

III. Using periods, write the abbreviations of the following words. (Score: 4)

6. Northwest _____**N.W.**_____   8. Wednesday _____**Wed.**_____

7. August _____**Aug.**_____   9. Virginia _____**Va.**_____

IV. Arrange the following words in alphabetical order, divide each word into syllables, and place an accent mark after each accented syllable: *apple, enter, enclose, about.* (Score: 12—3 for each word correctly placed, divided, and accented)

10. _____**a-bout'**_____   12. _____**en-close'**_____

11. _____**ap'ple**_____   13. _____**en'ter**_____

V. Underline the word or group of words in parentheses that properly completes the following sentences. (Score: 9)

14. Last summer (Mom and I, Mom and me) went to a Navaho village.

15. She has often (rode, ridden) to this village to visit.

16. She (took, taken) me (their, there) to see the beautiful sand paintings.

17. Anyone (who's, whose) interested in art should see (them, those) pictures.

18. An artist showed (Mom and I, Mom and me) how to paint with colored sand.

19. (Them, Those) dry colors are sprinkled over the sandy ground.

20. Navaho artists often destroy (their, there) sand paintings before dark.

Post Test 4

I. Fill each blank below with a word that will make each sentence give accurate information about writing letters. (Score: 4)

1. A _____**friendly**_____ letter has five parts.

2. A _____**business**_____ letter has six parts.

3. The greeting of a _____**friendly**_____ letter is followed by a comma.

4. The greeting of a _____**business**_____ letter is followed by a colon.

II. Write the following address as it should be written. (Score: 13)

5. mr f d lowenstein   **Mr. F. D. Lowenstein**

   36 west oak avenue   **36 West Oak Avenue**

   bozeman montana 59715   **Bozeman, Montana 59715**

III. Using periods, write the abbreviations of the following words. (Score: 4)

6. Michigan _____**Mich.**_____   8. November _____**Nov.**_____

7. Thursday _____**Thurs.**_____   9. Southeast _____**S.E.**_____

IV. Arrange the following words in alphabetical order, divide each word into syllables, and place an accent mark after each accented syllable: *mission, mistake, miser, mistreat.* (Score: 12—3 for each word correctly placed, divided, and accented)

10. _____**mi'ser**_____   12. _____**mis-take'**_____

11. _____**mis'sion**_____   13. _____**mis-treat'**_____

V. Underline the word or group of words in parentheses that properly completes the following sentences. (Score: 9)

14. Aesop was a Greek author (who's, <u>whose</u>) stories became famous.

15. Many of (<u>them</u>, those) told about animals that were able (<u>to</u>, too) talk.

16. (<u>Their</u>, There) purpose was to teach lessons about how people behave.

17. Aesop may have (took, <u>taken</u>) his ideas from the actions of people.

18. (<u>Nan and I</u>, Nan and me) like the fable "The Hare and the Tortoise."

19. Ms. Hill lent *Aesop's Fables* to (Nan and I, <u>Nan and me</u>).

20. (Your, <u>You're</u>) welcome to borrow it, (to, <u>too</u>, two).

Pretest 5

I. Underline each conjunction in the sentences below. (Score: 3)

1. Cindi went to the supermarket but forgot her money.

2. When she tried to pay at the store, Cindi couldn't find her purse.

3. Cindi returned the food and had to go back home.

II. Rewrite the following run-on sentence to make three better sentences. Leave out any *and* that is not needed. (Score: 3)

4. Kim and Rob made dinner and one stirred the spaghetti and sauce and who made the salad?

Kim and Rob made dinner. One stirred the spaghetti and sauce. Who made the salad?

III. Change the following singular nouns to plural possessive nouns. (Score: 4)

5. chef **chefs'**   7. guest **guests'**

6. child **children's**   8. sheep **sheep's**

IV. Draw a line under each adjective in the sentences below. (Score: 5)

9. The busy chefs put the spaghetti in a large, brown bowl.

10. Did the slippery spaghetti have a spicy sauce?

V. Write an antonym for each word below. (Score: 4)

11. graceful **awkward**   13. often **seldom**

12. late **prompt (or early)**   14. dangerous **safe**

VI. Write a synonym for each word below. (Score: 4)

15. difficult **hard**   17. seize **grasp**

16. genuine **real**   18. clumsy **awkward**

VII. In the sentences below underline the proper word form in parentheses. (Score: 8)

19. During early times people probably did not cook (there, their) food.

20. They didn't have (no, any) way to start fires for (theirselves, themselves).

21. Then someone (became, become) aware that sparks are (drew, drawn) with flint.

22. Perhaps a flint rock had (fell, fallen) against metal.

23. People (could, couldn't) hardly keep such a discovery a secret.

24. (Whose, Who's) food wouldn't taste better cooked?

Post Test 5

I. Underline each conjunction in the sentences below. (Score: 4)

1. Lonnie raced home <u>as</u> the sky grew darker <u>and</u> darker.

2. She didn't have much time <u>because</u> the rain was on its way.

3. <u>When</u> she finally arrived, it began to pour.

II. Rewrite the following run-on sentence to make three better sentences. Leave out any *and* that is not needed. (Score: 3)

4. Lonnie played records for hours and she read her new library book and staying in from the rain was fun.

Lonnie played records for hours. She read her new library book. _____

Staying in from the rain was fun. _____

III. Change the following singular nouns to plural possessive nouns. (Score: 2)

5. astronaut ____**astronauts'**____   6. deer ____**deer's**____

IV. Underline each adjective in the following sentences. (Score: 6)

7. The <u>tall</u> corn has <u>long</u>, <u>silky</u> tassels.

8. Will the <u>small</u>, <u>blue</u> blossoms become <u>delicious</u> vegetables?

V. Write an antonym for each word below. (Score: 4)

9. enemy ____**friend**____   11. ancient ____**new**____

10. careful ____**careless**____   12. cheap ____**expensive**____

VI. Write a synonym for each word below. (Score: 4)

13. every ____**each**____   15. rude ____**impolite**____

14. brief ____**short**____   16. remained ____**stayed**____

VII. In the following sentences underline the proper word form in parentheses. (Score: 8)

17. Ed had (became, <u>become</u>) so eager that he (couldn't, <u>could</u>) hardly wait.

18. He told (hisself, <u>himself</u>) that green sprouts would surely appear soon.

19. Rain had (fell, <u>fallen</u>) in (grate, <u>great</u>) showers all spring.

20. One morning he (<u>drew</u>, drawn) the curtain to look at the garden.

21. (Their, <u>There</u>) below he could see his flower bed.

22. Green shoots were pushing (<u>themselves</u>, theirselves) up through the moist earth.

Pretest 6

I. Listed below are some facts about the astronomer Nicolaus Copernicus. Use these facts to make an outline for two paragraphs. (Score: 20) **(Answers will vary.)**

Born in Poland in 1473   Recorded first observations of planets in 1497
Studied at University of Cracow, Poland   Proved that the earth was not the center
Studied at University of Bologna, Italy   of the universe
                                                              Proved that planets move around the sun

I.   Early years _____

   A.   Born in Poland in 1473 _____

   B.   Studied at University of Cracow, Poland _____

   C.   Studied at University of Bologna, Italy _____

II. Discoveries _____

   A.   Recorded first observation of planets in 1497 _____

   B.   Proved that the earth was not the center of the universe _____

   C.   Proved that planets move around the sun _____

II. Read the following sentences about writing a story. Write *T* beside true statements. Write *F* beside false statements. (Score: 6)

_____**T**_____   1.   A story should be planned before it is written.

_____**F**_____   2.   Unnecessary ideas may be included in the story.

_____**T**_____   3.   Arrange events in the order that they happen.

_____**T**_____   4.   Write the title in the center of the first line.

_____**F**_____   5.   Begin the story by repeating the title.

_____**T**_____   6.   Combine short, choppy sentences into more effective ones.

III.   Underline the proper word form in parentheses. (Score: 6)

  7.   Copernicus thought there were six planets (<u>in</u>, into) the solar system.

  8.   (Them, <u>Those</u>) six planets were the only ones that had been seen at that time.

  9.   Astronomers had no telescopes to help (<u>them</u>, those).

10.   Later, astronomers could look (in, <u>into</u>) telescopes that magnified the heavens.

11.   Through (them, <u>those</u>) telescopes they saw what Copernicus could not see.

12.   People (begun, <u>began</u>) to change their ideas about the solar system.

Post Test 6 (Final)

I.   Write *Yes* at the left of each group of words that is a sentence and *No* before each group that is not a sentence. Draw one line under each noun, two lines under each pronoun, and a circle around each verb. (Score: 16)

Yes   1.   Brenda had a new basketball

No   2.   Tucked under the arm

No   3.   Her hand on the ball

Yes   4.   She dribbled the ball down a street

II.   Place punctuation marks where they are needed, and underline each word that should begin with a capital letter. (Score: 31)

5.   Is it a red, blue, or orange ball?

6.   No, but i like those colors.

7.   "Shall I show you?" Jo asked.

8.   Jill shouted, "oh, please do!"

9.   We got it in detroit, michigan.

10.   Did mrs. b. rossi buy it in a sporting goods store?

11.   Jim, thursday is my birthday.

12.   How long the nile river is!

13.   on may 6, 1755, he arrived.

14.   Was "fog" an interesting poem?

III.   Write a synonym for each word below. (Score: 2) **(Answers will vary.)**

15.   enormous **huge**

16.   genuine **real**

IV.   Write an antonym for each word below. (Score: 2) **(Answers will vary.)**

17.   imaginary **real**

18.   quiet **noisy**

V.   Write a homophone for each word below. (Score: 2)

19.   hear **here**

20.   their **there (or they're)**

VI.   Write contractions of the following words. (Score: 2)

21.   will not **won't**

22.   you are **you're**

VII.   Arrange the following words in alphabetical order, divide each word into syllables, and place an accent mark after each accented syllable: *correct, cocoa, copper, convince.* (Score: 4—1 for each word correctly placed, divided, and accented)

23.   **co'coa**

24.   **con-vince'**

25.   **cop'per**

26.   **cor-rect'**

12

Post Test 6 (Final)

VIII. Write the plural form of each word in the first column below. Write the possessive form of each word in the second column. (Score: 6)

27. cherry ___**cherries**___   30. geese ___**geese's**___

28. knife ___**knives**___   31. Chris ___**Chris's**___

29. man ___**men**___   32. ponies ___**ponies'**___

IX. Write *T* beside the true statements below. Write *F* beside the false statements below. (Score: 5)

___**T**___ 33. The topic sentence of a paragraph usually introduces the subject.

___**F**___ 34. A paragraph must tell about two different subjects or main ideas.

___**T**___ 35. An outline is a written plan for a paragraph, a report, or a story.

___**T**___ 36. The inside address tells to whom the letter was written.

___**F**___ 37. The complimentary close tells who wrote the letter.

X. In the sentences below draw one line under each adjective and two lines under each conjunction. (Score: 5)

38. The thrilling game was over when the eager player caught the ball.

39. The crowd cheered as the happy team left the field.

XI. Underline the word or group of words in parentheses that properly completes the sentences below. (Score: 23)

40. (Was, Were) you there when Angie jumped (off, off of) the barn?

41. She (hardly, didn't hardly) hurt herself, for she (began, begun) to laugh.

42. She has (rode, ridden) a wild pony and climbed a windmill, (to, too, two).

43. Jeff tried to (teach, learn) her how to ride his unicycle.

44. Nothing (is, are) going to discourage Angie!

45. Do you remember when the roof was (blew, blown) off the chicken house?

46. (We, Us) saw her climb (in, into) the chicken house.

47. We thought Angie had (broke, broken) something.

48. She's always playing tricks on (Jeff and I, Jeff and me).

49. You can be sure it is (she, her) if there's any mischief done.

50. (Jeff and I, Jeff and me) once (saw, seen) her climb that tall tree.

51. She (don't, doesn't) like any of (them, those) quiet activities.

52. Once we (went, gone) to see if the pond had (froze, frozen).

53. We (sit, set) our lunches under a bush.

54. When we (came, come) back, (there, their) sat Angie eating every sandwich.